Fearon's
United States Geography

William Lefkowitz

Fearon Education
Belmont, California

Pacemaker Curriculum Advisor: Stephen C. Larsen
Stephen C. Larsen holds a B.S. and an M.S. in Speech Pathology from the University of Nebraska at Omaha, and an Ed.D. in Learning Disabilities from the University of Kansas. In the course of his career, Dr. Larsen has worked in the Teacher Corps on a Nebraska Indian Reservation, as a Fulbright senior lecturer in Portugal and Spain, and as a speech pathologist in the public schools. A full professor at the University of Texas at Austin, he has nearly twenty years' experience as a teacher trainer on the university level. He is the author of sixty journal articles, three textbooks and six widely used standardized tests including the Test of Written Learning (TOWL) and the Test of Adolescent Language (TOAL).

Subject Area Consultant: Shabnam Barati
Shabnam Barati holds a Ph.D. in Geography from the University of Sheffield, United Kingdom. She teaches at Chabot College in Hayward, California, and publishes regularly in journals for professional geographers.

Editor: Joseph T. Curran
Text Designer: Dianne Platner
Cover Design: Dianne Platner, Joe C. Shines
Graphics Coordinator: Joe C. Shines
Illustrators: Valerie Felts, Sherry Sheffield Boulton, Duane Bibby, Cletus Coble
Cartographers: Jean Ann Carroll, Sharon Johnson
Cover map: Copyright © 1988 by HAMMOND Incorporated, Maplewood, New Jersey
Photo Credits: Lick Observatory/University of California, Santa Cruz 2; Ron DiDonato 12; TSW/Click/Chicago Ltd. 20, 270; National Aeronautics & Space Administration 14, 114; The BETTMAN ARCHIVE 30, 40, 120, 150, 211, 250, 251, 253; United States Geological Survey 42, 45, 47, 49, 54, 57, 59, 61, 64, 163, 174, 202; Robert K. Byers 67; Florida State Archives 73, 149, 168, 210, 263; Steve Ringman/*San Francisco Chronicle* 76; Nova Scotia Tourism and Culture 81 (both); American Commercial Barge Line Company 87; Chicago Tribune Company, copyright, all rights reserved, used with permission 96; Florida Dept. of Commerce, Division of Tourism 105; Brant Ward/*San Francisco Chronicle* 124, 213; National Archives 128, 129, 209; James Danekas & Associates, Inc. 136; California Farm Bureau 148, 152; California Dept. of Water Resources 151, 153; Emma Rivera/Peace Corps 154; Stephen Feldman/Peace Corps 155; Bill Strassberger/Peace Corps 156, 157, 200, 256; Mobil Oil Corp./Courtesy API Photo Library 160; American Iron and Steel Institute 164, 165; Scale Models Unlimited 183; Library of Congress 190; Pete Breinig/*San Francisco Chronicle* 194; Frampton/Peace Corps 196; John Herr 197; Watson/Peace Corps 204; Gary Fong/*San Francisco Chronicle* 206; Susan Ehmer/*San Francisco Chronicle* 207; Vince Maggoria/*San Francisco Chronicle* 216; Dick Smith 225; Hewlett Packard Company 232; Richard Wheeler 243; REUTERS/BETTMAN NEWSPHOTOS 206; Paul Conklin/Peace Corps 265; U.S. Dept. of Agriculture/Soil Conservation Service 267; Don Tullous/The Oklahoma Publishing Co., Copyright 1975, from the May 21, 1975 issue of the *Oklahoma City Times* 281.

Copyright © 1990 by Fearon Education, 500 Harbor Boulevard, Belmont, CA 94002. All rights reserved. No part of this book may be reproduced by any means, transmitted, or translated into a machine language without written permission from the publisher.

ISBN 0-8224-0804-X

Printed in the United States of America
1. 9 8 7 6 5 4 3 2

Contents

Note from the Publisher	v

Unit One: Land and Water	**1**
1: Our Home in Space	2
2: Globes and Maps	12
3: Below and Above Earth's Surface	20
4: Earth Is Always Moving	30
Review	38
5: Earthquakes, Volcanoes, and Mountains	40
6: Other Forces That Change Earth	54
7: Landforms of the United States	64
8: Oceans, Lakes, and Rivers	76
Review	92

Unit Two: Climate, Vegetation, and Resources	**95**
9: Earth's Different Climates	96
10: Climate of the United States	114
11: Vegetation and Soil	124
12: U.S. Agriculture	136
Review	146
13: Earth's Renewable Resources	148
14: Earth's Nonrenewable Resources	160
15: How We Use the Land	174
Review	186

Unit Three: Industry, Transportation, and Population	**189**
16: Making, Buying, and Selling Things	190
17: Moving Goods, People, and Ideas	202
18: U.S. Resource Industries	216
19: Other U.S. Industries	232
Review	248
20: Earth Has Billions of People	250
21: People Live in Culture Groups	260
22: People of the United States	270
Review	286

Geography Skills

1:	Directions on Earth	10
2:	Countries of North America	11
3:	Dividing Earth into Hemispheres	26
4:	Locating States and Cities	28
5:	Finding Distance on a Map	29
6:	Reading a Table	52
7:	Finding In-Between Directions	53
8:	Reading a Landform Map	68
9:	Reading a Climate Map	106
10:	Reading a Bar Graph	108
11:	Dividing the United States into Regions	112
12:	Reading a Vegetation Map	132
13	Reading a Pie Graph	167
14:	Reading a Land Use Map	178

Atlas — **288**

North American Political Map	289
World Political Map	290
United States Political Map	292

Glossary — **294**
Index — **300**

**A Note from the Publisher
to the Student**

Think about this for a moment: Earth is the only planet we know of that has living things on it. There may be life somewhere else, but so far we haven't found it anywhere but here. What else makes Earth different from the other planets? That's one of the two main questions this book will help you answer. The other main question is this: What makes the United States different from other countries on planet Earth?

Studying geography is interesting as well as informative. Why are some regions of the United States crowded with people while others are not? Why are some places so rainy and others so dry? What makes mountains form? What makes them wear down? How does being near water affect the way people live? As you read through this book, you will find the answers to all these questions and many more like them. You will learn many important facts about our planet and our country. And you will know the story behind those facts.

In each unit you will learn something new about the people, the land, and the resources of the United States. And you will learn how to use maps, graphs, and tables—the tools of geography. By the end of the book you will be able to say where the country's major mountains and rivers are and what they are like. You will be able to tell what is grown on the land, where it is grown, and why it is grown there. And you will be able to describe who the people of the United States are, where most of them live, and how they came to live there.

Look for the notes in the margins of the pages. These friendly notes are there to make you stop and think. Sometimes they comment on the material you are learning. Sometimes they give examples. Sometimes they remind you of something you already know.

You will also find several study aids in the book. At the beginning of every chapter, you'll find **Learning Objectives**. Take a moment to study these goals. They will help you focus on the important points covered in the chapter. **Words To Know** will give you a preview of the geographic terms you'll find in your reading. And at the end of each chapter, a **summary** will give you a quick review of what you've just learned.

We hope you enjoy reading about our country and its people. Everyone who put this book together worked hard to make it interesting as well as useful. The rest is up to you. We wish you well in your studies. Our success is in your accomplishment.

Carol Hegarty
Publisher

Unit 1
Land and Water

Chapter 1
Our Home in Space
Directions on Earth
Countries of North America

Chapter 2
Globes and Maps

Chapter 3
Below and Above Earth's Surface
Dividing Earth into Hemispheres
Locating States and Cities
Finding Distance on a Map

Chapter 4
Earth Is Always Moving

Chapter 5
Earthquakes, Volcanoes, and Mountains
Reading a Table
Finding In-Between Directions

Chapter 6
Other Forces That Change Earth

Chapter 7
Landforms of the United States
Reading a Landform Map

Chapter 8
Oceans, Lakes, and Rivers

Chapter 1
Our Home in Space

Galaxies contain stars, suns, and planets. Our solar system is part of the Milky Way Galaxy.

Chapter Learning Objectives
1. Compare the sizes of Earth, the sun, and the moon.
2. Tell how much of Earth is covered with water and how much is covered with land.
3. Use a map to identify the continents.
4. Use a map to identify the oceans.
5. Describe plains, plateaus, mountains, valleys, hills, islands, and peninsulas.
6. Describe oceans, seas, gulfs, bays, lakes, rivers.
7. Find directions on a map.
8. Identify the countries of North America on a map.

Words To Know

continent a very large body of land; Earth is divided into seven continents
landform a feature of Earth's surface, such as a mountain, hill, plateau, plain, or valley
plain a large area of mostly flat land
sea level the point at which the ocean meets the land
plateau a large area of flat land that is higher than sea level
mountain a landform that rises very high above sea level and the surrounding land
valley a lowland between two mountains or mountain ranges
hill a landform that is similar to a mountain but not as high
island a landform that is surrounded on all sides by water
peninsula a piece of land that reaches out into the water from a larger body of land
ocean the largest body of salt water on Earth
sea a large body of salt water that is smaller than an ocean. Seas are partly surrounded by land.
gulf an inlet of an ocean or other large body of water, usually larger than a bay
bay an inlet of an ocean or other body of water, usually smaller than a gulf
lake a body of water surrounded on all sides by land
river a large stream of fresh water
mainland the largest part of a country that is separated from one or more other parts by water or land
compass rose an aid to finding directions on a map

Think of the hot sun hanging in space like a giant glowing ball. Think of the bright moon moving across the dark night sky. Think of the stars shining from far away. The sun, moon, and stars are all floating through space. And we, here on Earth, are floating along with them.

What is Earth like? To start with, we know that it is almost as round as a ball. But it is not perfectly round.

How big is Earth? Well, let's say you could walk around Earth at its widest point. And let's say you were to walk 20 miles a day. The trip would take you about 3 1/2 years!

Earth is almost four times as large as the moon. And the sun is 109 times as large as Earth.

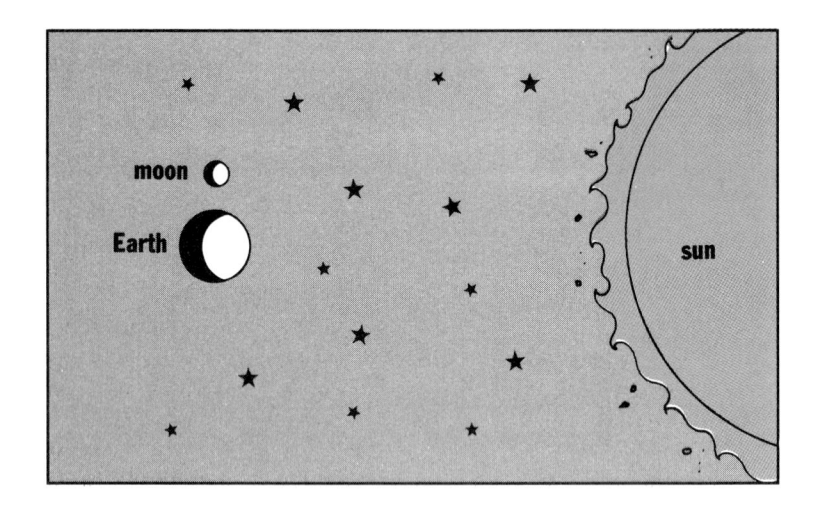

Earth is large when compared to the moon. But it is small when compared to the sun. Here's how you can compare the sizes of Earth, the sun, and the moon. Place a marble next to a basketball. Place a small stone next to the marble. Think of the basketball as the sun. Think of the marble as Earth. And think of the small stone as the moon.

Earth's Oceans and Continents

Long before anyone went up into space, sailors traveled all over Earth. They crossed the **oceans** and went up and down the coast of every land. They made drawings of what they saw. From these drawings, mapmakers drew maps of Earth. Today, mapmakers can use pictures taken from space when they draw maps. Their maps help us to better understand the world we live in.

Look at the map below. It shows how Earth is divided into ocean and land. Which is there more of, ocean or land?

More than two-thirds of Earth is covered by water. Less than one-third is land.

The land rises up from the water and divides it into four large oceans.

The land areas are called **continents**. A continent is a very large body of land. There are seven continents on Earth.

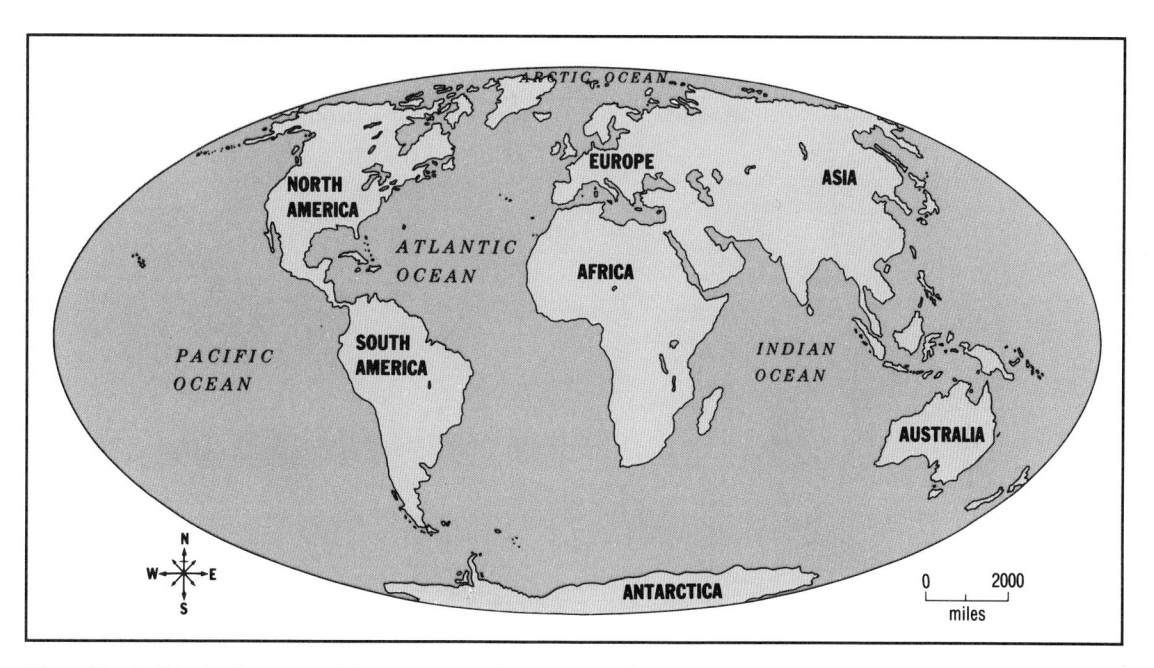

Map Study Study the map. Then answer these questions.
1. What are the names of the four oceans?
2. What are the names of the seven continents?
3. Which continent do you live on?

Earth's Landforms and Bodies of Water

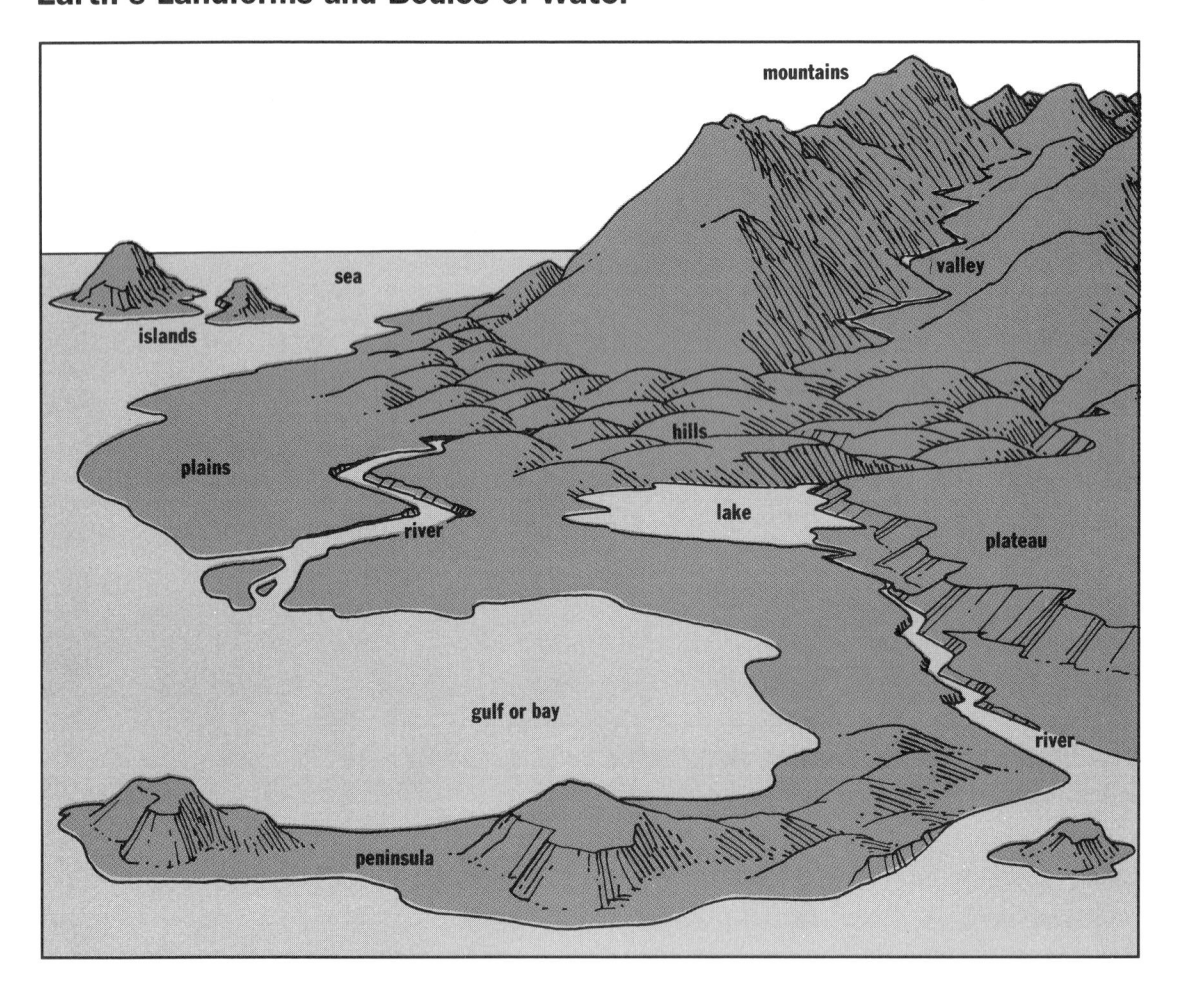

On Earth's Surface

Earth's surface is shaped into different **landforms** and bodies of water. Look at the landforms and the bodies of water in the drawing above. Then read about them on the next page.

Landforms

Plains are areas of mostly flat lands that often stretch for hundreds of miles. They may also be gently rolling land. They do not rise much above **sea level**. The ocean meets the land at sea level.

Plateaus are flat areas that are much higher than sea level. They often rise sharply from the lands around them.

Mountains rise very high above sea level and the surrounding land. The sides of mountains are very steep. Mountains may have rounded or pointed tops.

Valleys are low lands that lie between mountains.

Hills are similar to mountains, but they are not as high above sea level.

Islands are areas of land surrounded by water.

Peninsulas are areas of land that reach out into the water. A peninsula has water on three sides.

What kind of landform do you live on?

Bodies of Water

The oceans are the four largest bodies of salt water on Earth.

Seas are large bodies of salt water that are smaller than oceans. They are partly surrounded by land.

Gulfs and **bays** are bodies of salt water that reach into the land from an ocean or sea. Gulfs are larger than bays.

Lakes are bodies of water surrounded on all sides by land. Most lakes have fresh water. Fresh water can be used for watering crops and for drinking, cooking, and washing.

Rivers are formed by fresh water flowing from one place to another. Rivers flow into other rivers or into lakes, seas, or oceans.

Do you live closer to salt water or to fresh water?

Chapter One 7

Chapter Review

Summary

1. Earth floats in space as the sun, moon, and stars do. Earth is large compared to the moon. It is small compared to the sun.

2. About two-thirds of Earth's surface is covered with water. About one-third is covered with land.

3. Earth has seven large land areas called continents. They are North America, South America, Europe, Asia, Africa, Australia, and Antarctica.

4. Earth's four largest bodies of salt water are the Pacific Ocean, the Atlantic Ocean, the Indian Ocean, and the Arctic Ocean.

5. The main types of landforms are plains, plateaus, mountains, valleys, hills, islands, and peninsulas.

6. The main types of bodies of water are oceans, seas, gulfs, bays, lakes, and rivers.

Thinking and Writing

Answer these questions in complete sentences on a separate sheet of paper.

1. How many times larger is the amount of water that covers Earth than the amount of land?
2. How are plains and plateaus alike? How are they different?
3. How do mountains differ from hills?
4. How do islands differ from peninsulas?
5. How are gulfs and bays alike? How are they different?
6. How are lakes and rivers alike?

Questions to Discuss

1. How does the kind of landform your town is located on affect:
   - How easy or hard it is to build houses and other buildings?
   - How easy or hard it is to farm the land?
2. What bodies of water are nearby?
   - Do people travel or ship goods on any of them?
   - How would life be different if they weren't there?

Special Project

Write a report about the landforms and the bodies of water in your area. Take photos or draw pictures to show how they look. Add them to your report.

Geography Skills 1

Directions on Earth

Anytime you go from one place to another you are moving in a direction.

- If you are going toward the North Pole, you are going north.
- If you are going toward the South Pole, you are going south.
- If you are going toward the rising sun, you are going east.
- If you are going toward the setting sun, you are going west.

Let's say you were to fly from New York City to Quito. In which direction would you be flying?

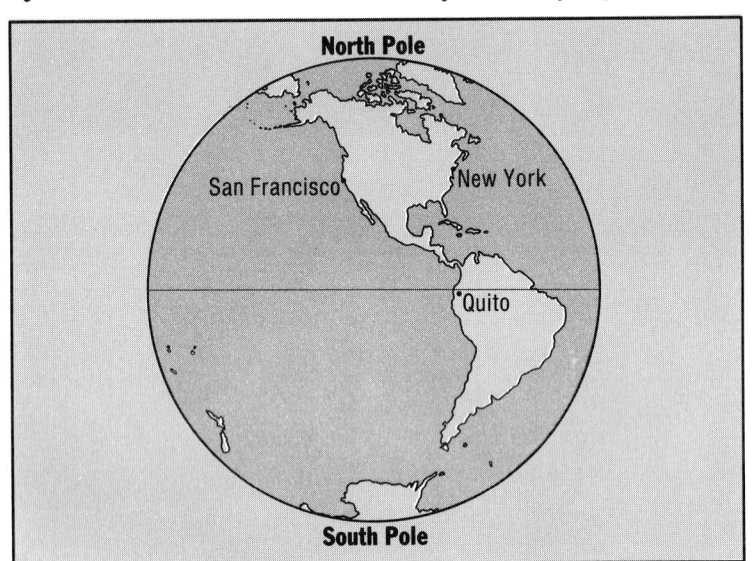

You'd be flying south. In which direction would you be flying on your return trip?

On your return you'd be flying north.

In which direction would you fly from New York to San Francisco?

Did you say west? In which direction would you fly on your return trip?

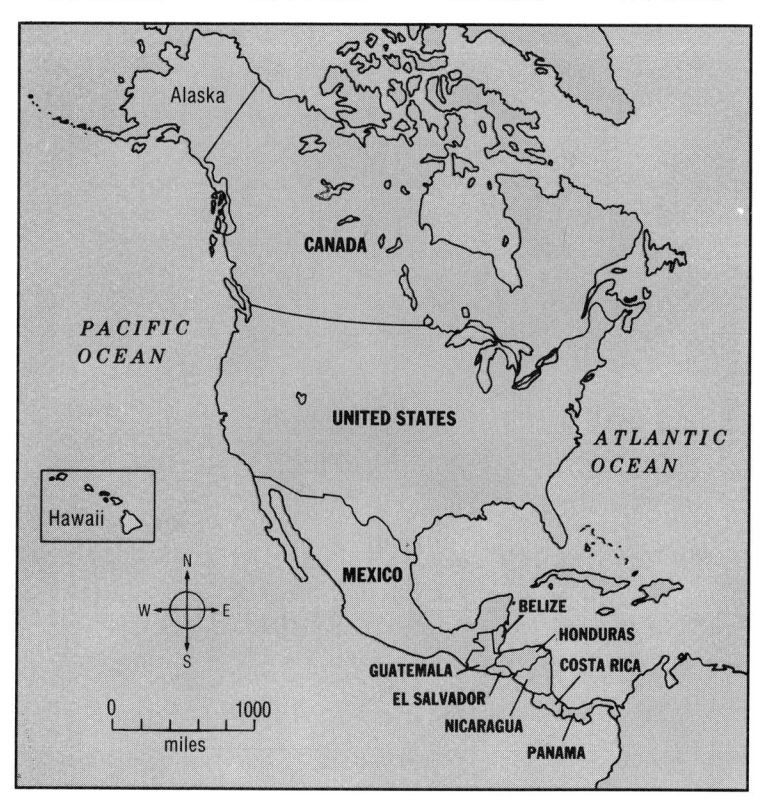

Geography Skills 2

Countries of North America

North America is divided into ten countries. Three are large. The seven smaller countries are known as Central America.

Read the names of the ten countries. Notice that the states of Alaska and Hawaii are separated from the United States **mainland**.

The **compass rose** on the left side of the map helps you tell direction.

N: north   S: south   E: east   W: west

Map Study
1. Which country is just north of the mainland United States?
2. In which direction would you go to get from the United States to Mexico?
3. Which ocean is west of the United States?

Chapter 2
Globes and Maps

Globes and maps are just two of a geographer's tools.

Chapter Learning Objectives
1. Tell three things you can learn from a globe about the land and water areas of Earth.
2. Define and locate the North and South Poles.
3. Define and locate the equator.
4. Define and locate the prime meridian.
5. Compare globes and maps.
6. Compare five kinds of map projections.

Words To Know

equator an imaginary line that circles Earth halfway between the North and South Poles; the line on a globe that stands for that imaginary line

prime meridian an imaginary line that circles Earth, running through the North and South Poles; the line on a globe that stands for that imaginary line

projection a way of showing all or parts of round Earth on flat paper

You can learn a lot about Earth from a globe. You can use it to:
- compare the sizes and shapes of continents, oceans, and countries;
- find out where these and other things, such as cities and rivers, are located;
- tell the distance from one place to another.

You can do the same things with many world maps. And maps can give you other kinds of information as well. Some maps will tell you:
- how many people live in a place,
- the kinds of food that are grown there,
- how much rain falls there every year.

You will find many maps in this book. As you read, study the maps carefully. Right now, look over the maps in the atlas at the back of this book. Later, use the maps in the atlas to locate places. If there is a globe in your classroom, use that as well.

Photograph of Earth **Drawing of a globe**

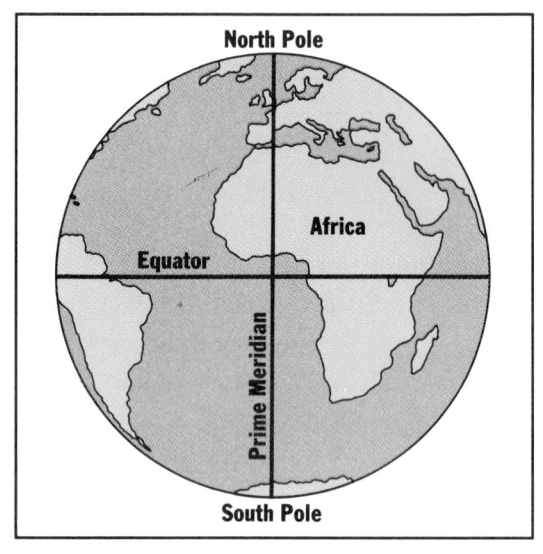

Globes

Look at the photo of Earth above. It was taken from out in space. Compare the photo of Earth with the drawing of a globe next to it. Both show the continent of Africa.

When you look at a globe you are looking at a small model of Earth. A globe shows where the continents and large bodies of water are located. It shows their shape and relative size.

Compare the relative sizes of Africa and Australia on the map in the atlas.

Relative size means the size of one thing compared to the size of another. When you compare the relative sizes of Africa and Australia, you can see that Africa is much larger.

Globes have certain markings that you should become familiar with. These include the North and South Poles, the equator, and the prime meridian.

The North and South Poles are points on Earth's surface. They help us tell directions. Globes show where those points are located. Find the North and South Poles on the drawing above. Notice that they are directly opposite each other.

14 Chapter Two

The **equator** is an imaginary line that circles Earth halfway between the North and South Poles.

Any place on Earth that is above this imaginary line is north of the equator. Any place that is below the imaginary line is south of the equator.

A globe shows where this imaginary line is located. Find the equator on the drawing on the facing page. Is most of Africa north or south of it?

The **prime meridian** is another imaginary line. But it circles Earth the other way. It passes *through* the North and South Poles.

Find the prime meridian on the drawing. Is most of Africa east or west of it? You will read more about the prime meridian in a later lesson.

Flat Maps

Globes are very helpful. But they can't be put into a book. And they aren't useful for showing a lot of the information people want to have. So flat maps are used instead.

Flat maps are not as accurate, or true, as round globes. When mapmakers try to show Earth on flat paper, some of the land or water areas get pulled or twisted out of shape.

Mapmakers have found a way to deal with this problem. They use different **projections**. A projection is simply a way of showing all or part of Earth on flat paper.

There are different kinds of projections. Each is accurate for some things but not for others. Mapmakers choose the best projection for showing the kind of information they want to give. On the next two pages you will learn about five main kinds of projections.

The main properties of maps are area, shape, distance, and direction. No one kind of map can show all of these accurately.

Compare the way Australia looks on a map with the way it looks on a globe. Notice the difference in shape.

Five Types of Projections
Mercator Projection

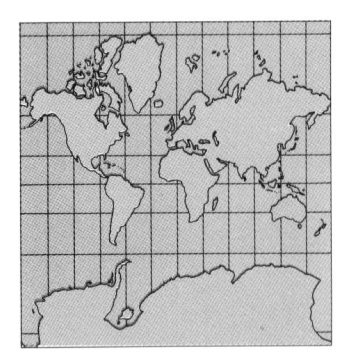

The Mercator projection shows true direction. It also shows the nearly correct sizes of places near the equator. Its main use is to set trade and travel routes between North America, South America, Europe, and Africa. But it greatly enlarges the sizes and shapes of land areas close to the poles.

Mercator projection

Why wouldn't a Mercator map be good for showing the true size and shape of Antarctica?

Equal-Area Projections

Look at the equal-area projection on the left below. This kind of projection is often used for making world maps that appear in textbooks. The reason is that it can accurately show the correct relationship between land and water areas. But there's a problem. Some of the continents come out looking as if they were pulled out of shape.

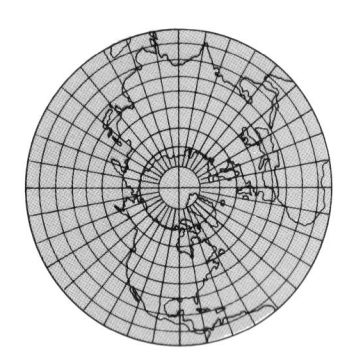

Equal area projection of Northern Hemisphere

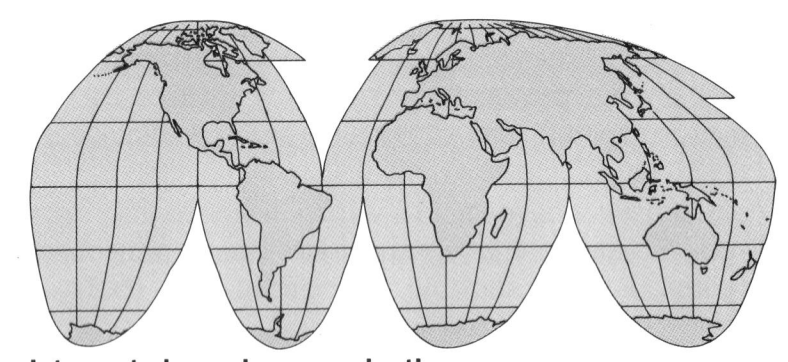

Interrupted equal area projection

Look at the equal-area projection on the right above. Notice that the oceans are cut apart. This is done to keep the size and shape of land areas more accurate. The problem with this kind of projection is that you can't tell distances across the oceans. So, this projection is often used to show only one continent.

16 Chapter Two

Polar Equidistant Projection

Polar equidistant projections accurately show directions and distances from each pole to other places. But they distort the shape of the continents.

Newspapers and TV news shows often use polar equidistant projections to show where world events take place. These projections are also good for showing air routes between Asia and North America or Europe. Planes flying between those continents pass over areas close to the North Pole.

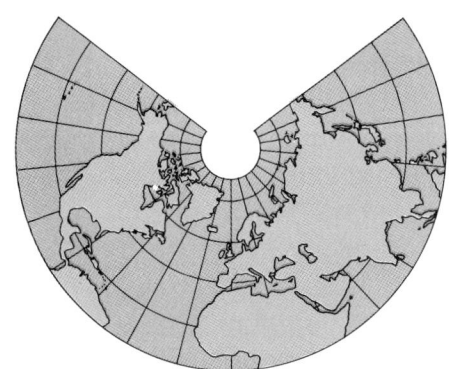

Polar equidistant projection

Conic projection of Northern Hemisphere

Conic Projections

Conic projections are often used to make maps of single continents. If they show only small areas of Earth, they are very accurate. In maps of larger areas, only part of the map is accurate.

Orthographic Projection

Orthographic projections are useful for showing half of Earth at a time. Areas closest to the center of the map are the most accurate.

Orthographic maps are often used in newspapers and on TV news shows. They are useful for showing where important events are happening. And they are useful for showing the correct distances of those places from the United States.

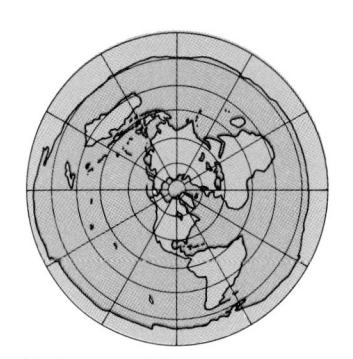

Orthographic projection

Chapter Two **17**

Chapter Review

Summary

1. Globes can be used to tell accurately:
   - the size, shape, and location of continents, countries, and large bodies of water;
   - the distance between one place and another;
   - what direction to go in to get from one place to another.
2. The North and South Poles are points on Earth. We can use them to help tell directions.
3. The equator is an imaginary line that circles Earth halfway between the North and South Poles.
4. The prime meridian is an imaginary line that circles Earth and passes through the North and South Poles.
5. Most flat maps are not as accurate as globes.
6. Different map projections have different uses.
   - Maps using Mercator projections are useful for showing shipping and air routes across the Atlantic Ocean. They distort areas close to the poles.
   - World maps based on equal-area projections are used in many books. If the projection shows land and water areas in their correct sizes, the shapes of some continents will be distorted.
   - Maps using polar equidistant projections are useful for showing where news events take place. They are also useful for showing air routes between Asia and North America or Europe. They do not show accurately the shapes of the continents.
   - Maps using conic projections can accurately show smaller parts of Earth, such as a single continent.
   - Maps using orthographic projections are useful for showing where world events take place. And they help us measure distances correctly.

Thinking and Writing

Answer these questions in complete sentences on a separate sheet of paper.

1. How is a globe like a model of Earth? Tell three things a globe shows.
2. If you were to add the North Pole to a map of the world, in which ocean would you place it?
3. On which continent is the South Pole?
4. Which projection might a ship captain use when sailing across the Atlantic Ocean?
5. Why are globes more accurate than most flat maps?
6. Why may some continents look different on one map than on another?

Questions to Discuss

1. How can maps and globes help you learn more about Earth and the places on it?
2. For which kinds of jobs might people often use maps? What do they use them for?

Special Project

Compare the shapes of the continents on a map with those on a globe. Make a list of the continents that seem distorted.

Chapter 3
Below and Above Earth's Surface

The surface of Earth as seen from within Arizona's Grand Canyon.

Chapter Learning Objectives
1. Describe the four layers below Earth's surface.
2. Define the atmosphere. Explain the importance of the troposphere.
3. Describe gravity.
4. Locate states and cities on a map of the United States.
5. Use global maps to locate Earth's four hemispheres.
6. Use a map to locate states and cities.
7. Use a map scale to find the distance between cities.

Words To Know

crust   Earth's outer layer
mantle   the layer of very hot rock between Earth's crust and outer core
core   the center of Earth
atmosphere   the layers of air above Earth's surface
troposphere   the layer of the atmosphere closest to Earth
oxygen   a gas that is released by plants and breathed in by animals
carbon dioxide   a gas breathed out by animals and taken in by plants

vapor   very tiny droplets of water or other liquid floating in the air
temperature   how hot or cold something is. In the United States, temperature is usually measured on the Fahrenheit scale.
gravity   a strong pulling force from inside Earth
hemisphere   half of a ball
scale   a number of evenly spaced points used for measuring

Below Earth's Surface

Would you like to take a trip to the center of Earth? Your trip would be 4,000 miles long. You would have to dig through solid rock. And you would have to swim through melted rock and metal.

The first part of your trip would be through Earth's **crust**. The crust is made of solid rock. The continents *and* the floor of the ocean are on the surface of this crust. Earth's crust is about five miles thick under the oceans. It is up to 25 or more miles thick under the continents.

Beyond the crust you would come to the **mantle**. Earth's mantle is 1,775 miles thick. This layer of Earth is made of very hot rock. Some of this rock is so hot it has melted.

Next you would come to the outer **core**. Scientists believe the outer core is made of melted iron and nickel. The outer core is 1,400 miles thick.

At the center of Earth, is the inner core. Scientists think the inner core is made of solid iron and nickel. The inner core is 800 miles thick.

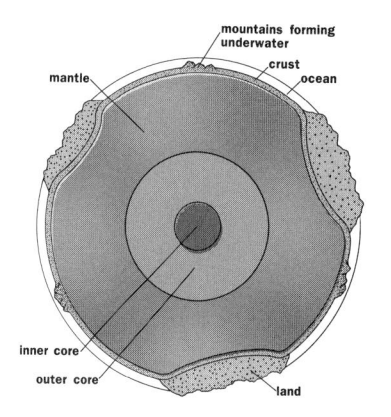

Cutaway view of Earth

Chapter Three   21

Above Earth's Surface

Earth is surrounded by layers of air that stretch for hundreds of miles above its surface. These layers are called the **atmosphere**. The atmosphere is the key to life on Earth. It contains gases that living things need. Most of these gases are found in the atmosphere's first layer, the **troposphere**.

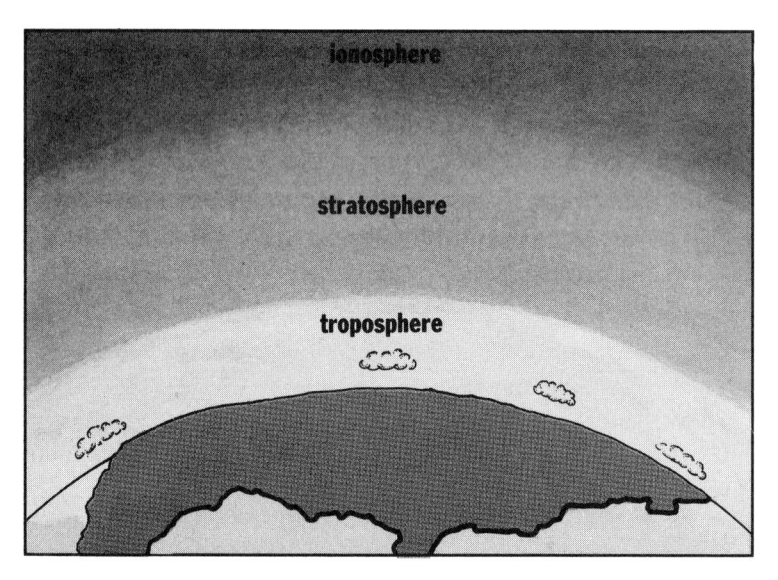

The troposphere, the atmosphere's first layer, stretches about 10 miles above Earth's surface. It helps keep all living things alive.

It is the release of oxygen by trees that helps make a walk in the woods so refreshing.

People and animals breathe in **oxygen**. Without it, they would die in a few minutes. They breathe out **carbon dioxide**.

Plants take in carbon dioxide and other gases. They release oxygen.

All living things need the water **vapor** found in the atmosphere. Water vapor is a gas made of tiny drops of water too small for us to see. It helps keep out some of the sun's heat. Without it, we would all burn up. When the sun is not shining, the water vapor keeps in heat that has built up during the day. If it didn't, we would freeze at night.

The atmosphere changes as we move higher above Earth's surface. **Temperatures** range from very hot to very cold. And as we rise higher in the atmosphere, the air becomes thinner and lighter.

What Holds Us Down?

What keeps air and oceans and us from floating into space?

Gravity holds us all in place. Gravity is a strong pulling force from inside Earth. The sun and the moon and other bodies in space also have gravity.

Think of how a magnet holds onto things made from iron. Gravity is like that. Earth's gravity pulls everything that is on or near Earth down to its surface. When you get far away from Earth, and other bodies in space, gravity has less force. That's why things float in space.

Earth's gravity is six times as strong as the moon's gravity.

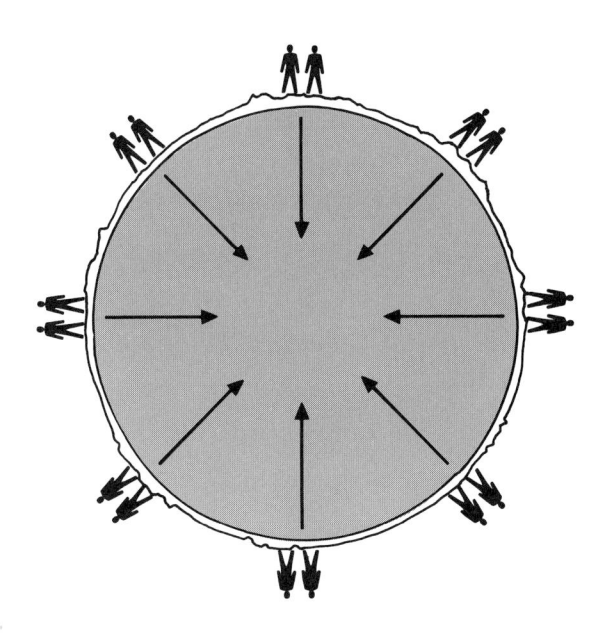

On and near Earth's surface, gravity pulls everything down. You can jump up, but gravity pulls you down again.

Chapter Three 23

Chapter Review

Summary

1. Earth is made of both solid and melted parts.
   - The crust is solid rock. It is from 5 to 25 or more miles thick.
   - The mantle is made of very hot solid rock and of melted rock.
   - Scientists think the outer core is melted iron and nickel.
   - They think the inner core is solid iron and nickel.

2. The layers of air that surround Earth are called the atmosphere. The lowest layer is called the troposphere.
   - It contains most of the water vapor and other gases we need.
   - In daytime, it helps keep out some of the sun's heat.
   - At night, it keeps in some of the heat that has built up during the day.

3. Gravity is a strong pulling force. It holds us to Earth.

Thinking and Writing

Answer these questions on a separate sheet of paper.

1. In terms of Earth's four layers, what do the continents and the oceans have in common?
2. How are the outer and inner cores alike? How are they different?
3. How do trees "breathe"?
4. What do oxygen, carbon dioxide, and water vapor have in common?
5. How does water vapor help regulate Earth's temperature?
6. An object that weighed one pound on the moon would weigh six pounds on Earth. Why?

Questions to Discuss

1. The troposphere is filled with dust and other tiny bits of matter. Where do you think these things come from?
2. Imagine that Earth's gravity suddenly had no effect on the people and things in your classroom. What would happen?

Special Projects

1. About 4,000 miles below you is the center of Earth. Draw a picture that shows you at the top and the four layers of Earth below you. Write the name of each layer on your picture.
2. Find out how some smoke from cars and factories is harmful to the atmosphere.

Geography Skills 3

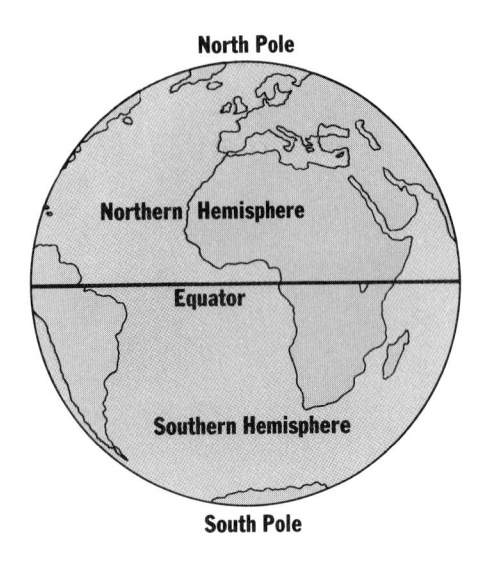

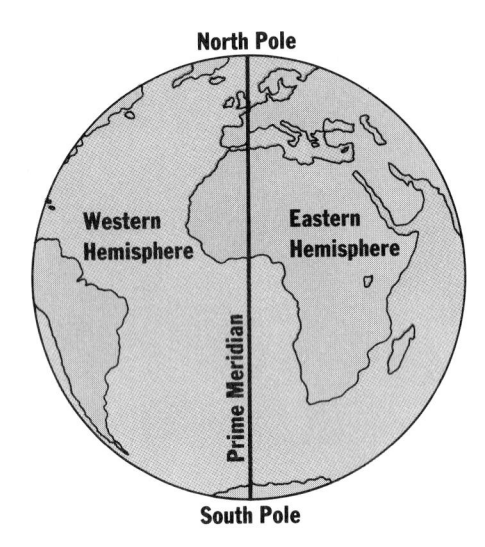

Dividing Earth into Hemispheres

It is often easier to study something large if we first divide it into smaller parts. When we study Earth, we can use the equator to divide it in half.

Everything above the equator is in the Northern **Hemisphere**. Everything below the equator is in the Southern Hemisphere. A hemisphere is half of anything that has a round shape.

We can also divide Earth from pole to pole. The prime meridian divides Earth into an Eastern Hemisphere and a Western Hemisphere.

Now look at the maps on the next page. They show what is in each of these four hemispheres.

26 Chapter Three

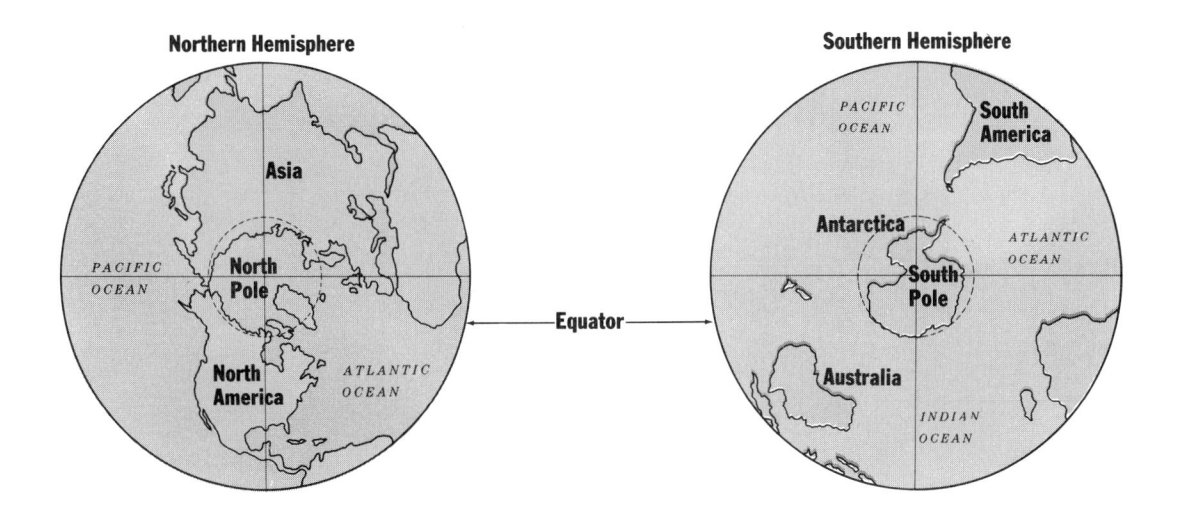

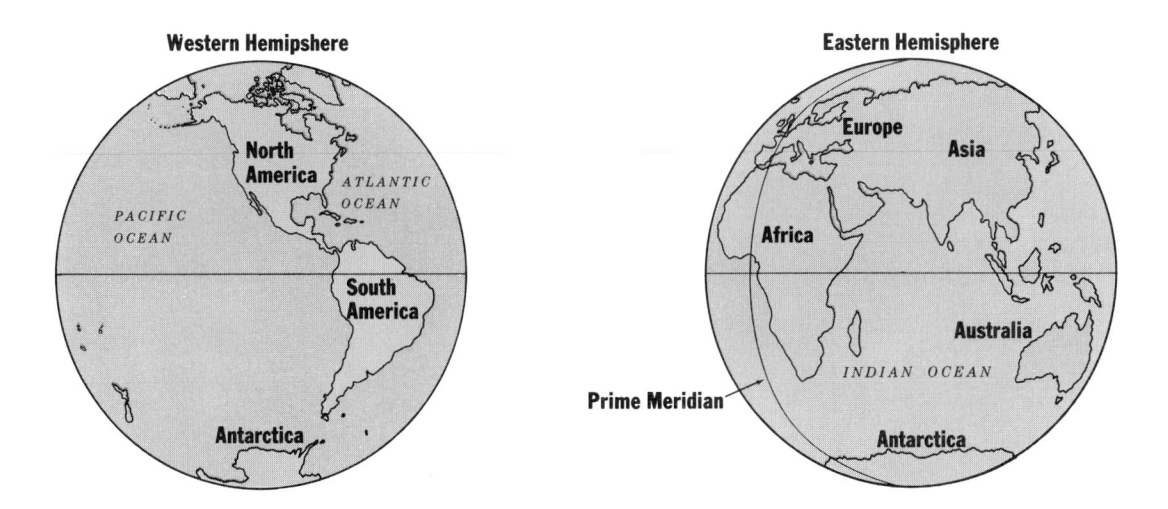

Northern Hemisphere

Southern Hemisphere

Equator

Western Hemisphere

Eastern Hemisphere

Map Study
1. Which line divides Earth into a Northern and a Southern Hemisphere? Which of these two hemispheres do you live in?
2. Which line divides Earth into an Eastern and a Western Hemisphere? Which of these two hemispheres do you live in?
3. Which two of the four hemispheres have the greatest amounts of land?

Chapter Three 27

Geography Skills 4

Locating States and Cities

The map below shows the United States of America. The United States is divided into 50 states. There are 48 states on the mainland. Hawaii is in the Pacific Ocean. Alaska is separated from the mainland by Canada.

The map shows all 50 states, but it names only nine of them. For a complete map of the United States, turn to the Atlas at the back of the book. This map below shows one city in each of the nine states. Small dots show where the cities are.

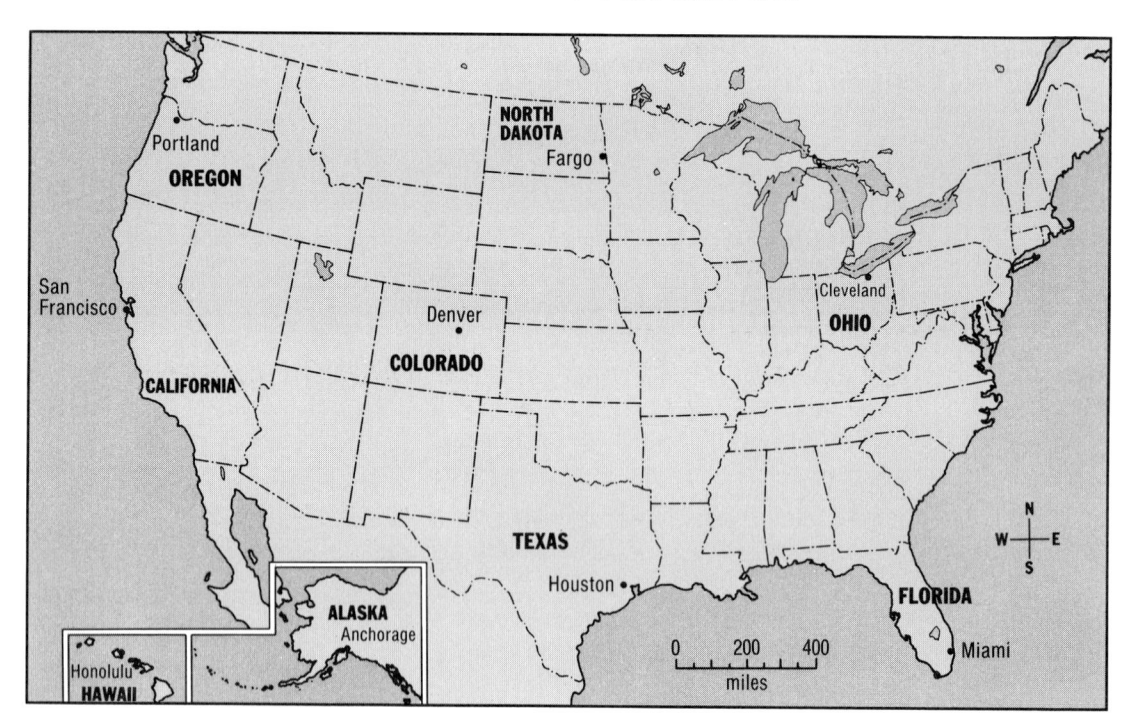

Map Study
1. In which state is each of these cities?
   a. Anchorage   b. San Francisco   c. Fargo   d. Miami
2. In which direction would you go to get from:
   a. Cleveland, Ohio, to Miami, Florida?
   b. Miami, Florida, to Houston, Texas?
   c. Houston, Texas, to Fargo, North Dakota?
   d. Fargo, North Dakota, to Cleveland, Ohio?

Geography Skills 5

Finding Distance on a Map

Map scales are used to measure distance.

The scale on the map below shows how much distance on the map equals 300 miles on land. It also shows shorter distances. Each mark after the 0 adds 50 miles to the mark before it.

Take a piece of paper and place it next to the dots that stand for Tampa and Miami. Mark dots on your paper next to the dots on the map. Then line up the dots on your paper with the marks on the scale.

The scale shows that the distance is 200 miles.

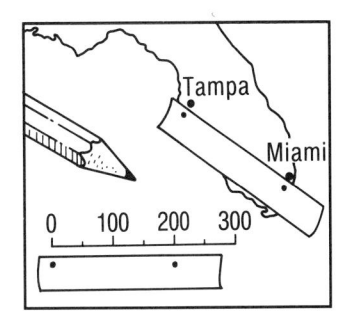

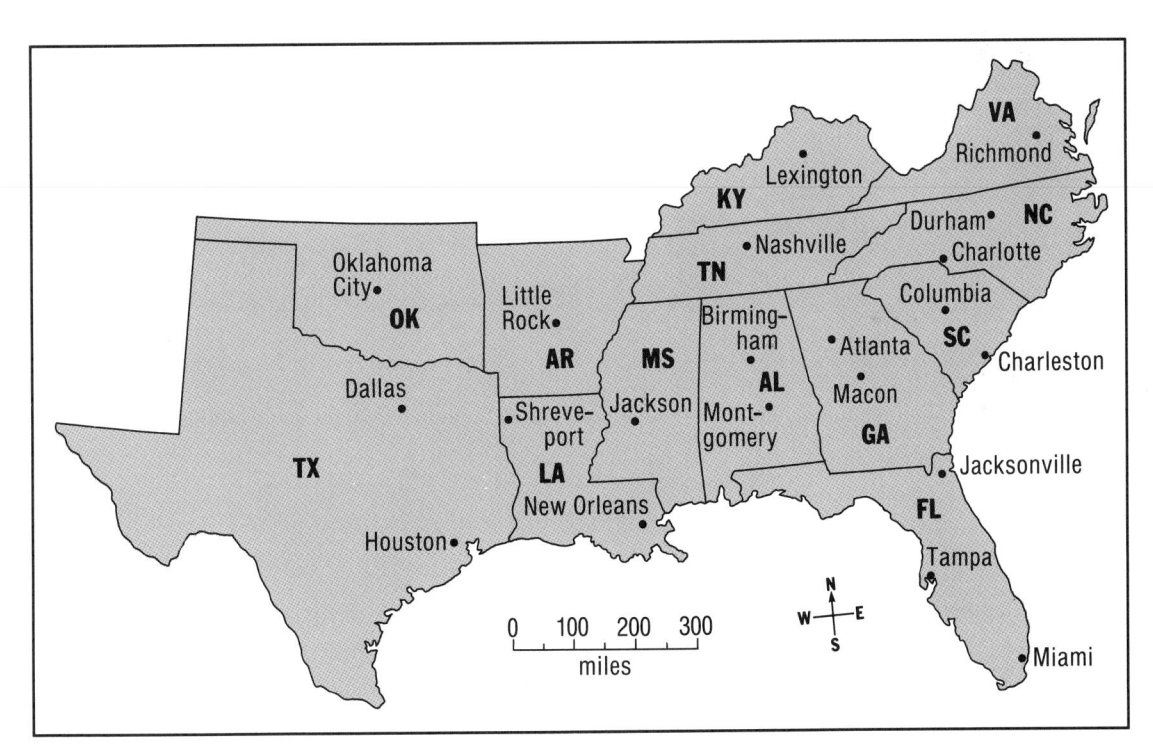

Map Study Find the distance between these cities:
1. Dallas and Houston (TX)
2. Atlanta and Macon (GA)
3. Birmingham (AL) and Charleston (SC)

Chapter 4

Earth Is Always Moving

Stonehenge is a 3,000-year old group of stones in Wiltshire, England. It was probably used as a calendar.

Chapter Learning Objectives

1. Tell why a day is 24 hours long.
2. Explain what causes daytime and nighttime.
3. Tell why a year is 365 days long.
4. Tell why Earth is heated unevenly.
5. Explain how the uneven heating of Earth affects temperatures in different places.

Words To Know

rotate to spin or turn around

planet any of the large bodies in space that circle the sun, such as Mercury, Venus, and Earth

season a time of year, such as summer or winter

average the most common or usual amount; to find the average of two numbers, add them and then divide the sum by two

---

Day follows night, and night follows day. But why? How does the sun's light come and go? Does the sun really rise and set?

Earth Rotates

The sun only *seems* to rise and set. It is Earth's movement, not the sun's, that gives us daytime and nighttime. Earth **rotates**, or spins, all the time. As it rotates, only half the **planet** faces the sun at any time.

In the drawing below, the Western Hemisphere is in daylight. On the other side of the world it is night.

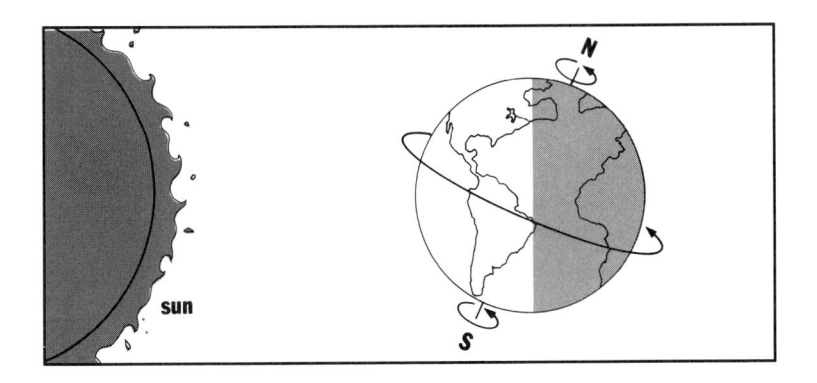

Earth tilts, or leans to one side, as it rotates.

The arrows show the direction in which Earth rotates.

Twelve hours later, Earth has rotated halfway around. Then the Western Hemisphere is in darkness.

Chapter Four **31**

Earth takes 24 hours to turn completely around. That's why we say that one day is 24 hours long.

Next time you see the sun come up or go down, remember this:

- Daytime comes when the part of Earth you are on moves into sunlight.
- Nighttime comes when the part of Earth you are on moves out of the sunlight.

High-Speed Spin

Earth rotates at a speed of more than 1,000 miles per hour. Why don't we feel it moving?

We don't feel Earth moving because we are moving along with it. And so is everything else on and near Earth, including the atmosphere.

Earth Moves Around the Sun

If Earth rotated at a slower speed, Earth's day would be longer.

You know that Earth rotates, or spins, and that it makes one complete turn every 24 hours. Earth moves in another way as well. While it is rotating, it is also moving around the sun. Earth takes 365 days to make a complete trip around the sun.

Earth's movement around the sun is what gives us our year. In the time between January 1 and December 31, Earth travels once around the sun.

Think About It

The further a planet is from the sun, the longer it takes to travel around it.

Mercury is closer to the sun than any other planet. Its year is only 88 Earth days long.

Pluto is the furthest planet from the sun. Pluto takes over 247 of our years to travel all the way around the sun.

Earth Is Heated Unevenly

Earth is heated unevenly as it makes its trip around the sun. Some parts of Earth are always warm. Some are always cold. Some parts have small changes in temperature during the year. Other parts have four different **seasons**. They have hot summers and cold winters. They have warm springs and cool falls.

The main reason for this uneven heating is the way Earth is tilted. The part of Earth that is directly facing the sun receives intense, or strong, rays of sunlight. That part is warm. The part of Earth tilted away from the sun receives less intense, or weaker, rays of sunlight. That part is cooler.

Look at the drawings. They show how light rays are weakened when they shine on a tilted surface.

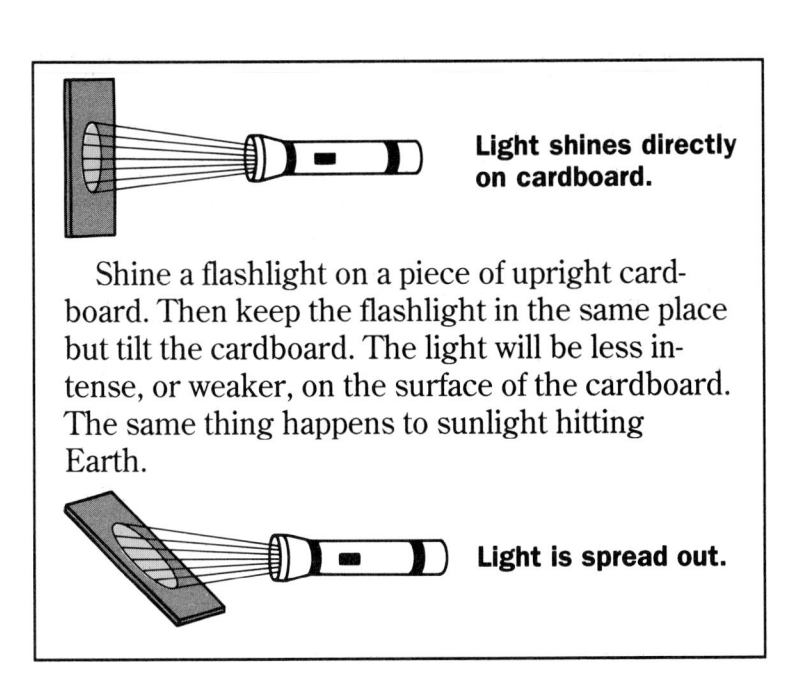

Light shines directly on cardboard.

Shine a flashlight on a piece of upright cardboard. Then keep the flashlight in the same place but tilt the cardboard. The light will be less intense, or weaker, on the surface of the cardboard. The same thing happens to sunlight hitting Earth.

Light is spread out.

Now look at the left side of the drawing on this page. In late June, the Northern Hemisphere is tilted toward the sun. It is getting more intense sunlight than the Southern Hemisphere. Summer is beginning in the Northern Hemisphere. And winter is beginning in the Southern Hemisphere.

Now look at the right side of the drawing. In late December, the Southern Hemisphere is tilted toward the sun. It is getting more intense sunlight than the Northern Hemisphere. Summer is beginning in the Southern Hemisphere. And winter is beginning in the Northern Hemisphere.

Winter and summer, of course, are not the only seasons. From late March to late June, the light that shines on the Northern Hemisphere is becoming more and more intense. The days are getting warmer. It is springtime. In the Southern Hemisphere, it is fall.

From late September to late December, the light that shines on the Northern Hemisphere is becoming less and less intense. The days are getting cooler. It is fall. In the Southern Hemisphere, it is spring.

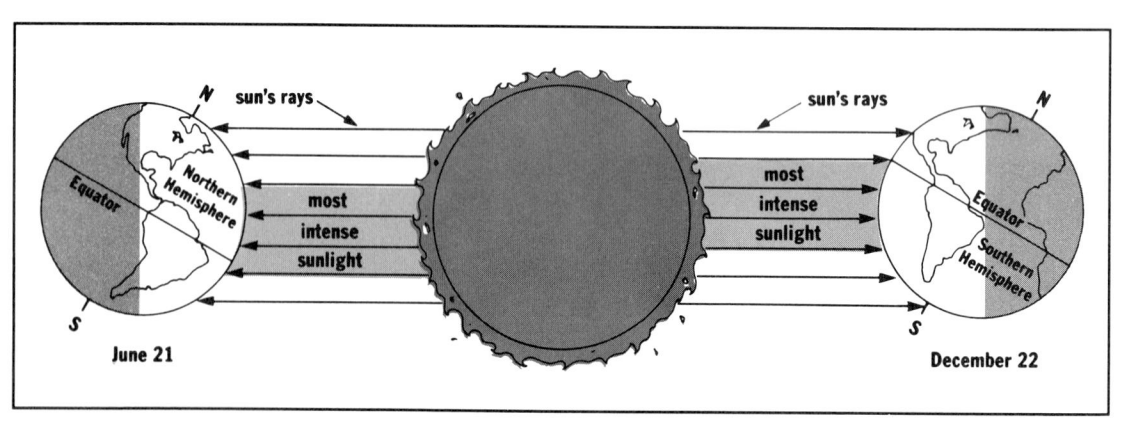

The sunlight over the Northern Hemisphere is most intense between late June and late September. It is least intense between late December and late March.

34 Chapter Four

At the Poles and the Equator

The areas on and near the equator receive intense sunlight all year long. Most places there are warm to hot all year.

The areas near the poles get little or no sunlight for part of the year. And the sunlight during the rest of the year is not very intense. The temperatures are low. It is cool to cold most of the year.

Think About It

Bismarck, North Dakota, for example, is one of the many places in the United States with four different seasons. In the course of a year, this city's temperatures can change quite a bit. Here is a list of Bismarck's **average** temperatures for each month of the year.

January	7°F	July	70°F
February	15°F	August	69°F
March	26°F	September	57°F
April	43°F	October	46°F
May	55°F	November	29°F
June	64°F	December	15°F

Note: The first day of each of the four seasons changes from year to year. In North America, they are as follows.

March 20 or 21: the first day of spring
June 20 or 21: the first day of summer
September 22 or 23: the first day of fall
December 21 or 22: the first day of winter

Your librarian can help you find the average temperatures in your area.

Chapter Four   **35**

Chapter Review

Summary

1. Earth rotates once every 24 hours, the length of a day.

2. At any one time, half of Earth is facing the sun. Earth's rotation causes daytime and nighttime.

3. Earth moves in a direct path around the sun. The trip takes 365 days, the length of a year.

4. Earth is heated unevenly as it moves around the sun. The main reason for this is Earth's tilt.

   - Places on and near the equator get intense sunlight all year. Most places are warm to hot year round.

   - The sunlight that falls on places near the poles is less intense than the sunlight falling anywhere else on earth. Most places there are cool to cold year round.

   - The sunlight that falls on other parts of Earth becomes more intense and less intense during the course of the year. These places have seasons.

Thinking and Writing

Answer these questions in complete sentences on a separate sheet of paper.

1. Why is each day divided into about 12 hours of light and 12 hours of darkness?
2. If Earth rotated at a faster speed than it does, how would the length of our day change?
3. How does a planet's distance from the sun affect the length of a planet's year?
4. How does the intensity, or strength, of the sunlight that falls on a place affect that place's temperature?
5. When summer comes to North America, winter comes to most of South America. Why?
6. Where would you be most likely to find places that do not have four very different seasons?

Questions to Discuss

1. What is really happening when you watch a sunrise or sunset?
2. Suppose Earth did not rotate. How would things on Earth be different?
3. Why do some parts of Earth have seasons?

Special Project

Write a report about seasons. Explain what causes them. Tell how seasons are different from each other. Add drawings, photos, or pictures from magazines to show the changes that take place.

Chapters 1–4

REVIEW

Answer these questions on a separate sheet of paper.

A. Key Words

atmosphere
equator
gravity
hemisphere
mainland
mantle
map scale
plateau
seasons
troposphere

Number your paper from 1 to 10. Then read each clue below. Find the word in the list on the left that matches the clue. Write that word next to the proper number on your paper.

1. The hot and melted rock below Earth's crust
2. A flat area of land high above sea level
3. Times of the year with different weather conditions.
4. The force that holds things down on Earth
5. All of the United States except Hawaii and Alaska
6. All the layers of air above Earth
7. The layer of air closest to Earth
8. One half of Earth
9. A numbered line that helps you tell distance
10. The line on a globe halfway between the poles

B. Key Facts

Number your paper from 11 to 20. Next to each number, write the letter in front of the words that best complete each sentence below.

11. The United States is on the continent of ___ .
    a. Europe   b. North America   c. Africa
12. The two oceans that wash the shores of the United States are the ____ .
    a. Atlantic and Pacific   b. Arctic and Indian   c. Indian and Pacific
13. Equal-area projections are good for showing ____ .
    a. the true shape of all the continents
    b. the relative size of the continents
    c. air routes across the poles

38   Review

14. To show where world events are taking place and how far away they are, newspapers often use ____ .
    a. Mercator projections   b. conic projections   c. orthographic projections
15. The distance from the surface of Earth to its center is about ____ .
    a. 3,200 miles   b. 4,000 miles   c. 13,000 miles
16. The gas in the atmosphere that animals breathe is ____ .
    a. carbon dioxide   b. hydrogen   c. oxygen
17. As you go higher in the atmosphere the air becomes ____ .
    a. dirtier   b. heavier   c. thinner
18. North America is in the ____.
    a. Northern and Western Hemispheres
    b. Eastern and Western Hemispheres
    c. Western and Southern Hemispheres
19. Earth rotates at a speed of more than ____ .
    a. 1,000 mph   b. 4,000 mph   c. 2,300 mph
20. When it is winter in the Northern Hemisphere, in the Southern Hemisphere it is ____ .
    a. fall   b. summer   c. spring

C. Main Ideas

Answer the five questions below.

21. How does the amount of land on Earth compare with the amount of water on Earth?
22. What is the main difference between mountains and plateaus?
23. Tell three things you can learn from globes and maps.
24. Why aren't flat maps always as accurate as globes?
25. What is Earth like beneath its crust?

Chapter 5

Earthquakes, Volcanoes, and Mountains

Some of the damage done by the 1906 San Francisco earthquake.

Chapter Learning Objectives

1. Describe the movement of the plates in Earth's crust.
2. Tell why and how earthquakes occur.
3. Tell why and how volcanoes erupt.
4. Tell how volcanoes build mountains.
5. Describe the formation of folded and block mountains.
6. Use a table to study the occurrence of earthquakes and volcanoes.
7. Use a map to find in-between directions.

Words To Know

earthquake   the shaking of part of Earth's crust caused by breaking or slipping rock within the crust

seismograph   a sensitive machine that records movements within Earth's crust

volcano   a break in Earth's surface through which melted rock flows

magma   the melted rock below Earth's crust

lava   melted rock from inside Earth that flows over the land when a volcano erupts

plate   a huge piece of Earth's crust that moves slowly across the mantle

fault   a deep crack in Earth's crust

Picture yourself shopping in a supermarket. Suddenly the building begins to sway. Apples and oranges roll out of their bins. Cans and jars tumble from the shelves.

What's going on?

It's an **earthquake**.

What Causes Earthquakes?

Earth's crust is made of rocks. Every day, some of these rocks shift or break below Earth's surface. This movement causes earthquakes.

Most earthquakes are too weak for us to feel. But strong earthquakes can destroy buildings, bridges, and highways.

Up, Down, and Sideways

During an earthquake, the ground may move up or down. Or it may move sideways. The movement can shake buildings apart.

When the ground moves down, buildings sink with it. When the ground moves sideways, anything built on it may be torn apart. Part of a fence or highway may be moved away from another part.

We can't tell exactly where or when an earthquake will happen. But scientists have a good idea of where they are *likely* to happen. And scientists are working on ways to tell when they will happen.

The scientists use very sensitive machines to keep track of every earthquake. The machines are called **seismographs**. A seismograph can record even very small movements within Earth's crust.

Volcanoes can release huge amounts of smoke and ash as well as lava.

Think About It
The waves of energy released by an earthquake can travel far and fast. In fact, they can move all the way through to the other side of Earth in 21 minutes. By studying such energy waves, scientists learn about the rocks that the waves pass through.

Volcanoes Release Pressure

Imagine that you are sleeping. Suddenly you are awakened by a loud roar. You rush to a window and look out. Huge flames and great clouds of smoke and ash are rising into the air. Something hot and thick is oozing out over the ground. You are watching the eruption of a **volcano**.

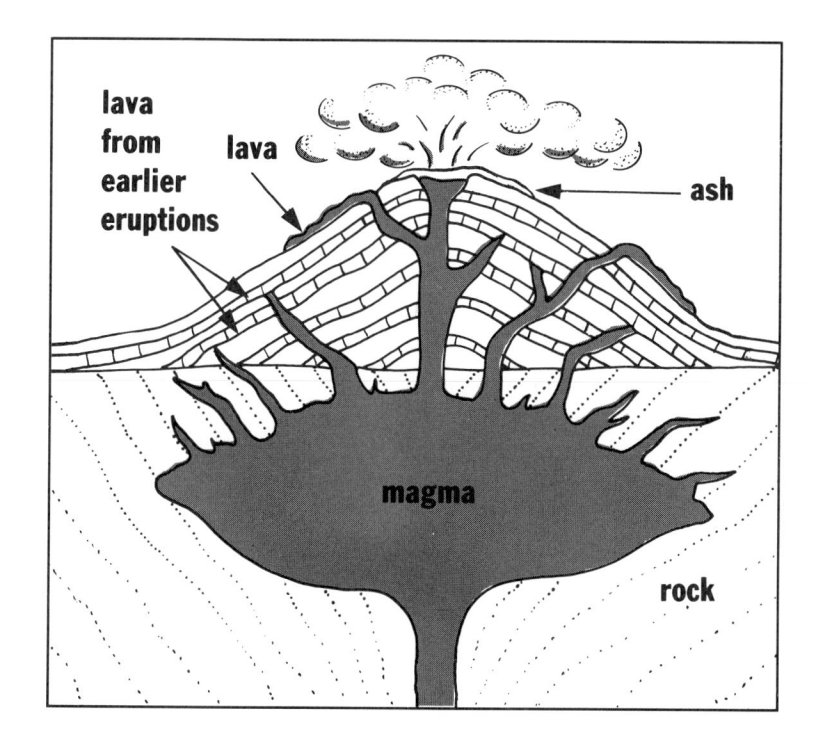

Lava eruption

What Causes Volcanoes?

Remember, part of the mantle, the layer below Earth's crust, is made of super hot melted rock. This rock is called **magma**.

Some of the magma melts openings in the solid rock of the crust above it. Magma rises up through the openings and forms large pools under Earth's surface.

Chapter Five 43

The weight of the solid rock around the pools presses on the magma. This causes the magma either to melt or to blast openings in the weak parts of the rock. The magma then pushes its way through the openings to the surface.

When the magma erupts onto the surface, it flows over the land. If the eruption is a strong one, smoke and ash can rise high into the sky. Winds may carry the ash far away before it falls to the ground.

After magma erupts, we call it **lava**. The lava cools and hardens into solid rock.

Once a volcano starts, it may go on erupting for a long time. Or it may stop erupting and then erupt again many years later.

Volcanoes Build Mountains

What do you think happens when a volcano erupts again and again, building up layers of lava?

Over long periods of time, the layers of hardened lava become mountains. A mountain thousands of feet high may take thousands of years to build.

Mount Saint Helens in Washington began erupting about 40,000 years ago. In 1980 it erupted with such force that it blew away part of its top. The mountain became shorter than it was before the eruption. However, if it keeps on erupting it will build a new top.

Sometimes the magma does not break through the crust. Sometimes it just pushes the crust upward. This action forms dome mountains. The Black Hills of South Dakota are dome mountains.

Volcanoes often erupt below the ocean floor. When that happens, the lava may rise above the water and form islands. Hawaii was formed in this way.

Volcanoes that are continually erupting are called "active volcanoes." Most of the eruptions are not violent. There are 850 active volcanoes in the world today.

Undersea volcanic eruption

Plates and Earthquakes

Slipping and breaking rock in Earth's crust causes earthquakes. But what causes the rocks to slip or break?

Here is what many scientists think is happening.

Scientists say that Earth's crust is made of a number of **plates**. The continents and oceans sit on these plates. And the plates "float" on Earth's mantle.

The plates are always moving. Some plates move toward each other. Some move apart. Some plates scrape past each other.

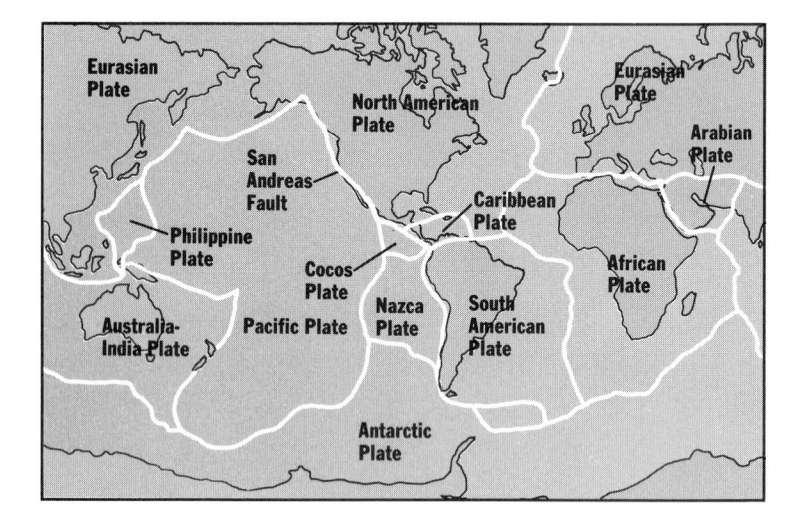

Earth's crust is made of a number of plates. The Pacific Plate is moving northward. This causes many earthquakes along the San Andreas Fault in California.

Scientists are not sure *why* the plates move. But they are quite sure the plates do move. They say the plates move between half an inch and four inches a year.

That may not seem like very much. But over millions of years, this movement causes great changes on Earth's surface.

Plates Put Pressure on Rocks

When two plates scrape past or press against each other for a long time, pressure builds up on the rocks of each plate. The pressure causes rock to suddenly slip or break. And this causes an earthquake.

Most earthquakes happen where there are **faults**, or deep cracks, in Earth's crust. The faults were also caused by the pressure of plate movement.

Most faults lie beneath Earth's surface and can't be seen. But some, such as the 600-mile-long San Andreas Fault in California, can be seen from the air.

The energy released by a major quake is about 10,000 times that of the first atom bomb.

Far below the San Andreas Fault are the edges of the Pacific and the North American plates. The Pacific Plate is slowly moving north of the North American Plate.

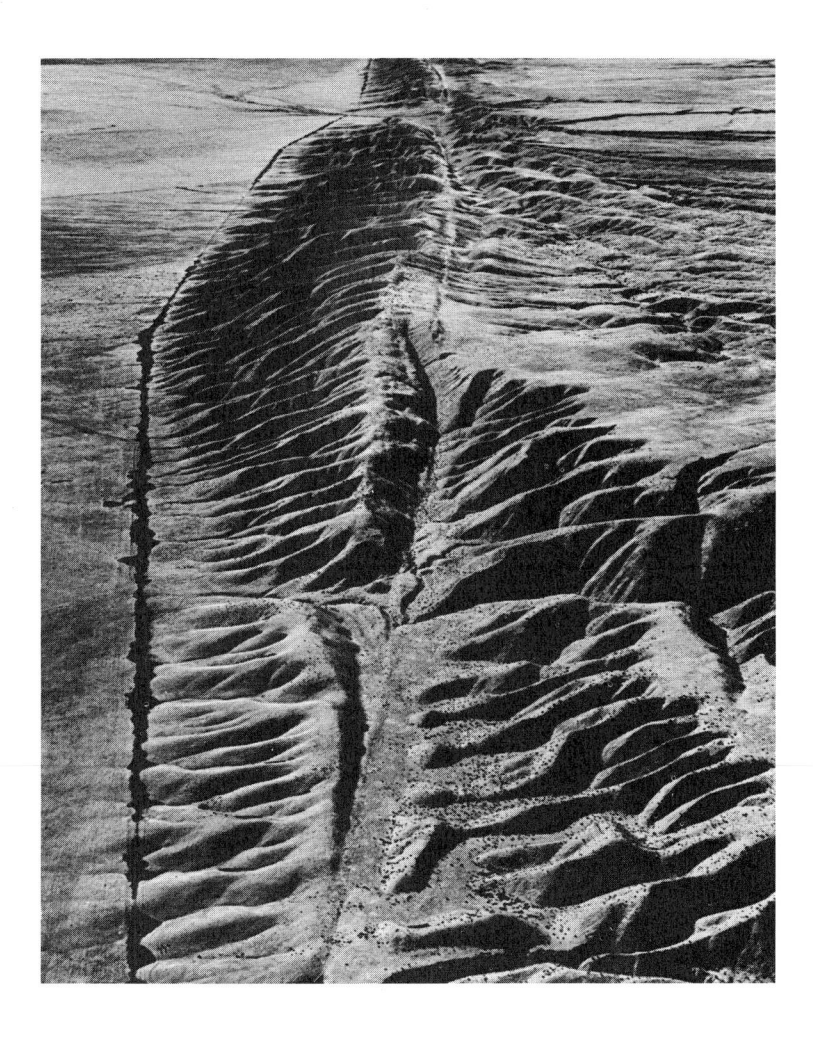

The San Andreas Fault

Part of the California coast sits on the Pacific Plate. What do you think is happening to that part of the coast?

That part of the California coast is moving toward Alaska. It is moving about two inches a year.

There are many earthquakes along the San Andreas and other nearby faults. A 1906 earthquake almost destroyed San Francisco. The Los Angeles area has had some bad earthquakes in recent times. And small earthquakes are felt along the San Andreas Fault every year.

Three Kinds of Mountains

Scientists say there are three main kinds of mountains. They are volcanic, folded, and block mountains.

The Sierra Nevadas

Volcanic Mountains

You have already read about how volcanoes can build mountains. But the first step in starting most volcanoes is plate movement.

When two plates collide, the edge of one may slide under the edge of the other. The lower edge sinks into Earth's hot mantle. Rocks in the sinking edge are melted by the heat and become new magma. The new, lighter magma rises upward. Some of it breaks through Earth's crust. It forms the kind of volcanic mountains you read about earlier.

Some volcanic mountains form under the ocean. This happens when plates carrying parts of the ocean floor move away from each other, leaving an opening in Earth's crust. Magma from the mantle rises up through the opening and becomes lava.

The lava spreads out on the ocean floor and hardens into new crust. Over millions of years, the oceans grow wider. In some places, the lava builds up into underwater mountains. The Mid-Atlantic Ridge is a chain of volcanic mountains that lies under the Atlantic Ocean. The tops of some of the higher mountains rise up above the water as islands.

Folded Mountains

When two plates collide, they press against each other for millions of years. This pressure can cause layers of rock on each plate to bend and fold into mountains and valleys. The high parts are called folded mountains. Scientists believe that the Appalachian Mountains were formed this way.

Mountainous areas are those that are 2,000 or more feet higher than the lands around them.

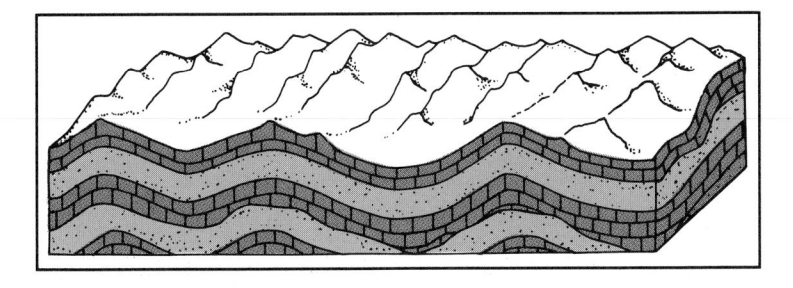

Folded mountains

Block Mountains

Some parts of Earth's crust have many faults. Sometimes, layers of rock between these faults break into huge blocks. Later, some of the blocks get pushed up and form mountains. Scientists believe that the Sierra Nevadas were formed in this way.

Block mountains

Chapter Review

Summary

1. Scientists believe that Earth's crust is made of a number of huge plates. The continents and oceans sit on these plates.

2. The plates move from half an inch to four inches every year. Sometimes the plates collide or scrape past each other. This pressure causes faults, or deep cracks, in Earth's crust. The pressure also causes rocks along the faults to slip or break. This slipping and breaking of rocks causes earthquakes.

3. Sometimes one plate slides under another plate. Rocks in the lower plate melt as the lower plate sinks into Earth's mantle. This adds more magma, or melted rock, to the mantle.

4. The new, lighter magma rises up through Earth's crust. It may erupt and form volcanoes and volcanic mountains, both on land and in the oceans. Or it may push the crust upward and form dome mountains.

5. Movement in Earth's crust also leads to the formation of folded mountains and block mountains.

Thinking and Writing

Answer these questions in complete sentences on a separate sheet of paper.

1. In terms of how they begin, how are earthquakes, volcanoes, and faults alike?
2. How does lava differ from magma?
3. Tell one way the San Andreas Fault differs from other faults.
4. Why is part of the California coastline slowly moving north?
5. How is the Mid-Atlantic Ridge like the Hawaiian islands?
6. How do the Sierra Nevada mountains differ from the Appalachians?

Questions to Discuss

1. What is an earthquake and what causes it?
2. What is a volcano and what causes it?
3. How is each of these kinds of mountains formed?
    - volcanic
    - folded
    - block
4. How do you think earthquakes and volcanoes affect people's lives?

Special Projects

1. Ask your librarian to help you find newspaper and magazine stories about earthquakes and volcanoes that have taken place in recent years. Write a report or tell the class about one or more of these events.
2. Do you live on or near a mountain? If so, find out how the mountain was formed.

Geography Skills 6

Reading a Table

Strong Earthquakes in North America 1964–1987

Year	Place	Strength
1964	Alaska	8.5
1971	California	6.5
1976	Guatemala	7.5
1985	Mexico City	8.1
1987	California	6.6
1987	Alaska	7.4

Table 1

Some Eruptions of U.S. Volcanoes 1984–1986

Year	Volcano	State
1984	Mauna Loa	Hawaii
1984	Veniaminof	Alaska
1984	Pavlof	Alaska
1980	Mount Saint Helens	Washington
1986	Kilauea	Hawaii
1986	Augustine	Alaska

Table 2

Tables often give useful information. Table 1 gives facts about some North American earthquakes. This table also shows how strong each earthquake was. Earthquakes are measured on a scale of one to ten. An earthquake measuring six or more can destroy buildings and roads. An earthquake measuring eight or more can destroy large parts of a city. Table 2 gives facts about some U.S. volcanoes.

Table Study
1. Which country had a 7.5 earthquake in 1976?
2. Which two earthquakes were the strongest?
3. In which two states did volcanoes erupt in 1986?

Geography Skills 7

Finding In-Between Directions

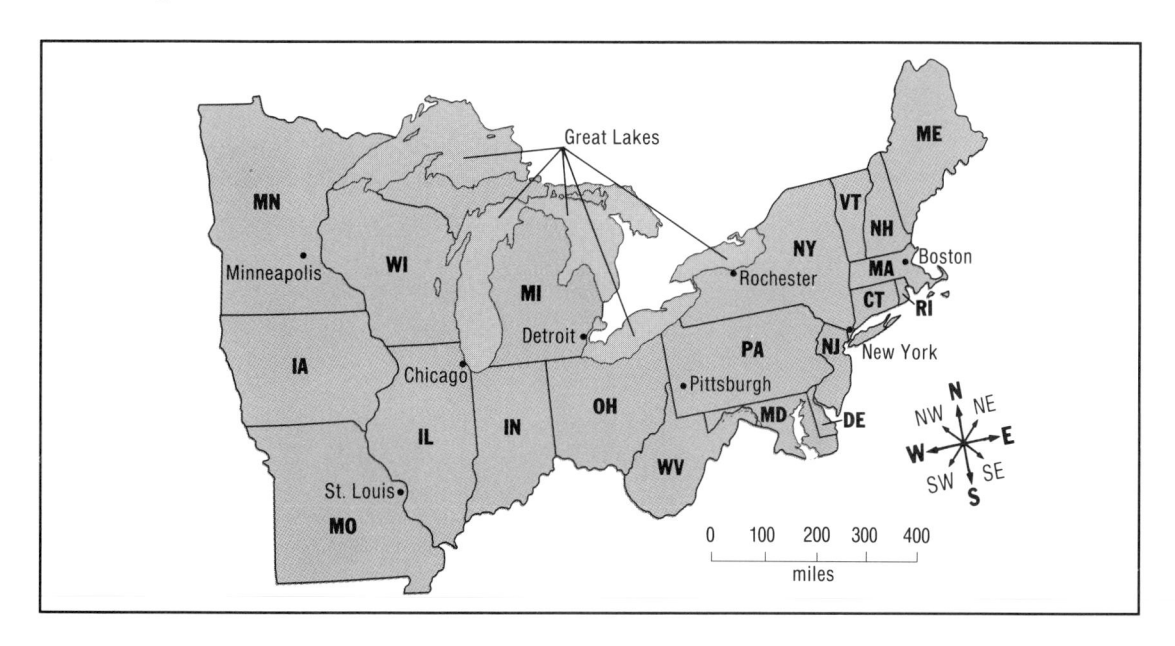

We do not always move directly north, south, east, or west. Sometimes we move in a direction that is in between these directions. Look at the map above. Find St. Louis, Missouri, and Chicago, Illinois. If you were to fly from St. Louis to Chicago, you would be flying both north and east. That is, you would be flying northeast.

The map's compass rose can help you figure out in-between directions. Here is what the in-between letters stand for:

NE: northeast   NW: northwest
SE: southeast   SW: southwest

Map Study In which direction would you fly from:
1. Chicago (IL) to St. Louis (MO)?
2. Minneapolis (MN) to Chicago (IL)?
3. Pittsburg (PA) to Detroit (MI)?
4. New York (NY) to Boston (MA)?

Chapter Five 53

Chapter 6
Other Forces That Change Earth

The power of moving water is one of the strongest forces on Earth.

Chapter Learning Objectives
1. Tell five ways in which water can weather or erode rock.
2. Tell how rivers can change the shape of the land.
3. Describe wind erosion.
4. Explain how glaciers can change the shape of the land.
5. Tell four ways people can cause erosion.

Words To Know

weathering the softening and wearing away of rock

erosion the carrying away of weathered rock

soil very fine bits of weathered rock mixed with living matter and the remains of plants and animals

sediment the loose rocks, stones, sand, and soil carried away by streams and rivers

delta islands and sandbars made from sediment dropped by a river

canyon a deep valley with very steep walls, such as the Grand Canyon

desert a barren, often sandy, area of land that receives very little rain

dune a hill of sand

glacier a very large moving body of ice and snow

fuel material that is burned to provide energy

mineral a usable substance, such as coal, oil, or iron, that is found in Earth's crust

You know how plate action and volcanoes help build mountains. Other forces wear down those mountains and make other changes on Earth's surface. These forces include water, wind, ice, and people.

Wearing Down Rock

Mountains are made of different kinds of rock. Some of these rocks are harder than others. But in time all can be softened and broken up. This is called **weathering**. It goes on above and below ground.

Some weathering is caused by the action of chemicals on the rock. The chemicals are in rain water that both runs off and seeps down into the ground. The chemicals are also in streams and rivers that flow over rocks.

The chemicals weaken or soften the rocks. Some rocks break apart. Some dissolve in the water.

Rocks are worn down in other ways, too. Steady, heavy rains wear holes in softer rocks. The rocks begin to break apart.

Sometimes rain fills cracks in rocks. During cold weather, the rainwater freezes. Freezing water expands, cracking the rocks apart.

Water Erosion

Streams break down weathered rock and then carry it away. This is called water **erosion**. Erosion is the carrying away of weathered rock. Fast-moving water slams one rock into another. Rocks are broken down into stones and stones into sand.

Streams twist and turn and wear away **soil** from their banks. Soil is very fine bits of weathered rock mixed with living matter and the remains of plants and animals. The rock, stones, sand, and soil carried by streams are called **sediment**. The streams run into rivers, carrying the sediment with them. Rivers flow across the land and they, too, wear away sand and soil and gather sediment.

When a river reaches flatter land, it slows down. The sediment begins to drop out. First, the heavy rocks fall. Then the stones, sand, and soil drop out.

Some sediment builds up new river banks. Some build sandbars and even islands. An area with a number of islands built from sediment is called a **delta**.

Most river sediment is carried out to the ocean. There it sinks to the ocean floor.

In time, weathering and erosion can greatly change the shape of the land.

Wearing Down Plateaus

Water also erodes plateaus. Rocks become weathered and broken down by rivers that carry them away.

The Grand **Canyon** in Arizona is an example of this. Over millions of years, the Colorado River has

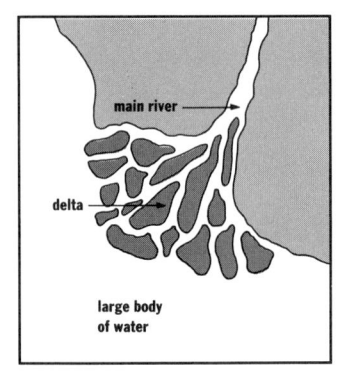

Deltas often form where a river flows into a lake or ocean.

The Grand Canyon carved out steep valleys in the Colorado Plateau. The valleys are a mile deep in some places.

Wave Erosion

Every day, waves full of sand and stone pound against ocean shores. Where there are high cliffs, the waves can break away pieces of the cliffs and cut out caves at the bottom of them. This weakens the cliffs. Sometimes large parts of them fall away into the ocean.

Waves also wear rock down into sand, making sandy beaches. Sand can come from the sediment brought down by rivers, too.

When water from a breaking wave rolls up onto a beach, it carries some sand with it. When the water rolls back, it takes some sand away. If the amount of sand taken away is the same as the amount brought in, the beach remains about the same size.

But during winter storms, the waves are larger than usual. They wash away more sand than they bring in. In time, a beach may be washed away.

In the summertime, gentle waves leave more sand than they take away. That's why beaches look wider in summer.

A very strong storm can destroy an entire beach and everything that is built along it.

Wind Erosion

Wind, too, can erode parts of Earth. In farmlands, wind blows away soil that has been loosened by plowing and dry weather. In **desert** and beach areas wind blows the loose sand around. It builds and moves sand **dunes**.

Fine bits of soil can be moved by even light winds. Strong winds remove far more soil. In some places, huge dust storms may blacken the daytime sky.

The soil may fall back to Earth far from where it was picked up. Over thousands of years, deep layers of wind-carried soil may form where the wind has carried it.

Much of America's corn is grown in wind-carried soil on the plains of Kansas, Iowa, and Illinois. Wheat is grown on wind-carried soil in Kansas, Nebraska, and Washington.

Erosion by Glaciers

Thousands of years ago, the temperatures in some places were much lower than they are today. In most of northern Asia, Europe, and North America, the snow didn't melt even in the summer. The same was true for the snow in high mountain areas elsewhere on Earth.

This buildup of snow took place during what is known as the last Ice Age.

Layers of snow built up over thousands of years. Tons of snow pressed down on the lower layers. These lower layers turned to ice, and then the huge bodies of ice and snow began to move. We call these bodies of ice and snow **glaciers**.

Some of the glaciers moved *very* slowly. Some moved as much as 30 feet a day. As they moved, they scraped or pushed at the rock and soil.

Glaciers that moved down mountains scraped away the sides of the mountains. They widened valleys.

Most glaciers carried big rocks and great amounts of soil with them. As the rocks moved they sometimes scooped out great chunks of land.

When the glaciers began to melt, they often left hills of rock and soil behind them. Water from the melting glaciers filled some of the scooped-out places and formed lakes. The Great Lakes were made in this way. In some places, the land was rubbed smooth by the passing glaciers.

Glaciers still form where snow does not melt from year to year. There are glaciers in the states of Montana, Washington, and Alaska. Glaciers are also found near the North and South poles and in South America, Europe, and New Zealand.

Most glaciers are between 300 and 10,000 feet thick.

A glacier in Alaska

Seeing It for Yourself

Today, most of Greenland and all of Antarctica lie under glaciers. But if you'd like to see a glacier close up, you don't have to travel quite so far.

Glacier National Park in northern Montana contains more than 50 glaciers. There are also beautiful lakes and mountains in the park.

In Washington, there are glaciers in the national park surrounding Mount Rainier.

If you live in or travel to Alaska, you can visit Glacier Bay National Park. Also in Alaska is Malaspina, the largest glacier in North America.

For free information on national parks in the United States, write to this address:

    Office of Public Affairs
    National Park Service, Room 3043
    Department of the Interior
    Washington, D.C. 20240

Erosion by People

Tree cutting, overuse of the soil, strip mining, and building roads and houses on hillsides are some of the ways people cause erosion.

We've been cutting down trees for thousands of years. We do it to clear the land for building and farming. We do it to get wood for **fuel** and for lumber and other wood products.

What do you think happens to a hillside when all its trees are cut down?

Trees break the force of raindrops. Fallen leaves soak up much of the water from rainfall and melting snow. So do the roots of trees. When the trees are cut down, there is nothing left to soak up the water. The soil turns to mud that may slide downhill. Sometimes houses and other buildings slide down with the mud.

Today, many logging companies plant new trees to replace the ones they've cut down.

Sometimes, farmers cause erosion when they overuse the soil. Planting the same crop year after year can wear out the soil so that crops can't grow in it. Then, in dry, windy weather, the soil may blow away because there are no plants to hold it in place.

Today, most farmers plant different crops from time to time so the soil won't wear out. Or they grow grass, clover, or other nonfood plants on part of their land for awhile. This helps preserve the soil.

Mining companies often cause erosion. They strip away land to get at coal, iron, and other **minerals** buried in the ground. This leaves bare rock and big holes.

Today, some mining companies replace and replant the soil in areas that they've mined.

In Chapter 14, you will read more about what can be done to keep the planet healthy.

Building on a hillside decreases the plantlife on that hillside. This decreases the amounts of soil and water the hillside can hold.

Chapter Six **61**

Chapter Review

Summary

1. Water can weather and erode rock:
   - Chemicals in the water weaken, soften, and dissolve rock.
   - Heavy rain makes holes in some kinds of rock.
   - Water freezes in cracks and expands, breaking the rock apart.
   - Streams break up rock and carry it away.
   - Waves wear down rock and wash away beaches.
2. Rivers form new banks, sandbars, and islands from the sediment they carry.
3. Wind blows away loose sand and soil. It builds sand dunes and moves soil to new places.
4. Glaciers can widen valleys and scoop out lake beds. They may leave behind hills of rock and soil. They may also smooth out the land.
5. People can cause erosion when they cut down trees, overuse the soil, mine, and choose poor building sites.

Thinking and Writing

Answer these questions on a separate sheet of paper.

1. Why might a winter rain lead to the breaking up of more rock than a summer rain?
2. How does erosion differ from weathering?
3. What is the difference between soil and weathered rock?
4. Why would you be unlikely to find soil full of large rocks on a delta island?
5. What does corn grown in Iowa have in common with wheat grown in Nebraska?
6. The last Ice Age took place many thousands of years ago. Yet there are still large glaciers in the world. Why?

Questions to Discuss

1. What are some ways that each of the following can change the land?
   - water
   - wind
   - glaciers
   - people
2. Think about where you live and the areas nearby. How have water, wind, and people affected landforms there? What changes are they making now?

Special Projects

1. Imagine you are a million years old. Tell a story about how your favorite mountain was formed and how it was worn down by weathering and erosion.
2. Find out about the last Ice Age, when glaciers covered much of North America. Report to the class.

Chapter 7
Landforms of the United States

Ship Rock is on the Colorado Plateau in New Mexico.

Chapter Learning Objectives
1. Describe the landforms of Hawaii and Alaska.
2. Describe the major landforms along the Pacific Coast of the United States.
3. Read a landform map.
4. Describe the landforms between the mountains of the Pacific Coast and the Rocky Mountains.
5. Describe the Rocky Mountains and the lowlands between them.
6. Explain how the central United States differs from the western United States.
7. Describe the Ozark-Ouachita and the Appalachian Highlands.
8. Describe the lowlands along the Atlantic and Gulf Coasts.

Words To Know

region a group of places that have one or more things that are alike
range a row or line of mountains; a large group of mountains
basin a wide area of land that dips downward from nearby mountains and plateaus
inlet any body of sea water that extends inland from the sea
interior the inland or central part of a country
pass a low gap, or opening, in a mountain range
gorge a narrow canyon
peak the highest part of a mountain
swamp an area of soft wet land

Suppose you could fly over the entire United States. What kind of landforms would you see below you?

You would see high snow-covered mountains and wide green valleys. You would see deep red canyons and broad grassy plains. You would see rocky coastlines and white sandy beaches.

The United States has eight major landform **regions**. A region is a group of places that are similar to each other in one or more ways. Moving from west to east, the eight landform regions of the United States are:

- Hawaii and Alaska
- Pacific **Ranges** and Lowlands
- Western Plateaus, **Basins**, and Ranges
- Rocky Mountains
- Interior Plains
- Ozark-Ouachita Highlands
- Appalachian Highlands
- Coastal Lowlands

In this chapter, you will learn what makes each region different from the others. The maps in this chapter will help you form a picture of the whole United States.

Hawaii and Alaska

Hawaii

The state of Hawaii is made up of eight islands. The largest island is also called Hawaii. The islands have a number of volcanic mountains, the highest being Mauna Kea. Mauna Kea is on the island of Hawaii. It rises 13,796 feet above sea level.

Between the mountains there are many green valleys. Around the edges of the islands there are many beaches. Some of them have black sand that was made from weathered lava.

Alaska

Most of Alaska's surface is covered by two mountain ranges—the Brooks Range and the Alaska Range. The wide Yukon River Valley divides these two groups of mountains.

Mount McKinley's height is equal to the length of about 80 city blocks.

The highest mountain in North America, Mount McKinley, is found in the Alaska Range. Mount McKinley rises 20,320 feet above sea level. That's almost four miles high!

Alaska has a very long coastline broken by many inlets and bays. North of the Brooks Range there is a wide coastal plain. The southern coast has many steep cliffs. A peninsula and a long chain of islands jut out into the Pacific Ocean. As in Hawaii, many of these islands have active volcanoes.

Pacific Ranges and Lowlands

Three mountain ranges cover most of the Pacific Coast States. They are the Coast, Cascade, and Sierra Nevada Ranges. Some of the mountains in the Coast Range rise straight up from the sea. In other places there are coastal plains with sandy beaches between the mountains and the ocean.

Big Sur, in northern California, is part of the Coast Range.

The other two ranges are further inland. The Cascades are volcanic mountains. Mount Saint Helens, which you read about in Chapter 5, is one of them.

The other range, called the Sierra Nevada, contains the highest mountain on the U.S. mainland. It is Mount Whitney, which rises 14,495 feet above sea level.

Between the coastal and inland mountain ranges there are long, wide valleys. The largest of these is the Central Valley of California. It is about 40 miles wide and 400 miles long.

The long coastline of the western United States is broken in places by deep bays and other **inlets** from the sea. These include Puget Sound, San Francisco Bay, and San Diego Bay.

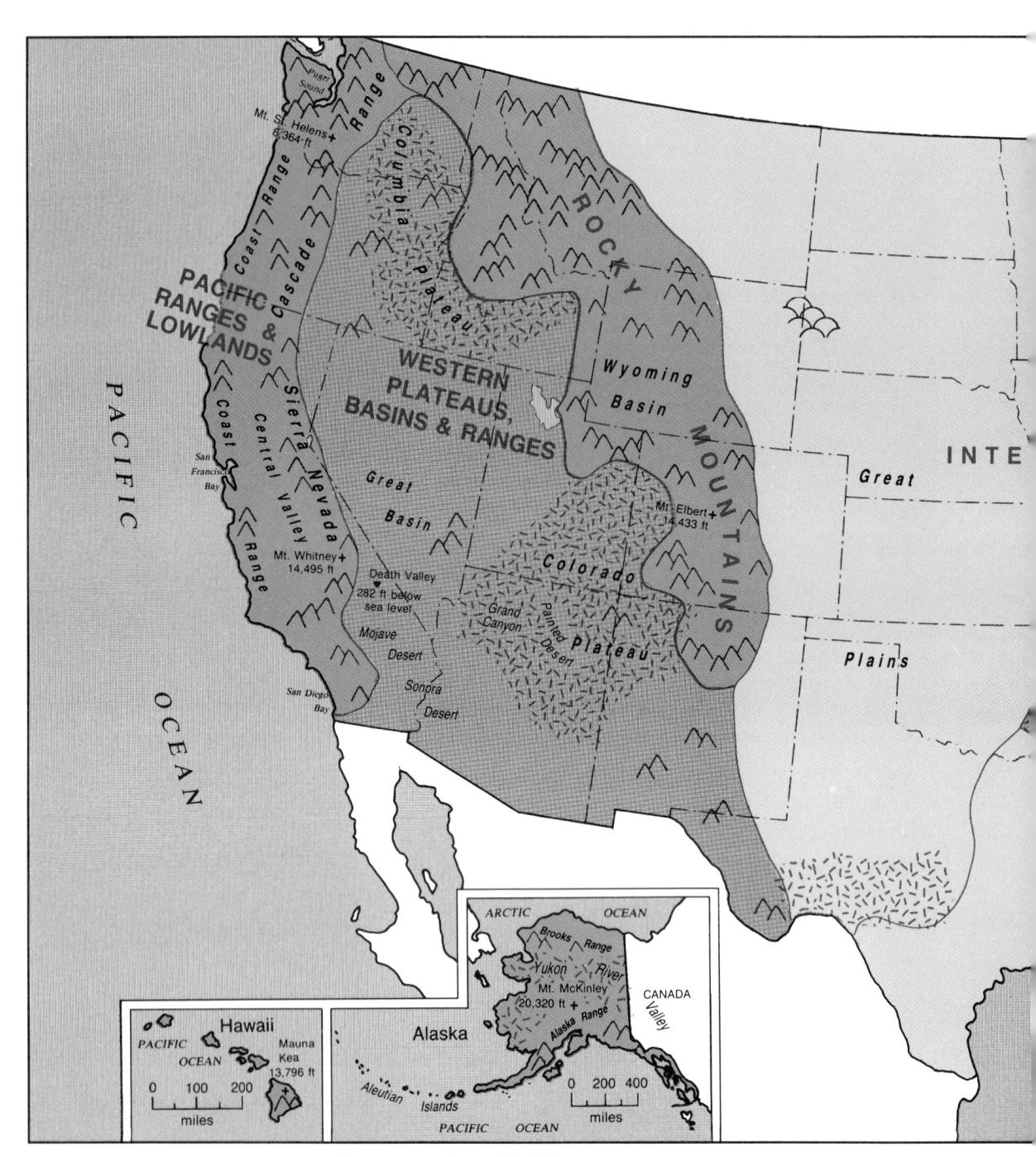

Geography Skills 8
Reading a Landform Map

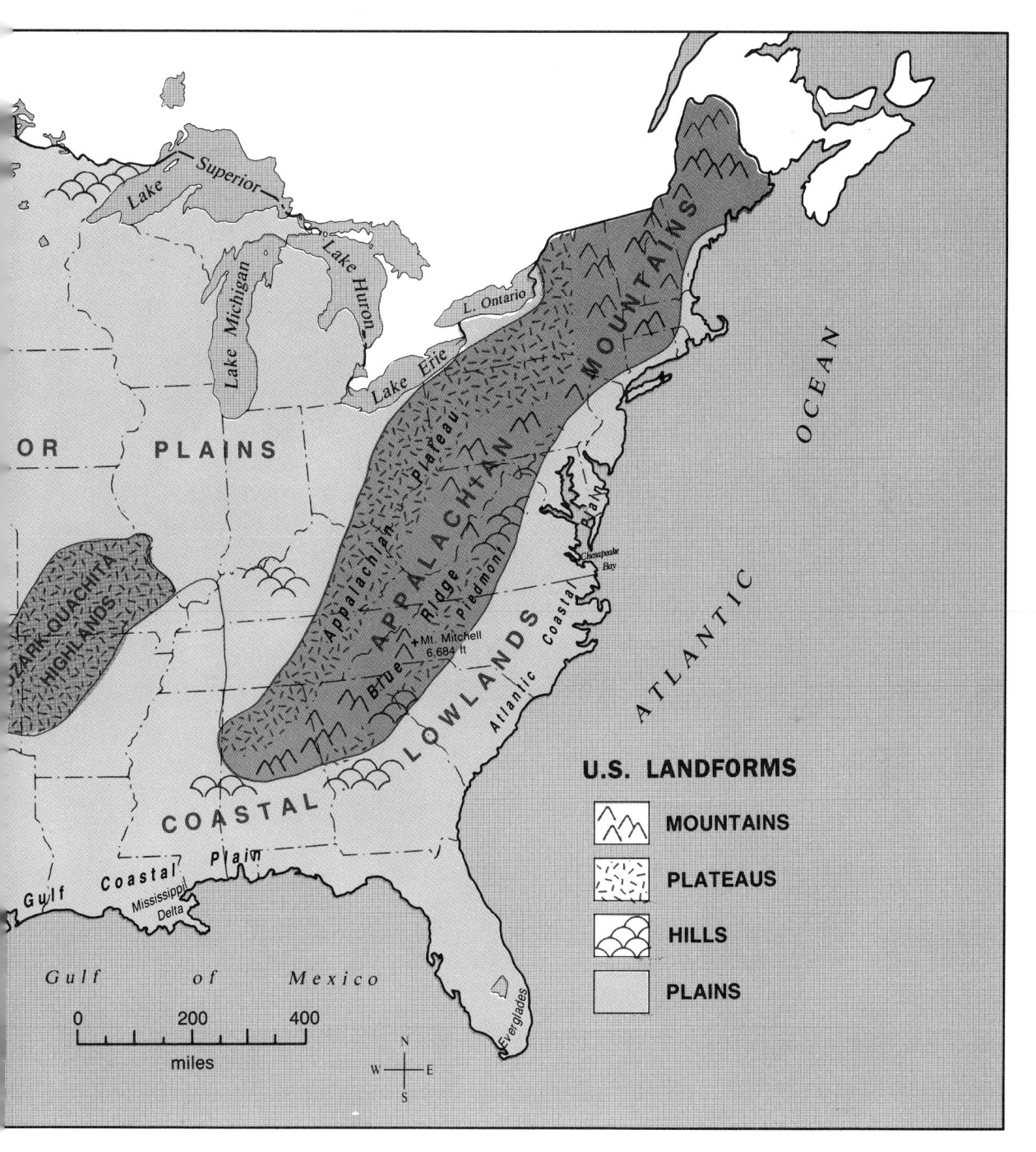

Map Study
1. Which basin forms a pass between the Rocky Mountains?
2. Is most of the **Interior** Plains mountainous or flat?

Western Plateaus, Basins, and Ranges

East of the Pacific Coast Ranges is a region of high plateaus, low basins, and mountains. The region extends from Washington, south to Mexico. A basin is a wide area of land that dips downward from nearby mountains and plateaus.

The Columbia Plateau is in the northern part of the region. It was formed thousands of years ago when hot lava seeped out of cracks in Earth's crust. Since then, streams have cut many deep canyons into the land.

The Colorado Plateau is in the southern part of the region. Long ago it was pushed up higher than the lands around it by forces below Earth's crust. The plateau has many strange landforms, including the deep canyons you read about in Chapter 6. Besides the canyons, there are natural bridges, arches of solid rock, and flat-topped rock formations.

Between the two plateaus there is a huge area of basins. Among them is the Great Basin. In the basins there are both desert lowlands and mountains. The lowest place in the United States is in the Great Basin. It is called Death Valley, and it is 282 feet *below* sea level.

In the state of Colorado, the Colorado Plateau takes up about a fifth of the land area.

Rocky Mountains

The Rocky Mountain Range begins in Alaska. It continues through Canada and runs all the way south to New Mexico. Most of the mountains in the range are high and rugged.

Some of the highest **peaks** of the range are in Colorado. A peak is the highest part of a mountain. Many of the peaks rise more than 14,000 feet.

Valleys of many sizes and shapes lie between the mountains. There are also some large basin areas. The Wyoming Basin forms a wide **pass** between the northern and southern parts of the Rockies. A pass is a gap, or opening, in a mountain range. Some trains cross the region through this pass. Trains and autos also travel through other passes and through tunnels cut into the mountains.

Strange Southwestern Landforms

Arizona. *Meteor Crater* is 4,150 feet wide and 570 feet deep. It was dug out by a huge object from space that hit Earth long ago.

Oak Creek Canyon, near Sedona, has beautiful red rock formations.

The *Painted Desert* has colorful rock and sand stretching 200 miles along the Little Colorado River.

Colorado. The *Garden of the Gods* is a beautiful cluster of huge sandstone rocks. Thousands of people gather there for sunrise services on Easter Sunday. It is near Colorado Springs.

Red Rocks Park, near Denver, is an open-air theater seating 9,000 people at concerts and stage shows. Around the park are huge red rocks that help keep in the sound.

Royal Gorge is a deep canyon cut by the Arkansas River. It is crossed by a bridge 1,053 feet above the water. Trains run on tracks built along the sides of the gorge. The tracks provide a water-level route through part of the Rockies. The gorge is near Canon City.

New Mexico. The *Carlsbad Caverns*, in the southwestern part of New Mexico, are gigantic caves with fantastic rock formations. Every evening, tens of thousands of bats fly out of the caves in search of food. At dawn, they return.

Pueblo Benito is a 500-room apartment house built by Native Americans on the side of a cliff. It is near the town of Farmington.

Interior Plains

Almost 1,000 miles of flat or gently rolling land lie between the western and eastern mountains of the United States. This is the Interior Plains.

The western part of the region is called the Great Plains. It starts off as low plateaus and hills and then levels off into flat land. The flat lands extend to the Great Lakes area, where there are rolling hills.

Herds of wild buffalo once roamed freely on the Great Plains. Today the area is covered mostly by ranches and wheat farms.

As you read in Chapter 5, glaciers carved out the Great Lakes and thousands of smaller lakes.

Ozark-Ouachita Highlands

East of the flat plains of Oklahoma is a small range of high, rugged hills. This area is called the Ozark-Ouachita Highlands. Rivers have cut many deep canyons into the highlands. There are also many underground caves. They include the Blanchard **Caverns** in Arkansas, which are among the largest caves in the United States.

Appalachian Highlands

After you cross the Ozark-Ouachita Highlands, the land is mostly low and flat again. But soon you reach the Appalachian Highlands, which include the Appalachian Mountains.

The low mountains of this region run from Alabama all the way north to Canada. The highest of them, Mount Mitchell, rises 6,684 feet above sea level.

How does the height of the Appalachians compare with the height of the Rockies?

Getting across the Appalachian Highlands is a problem. But in a number of places rivers have cut gaps in the mountains and leveled the land. Daniel Boone led early settlers through the Cumberland Gap to Kentucky. In later times, roads and railroads were built in the Cumberland and other gaps.

The southern part of the Appalachian Highlands includes the Blue Ridge Mountains. They are among the oldest mountains in the country. The tops of many are well worn and rounded.

Coastal Lowlands

The Coastal Lowlands extend along the Atlantic and Gulf Coasts from Maine to Texas. They include the Atlantic Coastal Plain and the Gulf Coastal Plain.

A swamp in Florida's Everglades

In Maine and New Hampshire the region is only about 10 miles wide. In other places it forms a wide belt of land which includes all of Florida.

The highest part of the region is called the Piedmont. The Piedmont is an area of rolling hills to the east of the Blue Ridge Mountains. It reaches from New York to Alabama.

Most of the coastal lands rise less than 100 feet above sea level. In many places they are only a few feet high.

Hundreds of sandy beaches line the shores of the coastal plains. Offshore there are hundreds of small islands.

Thousands of years ago, much of the coastal plains were covered by water. Today, some of the land is still covered by **swamps**. A swamp is an area of soft land that is always wet.

One of the largest swamps in the United States is found in southern Florida. It is called the Everglades. The area is home to thousands of alligators and colorful birds.

The coastal plains also include delta lands. The Mississippi Delta is the largest of these.

Chapter Review

Summary

1. Hawaii's eight islands have many volcanic mountains. At 13,796 feet, Mauna Kea is the highest of these. Most of Alaska is covered by two large ranges of mountains—the Brooks and the Alaska Ranges. Mount McKinley is the highest mountain in North America. It is 20,320 feet high and is part of the Alaska Range.

2. The Coast, Cascade, and Sierra Nevada Ranges cover most of the Pacific Range and Lowlands region. Between the ranges there are large valleys. The region's mostly mountainous coastline has hundreds of sandy beaches.

3. The Columbia Plateau is a high area formed by lava that seeped up through cracks in Earth's crust. The Colorado Plateau is land that was uplifted by forces below the crust. Streams have dug out deep canyons in both plateaus. Between the plateaus are low basin lands with deserts and mountains.

4. The Rockies are high, rugged mountains that run all the way from Alaska to New Mexico. The region has many valleys of different sizes and shapes. The Wyoming Basin forms a wide pass between the northern and southern Rockies.

5. The Interior Plains are about 1,000 miles wide. They contain mostly flat or gently rolling land.

6. The Ozark-Ouachita Highlands are high rugged hills with canyons and caves. The Appalachian Highlands run from Alabama north to Maine. They are lower than the mountains in the western part of the United States. They include the country's oldest mountains.

7. The Coastal Lowlands include the rolling hills of the Piedmont and the mostly flat lands of the Coastal Plains. The Coastal Plains include beaches, swamps, deltas, and offshore islands.

Thinking and Writing

Answer these questions in complete sentences on a separate sheet of paper.

1. Tell one way in which the landforms of Hawaii and Alaska are alike and one way in which they are different.
2. In what way are the mountains of the Cascade Range similar to the mountains of Hawaii?
3. How does the way the Columbia Plateau was formed differ from the way the Colorado Plateau was formed?
4. Tell one way the Blue Ridge Mountains differ from the Rockies.
5. What makes the Interior Plains different from the lands east and west of it?
6. Look carefully at all the coastal lands in the map on pages 68–69. How do the lands along the Pacific Coast differ from most of the lands along the Atlantic and Gulf Coasts?

Questions to Discuss

1. What kinds of problems do mountains present for traveling and moving goods? What are some ways people and goods get across the Rocky Mountains and the Appalachian Highlands?
2. Many more people live on the Interior Plains and the Coastal Lowlands than in the mountain regions of the United States. Why do you think this is so?

Special Project

Write or tape record a story about an auto trip across the United States. Describe the changes as you move from one landform to another.

Chapter 8
Oceans, Lakes, and Rivers

The Sacramento Delta

Chapter Learning Objectives
1. Tell why sea water can't be used for drinking or for watering crops.
2. Explain what waves, tides, and currents are.
3. Describe what the ocean floor is like.
4. Describe life in the sea.
5. Describe the Mississippi River system.
6. Tell how ships are able to sail between the Great Lakes and out to sea.

Words To Know

continental shelf land at the edge of a continent that gently slopes beneath the ocean

tsunami a fast moving wave started by an earthquake or a volcanic eruption

tide the rise and fall of the surface of the sea. It is caused by the pull of the moon's and the sun's gravity.

current a part of a large body of water that moves in a particular direction

source the place where a river begins

mouth the place where a river flows into a larger body of water

tributary a river or stream that flows into a larger river or stream

barge a flat-bottomed boat used to carry heavy loads, such as coal or oil

electricity a form of power used to make light and heat and to run machines

irrigation the use of water from a river or well to raise crops

canal an inland waterway that has been dug by people rather than by nature

lock the part of a canal used to raise or lower ships from one height to another

ore rock that contains metals such as iron, copper, or gold

port a city where ships pick up and deliver goods

As you read in Chapter 1, about two-thirds of Earth's surface is covered by water. This includes oceans, lakes, and rivers. In this chapter, you will learn more about these bodies of water.

Water has played an important part in the growth of the United States. Long ago, Native Americans used the rivers and lakes for traveling long distances. Later, explorers and settlers crossed the Atlantic Ocean from Europe. They too used the rivers and lakes to travel inland.

Besides providing a means for travel, the oceans, rivers, and lakes also provided food. Fish and shellfish were plentiful. Later, streams and rivers provided power to run machines. Oceans, lakes, and rivers are still providing us with food, water power, and ways of moving people and goods.

The Oceans Are One Big Salty Sea

Turn to the maps of the Northern and Southern Hemispheres on page 27. Look at the water areas in each hemisphere. Notice that the water spreads out over the globe and forms one world ocean.

What we call the Atlantic, Pacific, Indian, and Arctic Oceans are really just parts of this one giant ocean. And when we talk about seas, gulfs, and bays, we are talking about smaller parts of this giant ocean. However, the word *sea* is also used to mean any large body of salt water other than a lake.

All sea water is salty. Most of the salt in the water is similar to table salt.

Have you ever tried floating in both fresh water and salt water? If so, you know it is easier to float in salt water. The salt helps to hold you up.

Because of the salt, sea water is unfit to drink or to be used for watering crops. Ways have been found to remove the salt, but it is very costly to do so.

Beneath the Sea

What do you think the bottom of the sea is like? Is it flat like a plain or rugged like a mountain range?

It is both. The bottom of the sea is like the surface of the continents. It has mountains, plains, and plateaus. And there are canyons in the sea that are as deep as the Grand Canyon.

Some parts of the ocean bottom are much deeper than others. The depth varies from a few inches near shore to over six miles in some places.

The deepest spot in the sea that we know about is in the Mariana Trench. This long, deep trench is on the floor of the Pacific Ocean. At one point, the bottom of the trench is more than 36,000 feet deep.

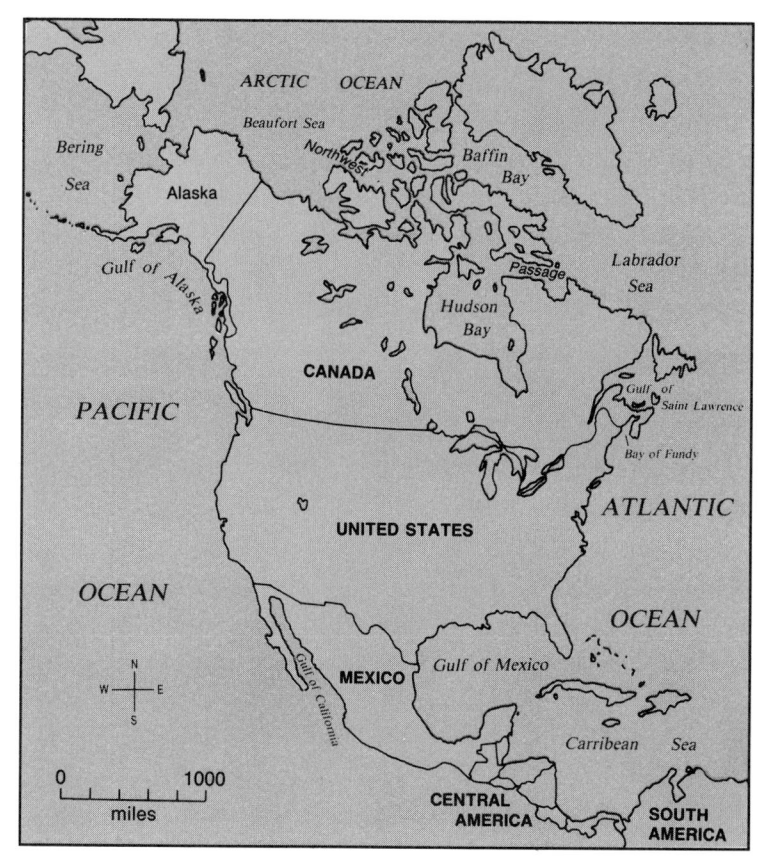

North American Bodies of Sea Water

Map Study
1. What is the name of the sea that is west of Alaska?
2. What is the name of the gulf on the eastern side of Canada?
3. What is the name of the sea that is east of Central America?

Have you ever walked out into the ocean? If so, then you know that the land usually slopes gently downward beneath the water. Most often, it continues to slope gently downward, sometimes for hundreds of miles. Then it suddenly drops off.

These gentle underwater slopes are the edges of the continents. They are called **continental shelves**. In some places, there is no shelf. Instead, the coastline drops off suddenly into deep water.

Imagine that you could place the world's highest mountain in the deepest part of the Mariana Trench. The top of the mountain would still be a mile below the ocean's surface.

Chapter Eight 79

Waves

Most of the high waves that surfers like to ride were started far out at sea by strong winds. During strong wind storms, waves may rise 40 feet or more. Such large waves can crash down on a ship and sink it. Sometimes they smash ships against rocks, breaking them apart.

Waves are also started by earthquakes and volcanic eruptions.

A wave started by an earthquake or volcanic eruption is called a **tsunami** (*soo NAHM ee*). Tsunamis can travel across the open ocean at speeds of 400 to 500 miles per hour.

The wave may be hard to see as it crosses the ocean. But when it reaches a bay it can form a high wall of water. The water then comes crashing down on shore.

Tsunamis have destroyed towns and drowned thousands of people. In 1946, an earthquake off the coast of Alaska caused a tsunami that wrecked Hilo, Hawaii. The tsunami had traveled almost 5,000 miles before it reached Hilo.

A 40-foot wave is about as high as a four-story building.

The Shape of a Wave

An ocean wave is a force that travels through the water. The wave moves up and down. This makes the water it passes through move up and down also.

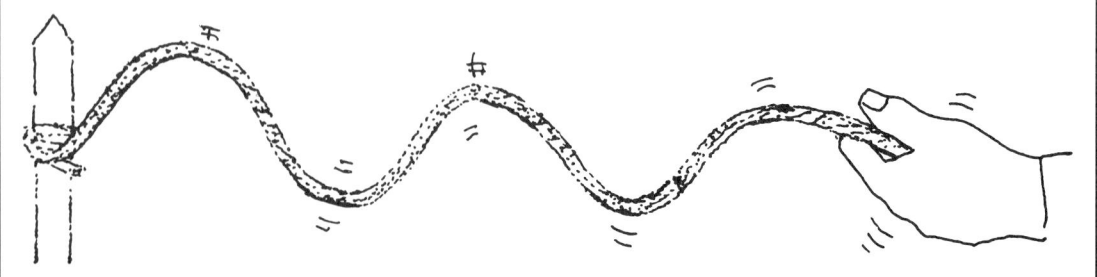

To get an idea of the way a wave moves, tie one end of a rope to a post. Snap the other end up and down to make waves travel through the rope.

Low tide in the Bay of Fundy

High tide in the Bay of Fundy

Tides

Have you ever spent a few hours at an ocean beach? If you have, you know that the water's edge keeps moving up and down the width of the beach. It slowly creeps higher and higher up the beach for about six hours. Then it slowly falls back for the next six hours. This rising and falling of the ocean's surface is called **tides**.

Tides are caused mainly by the pull of the moon's gravity. When the pull is strongest, it forces water to rise higher on the shore. This is called high tide. When the pull is weakest, the water flows back again. This is called low tide. The timing of the tides depends on the movements of Earth and the moon.

Along most coastlines, tides rise six to eight feet. Inside a bay, they may rise 20 feet or more. The longer and narrower the bay, the higher the tides. Tides in Canada's Bay of Fundy, which in parts is very long and narrow, can rise more than 40 feet.

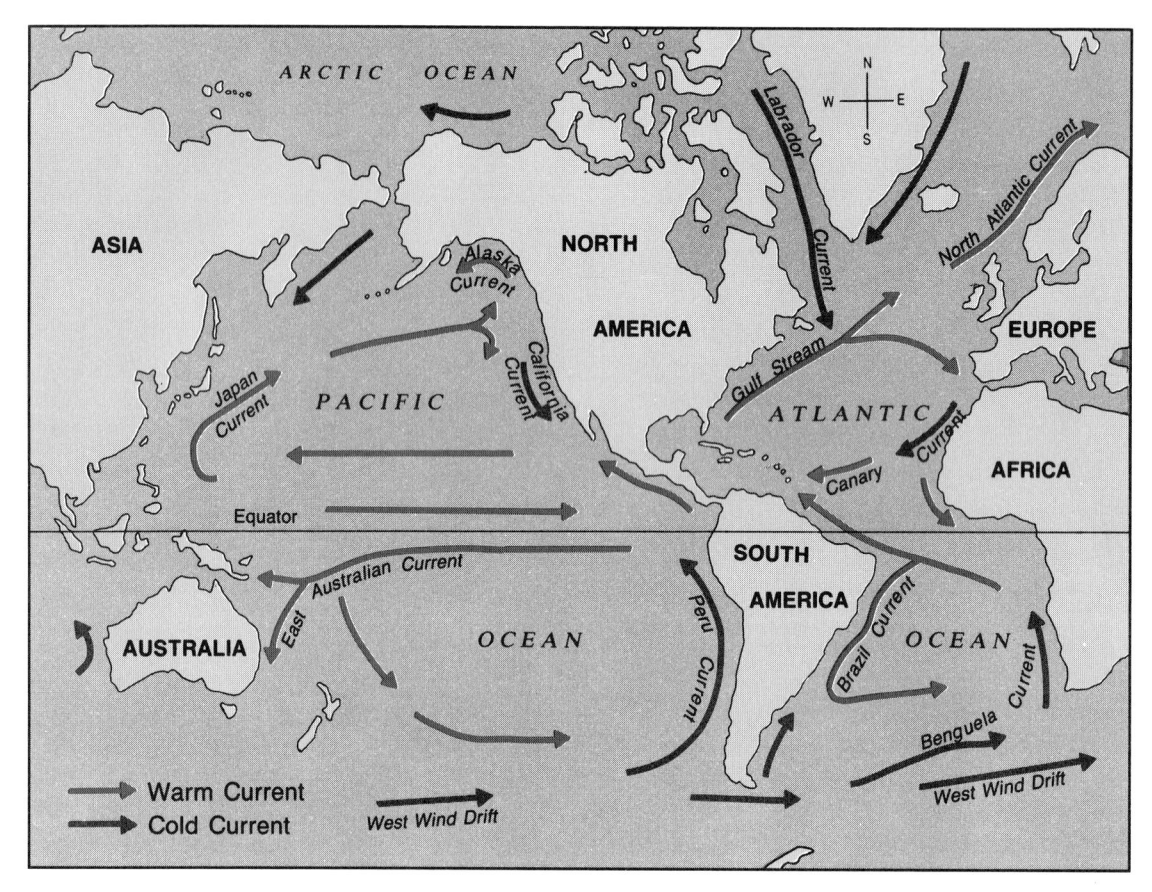

Map Study

1. What is the name of the current that flows past the west coast of the United States mainland? Is it a warm or a cold current?
2. What is the name of the current that flows past the east coast of the United States? Is it a warm or a cold current?

Pacific and Atlantic Ocean Currents

Currents

The sea is never still. Besides the waves and tides there are **currents** in the ocean. These currents are like huge rivers of water that flow in different directions within the ocean. Compared to an ocean current, the mighty Mississippi River is a tiny stream.

Some currents flow near the ocean's surface. Others flow deep below the surface. The currents travel in paths away from and toward the equator.

Surface currents are set in motion by winds. They carry warm water away from the equator. As a warm current gets further from the equator, it cools. By the time the current turns back toward the equator it is a cold current.

Ocean currents are important. They bring food to animals in the sea. They help ships travel faster. And they affect the weather.

Sea Life

The sea is full of life. Plants grow as deep as sunlight can reach. But animals live everywhere in the sea, even in the deepest parts. The largest animals are gray whales. They often reach a length of 95 feet. The smallest animals are too small to see without a microscope.

95 feet is about as long as three classrooms.

All the plants and animals in the sea are part of a food chain. The tiniest animals eat the tiniest plants. Other animals eat the animals that eat the tiny plants. Larger animals eat those animals. And so it goes. For the most part, bigger animals eat smaller animals.

There are three main types of sea animals. First, there are the microscopic animals. They and the tiny plants they feed on are carried along by the currents.

The second type are those that swim in search of their food. These include fish, otters, sea lions, and whales.

The third type live on the ocean bottom. They include shellfish that can move in search of food— such as clams, crabs, and lobsters. They also include shellfish that are fixed to one spot, such as oysters. This kind of shellfish gets its food from passing currents and from food that drifts down from above.

The Mississippi River System

As you know, many rivers empty into ocean waters. On most days, the Mississippi River empties about 33,000 gallons of water *per second* into the Gulf of Mexico.

The Mississippi River is the longest river in the United States. From its **source** to its **mouth** it is 2,348 miles long. The source of a river is the place where it begins. The mouth is where the river empties into a larger body of water.

The source of the Mississippi is a small stream that flows out of a lake in northwestern Minnesota. As it flows south, the river is joined by many **tributaries**. Tributaries are the smaller rivers that feed into a large river.

As the waters from other rivers join the Mississippi, it gets wider and wider. By the time it reaches Cairo, Illinois, it is almost a mile wide.

The Mississippi starts out as a clear stream. But the Missouri River pours tons of mud into it. The Mississippi carries most of this mud all the way to its mouth, near New Orleans. There it dumps the mud and other sediment it has been carrying. This adds new land to the Mississippi Delta.

Draining the Land

Streams and rivers carry away most of the water that falls each year as rain or snow. Without them, the land would become flooded.

The Mississippi and its tributaries make up the largest drainage system in the United States. This system drains the eastern side of the Rocky Mountains and the western side of the Appalachian Highlands. And it also drains most of the plains in between them.

Use a finger to trace the paths of the Mississippi River and all its tributaries on the map.

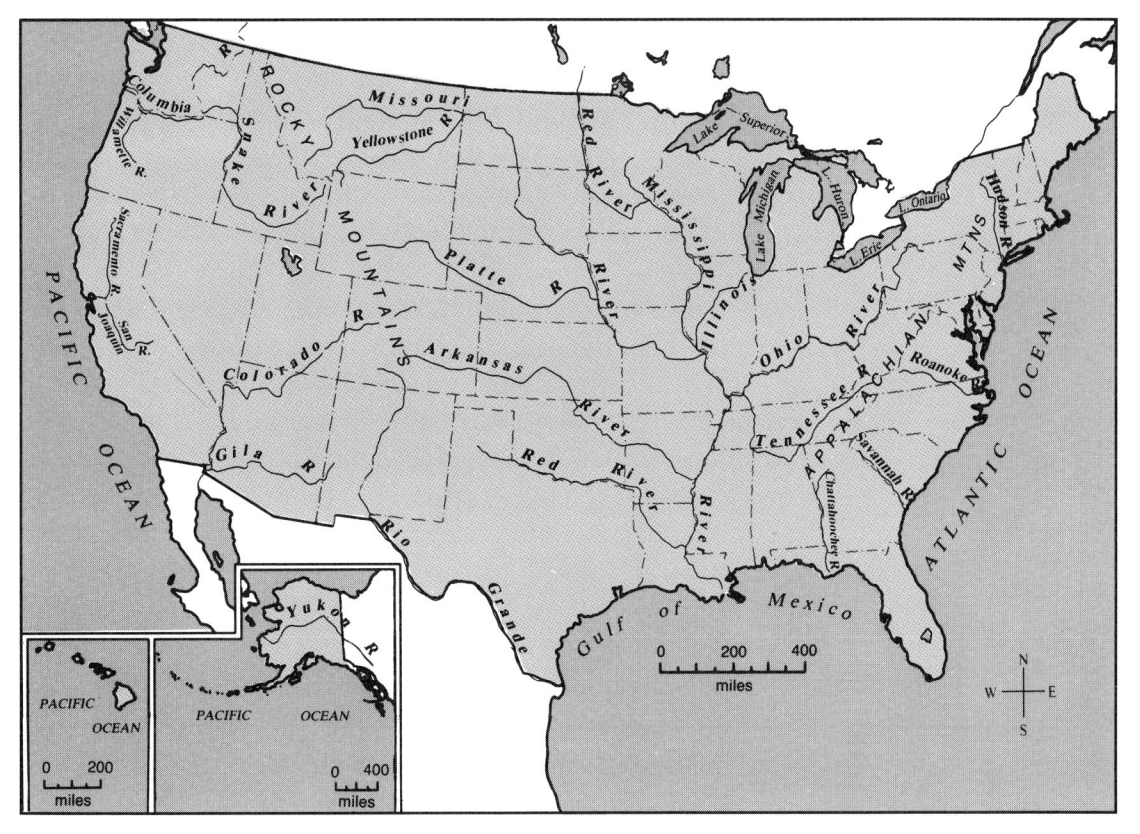

Map Study
1. In what mountain range does the Missouri River begin?
2. Name one tributary of the Mississippi River.
3. What body of water does the Savannah River flow into?

Major Rivers of the United States

Other river systems drain other parts of the country. The Columbia and its tributaries drain the Northwest. The Colorado and Rio Grande Rivers drain the Southwest. A number of small rivers drain the land east of the Appalachians. These include the Hudson River in the north and the Savannah River in the south.

Which of the rivers on the map, if any, drain your part of the United States?

Chapter Eight   85

Making Use of U.S. Rivers

Rivers are not as important today as they once were for moving people. But they are still very important for moving goods.

Find the Mississippi and Ohio Rivers on the map on page 85. These rivers and their tributaries form the busiest inland waterway in the United States.

Ships can travel the Mississippi for 1,800 miles from the Gulf of Mexico to Minneapolis. But most of the traffic on this waterway comes from long lines of oil and coal **barges**. A barge is a large flat-bottomed boat. It is usually towed or pushed by a tugboat.

Many U.S. rivers, or parts of them, are not deep or wide enough to handle heavy shipping. The waters of others are too rough for shipping. Still, these rivers are important for other reasons. They provide water for drinking, cooking, cleaning, and watering crops. They also provide water power for making electricity. You will learn more about how rivers help produce **electricity** in Chapter 13.

Western Rivers

The Columbia River in Washington is an important waterway in the Northwest. It is used for shipping, **irrigation**, water power, and fishing. Irrigation is the use of water from rivers or wells for raising crops.

In California, the San Joaquin and Sacramento Rivers supply much of the water needed for irrigation.

Further east, the Snake and Colorado Rivers provide water for irrigation. Many people fish in these rivers. Some people ride the rivers' wild rapids in kayaks or rafts.

The Rio Grande flows between Texas and Mexico. It makes farming possible in this otherwise dry area.

Barge traffic on the Mississippi River

Eastern Rivers

The Ohio, the Cumberland, and the Tennessee Rivers are in the southeastern part of the country. Before the 1930s, the Tennessee River often flooded. Then dams were built to control the flooding and to use the river's flowing water for making electricity. Water held by the dams is also used for irrigation.

Important rivers in the Northeast include the Connecticut, the Hudson, and the Susquehanna. These rivers have helped produce rich farmlands. They also provide waterways for inland shipping.

See the photo of a dam on page 152.

Chapter Eight **87**

The Great Lakes

The five Great Lakes are the largest group of freshwater lakes in the world. Only Lake Michigan is entirely within the United States. The other four lakes are shared with Canada.

Lake Superior is the largest of the lakes. It is a little larger than the state of South Carolina. Lake Ontario is the smallest of the lakes. It is a little smaller than the state of New Jersey.

The lakes are not all the same height above sea level. Lake Superior is 600 feet above sea level. Lake Ontario is only 245 feet above sea level. In spite of this, large ships can travel from lake to lake.

Canal Connections

Workers have dug **canals** to connect the lakes. A system of **locks** within the canals raises and lowers the ships when necessary.

A lock is like a huge pool. There are giant gates at both ends of it. Suppose a ship has to move from a higher lake to a lower lake. The ship sails up to the lock. The lock is filled with water to the same height as the water the ship is floating on. Then the gates closest to the ship are opened. The ship sails into the lock. The gates close behind it.

Next, water in the lock is lowered to the level of the water in the lower lake. As the water comes down, so does the ship. When the water levels are equal, the gates in front of the ship are opened. The ship then sails into the lower lake.

The opposite happens if the ship needs to be raised.

With the help of canals and locks, ships can travel all the way from Lake Superior to Lake Ontario.

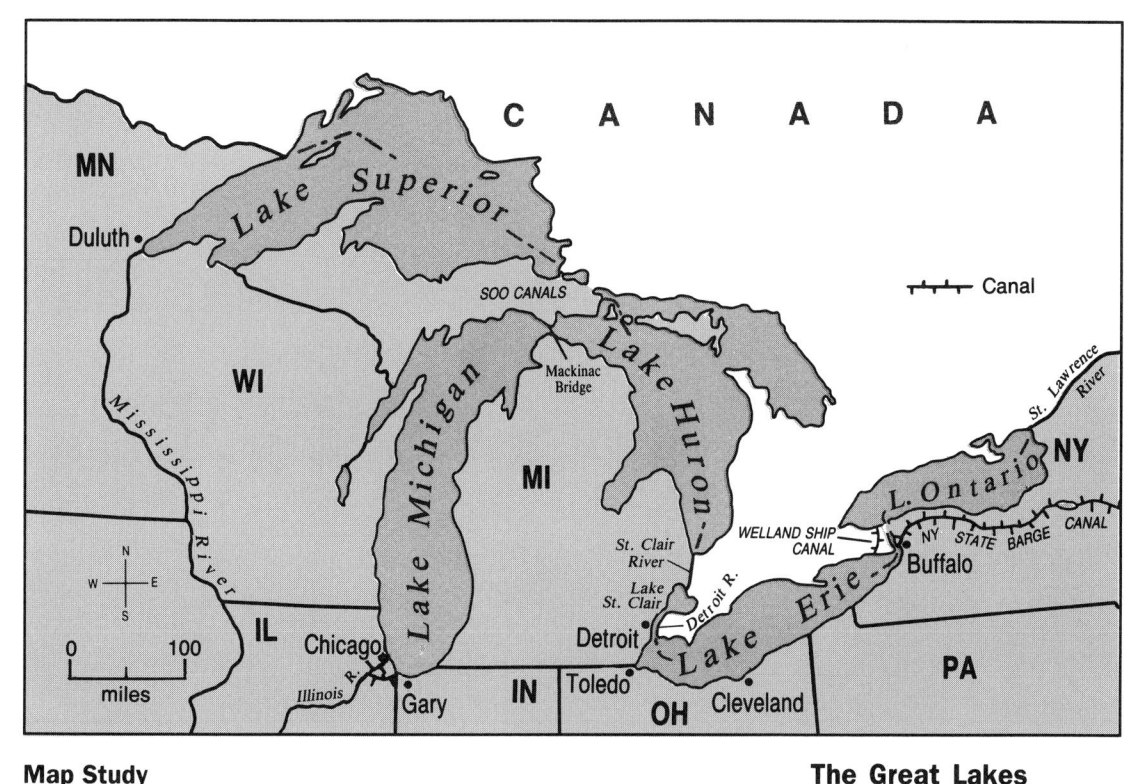

Map Study

The Great Lakes

1. Which canals connect Lakes Superior and Huron?
2. What three bodies of water connect Lakes Huron and Erie?
3. What is the distance between Toledo and Buffalo?

A Route to the Sea

From Lake Ontario, ships can travel through another set of canals to reach the Saint Lawrence River. This group of canals is called the St. Lawrence Seaway. Once on the river, ships can sail straight out to the Atlantic Ocean.

Most of the ships that travel from the Great Lakes to the sea carry wheat and iron **ore** to Europe. Coal, oil, steel, and automobiles are also shipped to Europe from lake **ports**. Major U.S. lake ports include Buffalo, Cleveland, Detroit, Chicago, and Duluth.

Look at the map above. Find Duluth. Run your finger along the route a ship would travel to get from Duluth to the Atlantic Ocean.

Chapter Eight 89

Chapter Review

Summary

1. There is really only one giant ocean, but we give different parts of it different names. We often call the waters of this giant ocean the sea. Sea water is salty. It is unfit for drinking or for watering crops unless it is specially treated.

2. Ocean waves may be started by winds, earthquakes, or volcanic eruptions. The pull of the moon's gravity is the main cause of high and low tides. Warm and cold currents flow like huge rivers through the ocean.

3. The bottom of the sea has plains, mountains, and plateaus. Its depth ranges from a few inches to more than six miles.

4. There are three kinds of animals in the sea. The smallest ones float with the currents. They eat microscopic plants that are also carried by currents. Others swim in search of food. The third kind live on the ocean floor, moving about or staying in one spot. All sea life is part of a food chain.

5. The Mississippi River system drains most of the United States. Other river systems drain other parts of the country. The Mississippi and Ohio Rivers and their tributaries form the busiest inland waterway in the United States.

6. A system of canals and locks allows ships to travel across the Great Lakes and out to sea.

Thinking and Writing

Answer these questions in complete sentences on a separate sheet of paper.

1. In what way is the bottom of the sea like the land above the sea?
2. Why is it true to say that the sea is never still?
3. What do we mean when we say that all living things in the sea are part of a food chain?
4. What kind of workers do you think need to know a lot about waves, currents, and tides?
5. Tell two things that can be done with river water that can't be done with ocean water.
6. Why are canal locks important to shipping on the Great Lakes?

Questions to Discuss

1. What are some ways that waves and tides may affect the lives of people living along a seacoast?
2. What part have oceans, rivers, and lakes played in the growth of the United States?

Special Projects

1. Make a poster showing ways in which we depend on oceans, rivers, lakes, or all three. Use your own photos or cut pictures out of magazines.
2. Go to the library. Ask the librarian to help you find the names of the five longest rivers in the world. Write down their names, their lengths, and their locations. Back in class, find the rivers on a globe or map of the world.

Chapters 5–8

REVIEW

Answer these questions on a separate sheet of paper.

A. Key Words

canyon
current
erosion
irrigation
lava
mineral
peak
region
sediment
swamp

Number your paper from 1 to 10. Then read each clue below. Find the word in the list on the left that matches the clue. Write that word next to the proper number on your paper.

1. The carrying away of weathered rock
2. The loose rock, soil, and sand carried away by rivers
3. A deep valley with very steep sides
4. Iron or other substances found in Earth's crust
5. Giant stream of water that flows within the ocean
6. What magma is called after it erupts above ground
7. An area of soft, wet land
8. The highest part of a mountain
9. A group of places that are similar in some ways
10. The watering of crops with river or well water

B. Key Facts

Number your paper from 11 to 20. Next to each number, write the word in the parentheses that best completes each sentence below.

11. In recent times, most of the strong earthquakes in the United States have occurred in California and (Texas / Alaska).
12. The islands of Hawaii are the tops of (volcanic / folded) mountains.
13. There are active volcanoes today in the states of Alaska, Hawaii, and (Washington / Maryland).
14. The steep valleys of the Grand Canyon were carved out by the (Mississippi / Colorado) River.
15. The Mississippi Delta was formed from (lava / sediment) carried by the Mississippi River.
16. The Great Lakes were carved out by (glaciers / rivers).
17. The Sierra Nevadas are an example of (folded / block) mountains.
18. The Appalachian Mountains are an example of (volcanic / folded) mountains.
19. Ocean (tides / waves) change every six hours.
20. The Mississippi and (Columbia / Ohio) Rivers form the busiest inland waterway in the United States.

C. Main Ideas

Answer any five questions below. Number your paper with the same numbers as the questions you choose.

21. What can happen on the surface of Earth when rocks below it slip and break?
22. What happens on the surface of Earth when hot magma is forced upward by pressure from below?
23. Explain one way in which either chemicals or rainwater break up and wear down rock.
24. Name two ways in which people cause erosion.
25. Name the major landforms in the western, central, and eastern parts of the United States.
26. Explain how automobiles and trains can pass through either the Rocky or the Appalachian Mountains.
27. Tell how the bottom of the sea is like the land above the sea.
28. Name three ways in which rivers help us.

Unit 2
Climate, Vegetation, and Resources

Chapter 9
Earth's Different Climates
Reading a Climate Map
Reading a Bar Graph
Dividing the U.S. into Regions

Chapter 10
Climate of the United States

Chapter 11
Vegetation and Soil
Reading a Vegetation Map

Chapter 12
U.S. Agriculture

Chapter 13
Earth's Renewable Resources

Chapter 14
Earth's Nonrenewable Resources
Reading a Pie Graph

Chapter 15
How We Use the Land
Reading a Land Use Map

Chapter 9
Earth's Different Climates

The North Central Region of the United States is known for its heavy winter snowfalls.

Chapter Learning Objectives
1. Describe the three major temperature regions.
2. Explain how large bodies of water, ocean currents, elevation, and winds can affect temperature.
3. Explain precipitation and how high mountains may affect it.
4. Contrast the climates of Alaska, Kansas, and Florida.
5. Use a map key to read a climate map.
6. Read a temperature bar graph.
7. Use a map to divide the United States into geographical regions.

Words To Know

weather day-to-day changes in air temperature, winds, and precipitation
climate the usual yearly weather of a place
elevation the height of the land above sea level
tropical having to do with the tropics, the warm moist regions around the equator
polar having to do with areas near the North or South Poles
temperate not too hot and not too cold
precipitation wetness that falls from the sky as rain, snow, sleet, and hail; fog is also a form of precipitation
sleet rain that has partially frozen
hail small balls of ice
evaporate to turn into tiny droplets that are too small to be seen
moisture wetness
hurricane a strong storm that has fast-moving winds and often heavy rain
tornado a violent, fast-moving column of air that extends downward from a cloud

---

What is the **weather** usually like where you live? Is it about the same all year? Or is it sometimes hot, sometimes cold, and sometimes in between? Do you get a lot of rain or snow, or is it usually dry?

The kinds of weather a place has is usually the same from year to year. This usual yearly weather is called **climate.** Different places in the world have different climates.

Climate has a big effect on people's lives. It affects the kinds of food they can grow. It affects the kinds of clothing they wear. It affects the kinds of houses they live in. What else might it affect?

Did you think about the kinds of outdoor activities they can enjoy?

Chapter Nine

Temperature Regions

Several things affect air temperature where you live. They include:
- intensity, or strength, of sunlight;
- nearness to large bodies of water;
- **elevation**;
- wind.

In this unit, we will study each of these. Let's start with the first one, intensity of sunlight.

There are three main temperature regions on Earth.

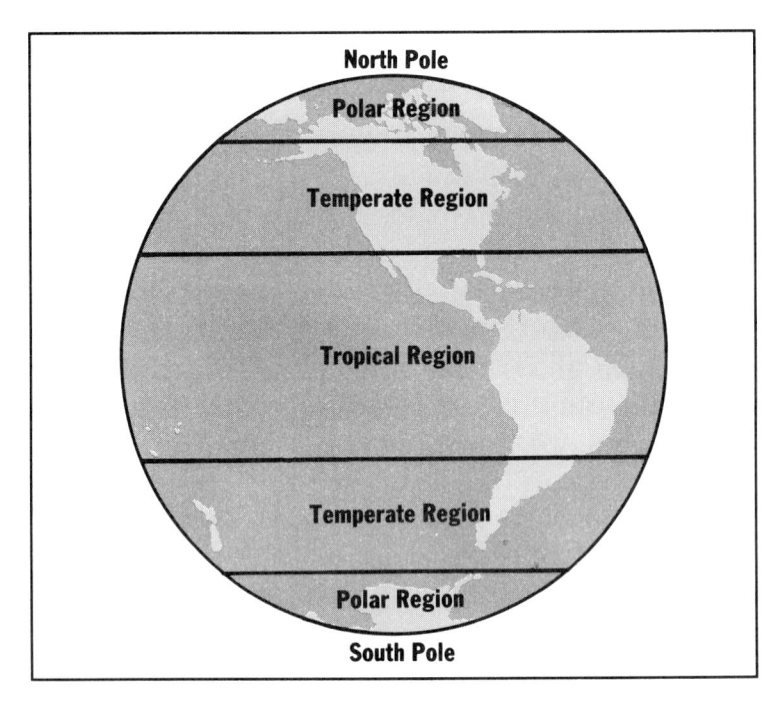

Map Study The lines running east and west show where each temperature region begins and ends.
1. What are the names of the three regions?
2. Which regions is North America in?

In a temperature region, most places in the region have similar temperatures. This is because the sunlight falls with about the same intensity everywhere in the region.

The temperature of most places in the **tropical** region is usually warm to hot.

The temperature of most places in the two **polar** regions is usually cold to very cold.

The temperature of most places in the two **temperate** regions changes as Earth moves around the sun. It is usually cool to cold in winter. It is usually warm to hot in summer.

Oceans Affect Temperature

Large bodies of water can help raise or lower air temperature over nearby lands. Here is an example.

Kansas City, Missouri, and San Francisco, California, both get about the same intensity of sunlight. But San Francisco is much warmer in the winter than Kansas City. And San Francisco is cooler in the summer.

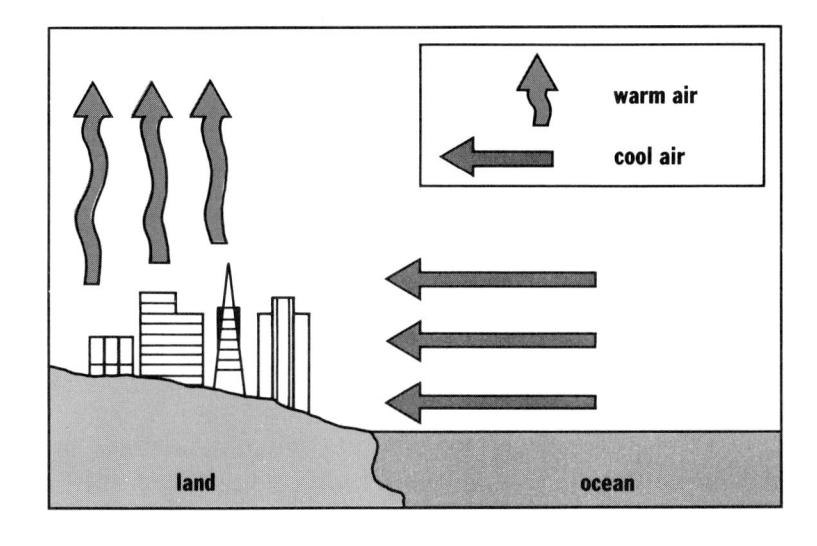

In summer, warm air over the coast rises up. Cooler air from over the ocean takes its place. This helps keep coastal temperatures lower than those farther inland.

Kansas City is far from any ocean. But San Francisco is next to the Pacific Ocean. Oceans and other large bodies of water take longer to warm up than land does. They also take longer to cool off.

In winter, the ocean near San Francisco is warmer than the nearby land. The ocean helps warm the air over the land.

What large body of water is closest to where you live?

In summer, the ocean near San Francisco is colder than the nearby land. The ocean helps cool the air over the land.

Ocean Currents

There is another way that oceans affect temperatures along a coast. Cool ocean water flows from cool regions to warm regions. Warm ocean water flows from warm regions to cool regions. The water flows in currents that are like giant streams within the oceans.

Winds passing over the currents are either heated or cooled. Later, when these winds pass over a coastal area, they heat or cool the land there.

Elevation Affects Temperature

Have you ever hiked up a mountain? If so, you may have felt the air get cooler as you climbed higher. This happens everywhere, even in the hot tropics.

For each 1,000 feet you climb above sea level, the temperature drops about 3 1/2 degrees Fahrenheit.

Look at the drawing on the next page. Suppose it is 80° F at the foot of a mountain. People there might wear T-shirts and shorts to play a game of volleyball.

Is there enough change in elevation to affect temperatures where you live?

About 8,000 feet up the mountain, the temperature may drop to 52° F. Hikers need warm shirts to be comfortable there.

At the same time, the temperature at 15,000 feet may be only 27° F. Mountain climbers have to bundle up in parkas to keep out the cold.

How Elevation Affects Temperature

15,000 feet
27° F

8,000 feet
52° F

sea level
80° F

Precipitation

Rain, snow, sleet, and hail are all forms of **precipitation**. Where does this wet stuff come from?

The sun beats down on Earth's lakes and oceans. The water begins to **evaporate**. It turns into a gas called water vapor. Plants and soil also give off water vapor when they are heated by the sun.

When the heated air rises, the water vapor rises up with it. As the air rises, it starts to cool down. Cool air

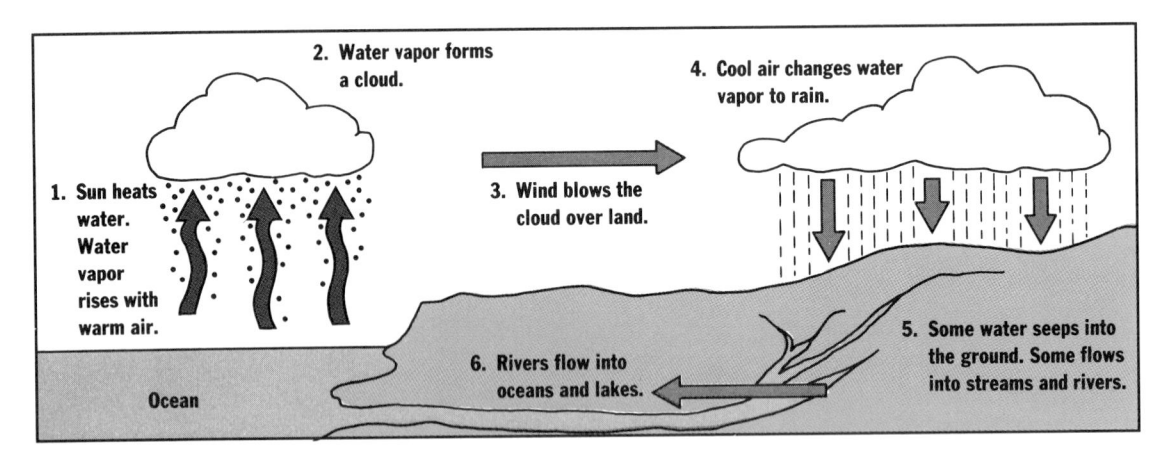

The Water Cycle

1. Sun heats water. Water vapor rises with warm air.
2. Water vapor forms a cloud.
3. Wind blows the cloud over land.
4. Cool air changes water vapor to rain.
5. Some water seeps into the ground. Some flows into streams and rivers.
6. Rivers flow into oceans and lakes.

Ocean

can't hold as much water vapor as warm air can. The water vapor mixes with tiny bits of dust and other matter in the air and forms into droplets of water. The droplets form clouds.

What Makes the Drops Fall?

If there is a lot of **moisture** and the air continues to cool, the droplets in the clouds come together and form larger drops. If the drops become heavier than the air, they start falling to the ground.

When the air is not too cold, the drops fall as rain. If the temperature of the air is below freezing (32° F), the drops fall as snow, **sleet**, or **hail**. Sleet is frozen raindrops. Hail is balls of ice. Sleet is smaller and wetter than hail. Balls of hail are usually small. But sometimes they can be as large as baseballs.

Some of the water that falls soaks into the ground. But much of it flows into streams and rivers. The rivers flow into lakes and oceans.

In this way, Earth's water moves in an endless cycle. A cycle is something that goes around and around. It repeats itself.

Different places on Earth get different amounts of precipitation. Some deserts get no precipitation at all. Some tropical forests get over 400 inches per year.

Winds

As heated air rises, cooler air moves in to take its place. This movement of air is what makes wind.

Winds blow across the continents and oceans every day. When wind from a cool place passes over a warmer place, the temperature there will drop. When wind from a warm place passes over a cooler place, the temperature will rise.

Winds also affect precipitation. They carry water vapor and storms from one place to another.

Windstorms

Hurricanes are strong storms with wind speeds that sometimes reach 150 miles per hour. They usually start over oceans. Then they may move inland. Often they carry much rain with them.

Hurricanes sink ships. They whip up huge waves that wash away beaches. They blow away trees and houses.

Tornadoes start over land. They move quickly over small areas. They toss cars and trucks about as if they were toys. They destroy houses and other buildings.

One side of a mountain may get more precipitation than the other.

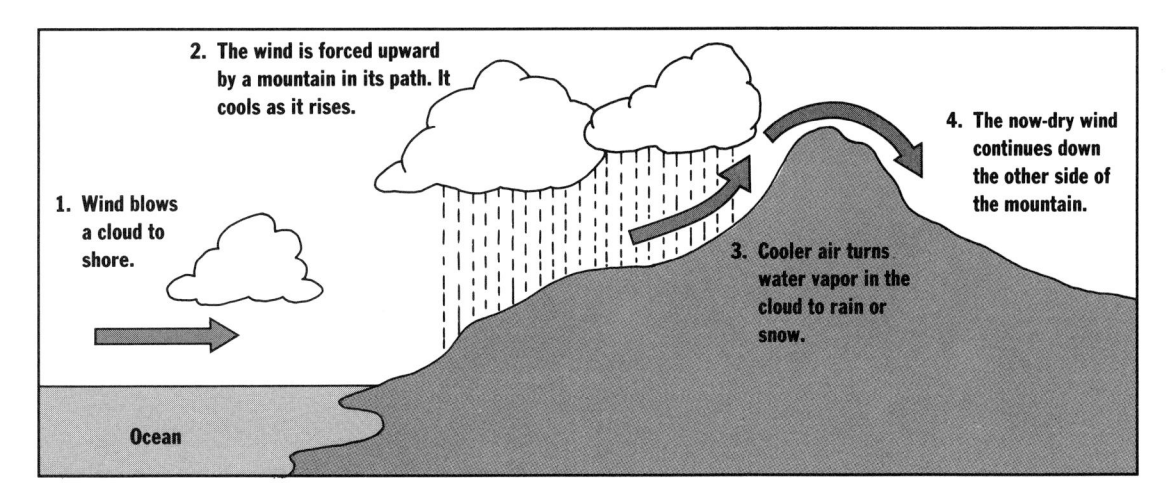

1. Wind blows a cloud to shore.
2. The wind is forced upward by a mountain in its path. It cools as it rises.
3. Cooler air turns water vapor in the cloud to rain or snow.
4. The now-dry wind continues down the other side of the mountain.

Ocean

Chapter Nine

Three Different Kinds of Climate

You have been reading about different things that can affect the climate of a place. Read now how these things affect the climate of three different places in the United States.

North Coast of Alaska: Polar

The north coast of Alaska is in the polar region. The sunlight there is much less intense than places further south. The ocean waters nearby are frozen over for most of the year. Sea winds blowing over the land are cold.

Winters are long and bitterly cold. Temperatures often drop well below 0° F. Summers are short and cool. Temperatures seldom go above 50° F.

Summer days are long. But the intensity of the sunlight is weak. The ground below the surface stays frozen all year. Only tiny plants are able to grow.

The air is usually so cold it cannot hold much water vapor. In the town of Barrow, only about five inches of precipitation fall each year.

Kansas: Temperate

Kansas is in the temperate region. The intensity of the sunlight there changes during the year. There are no large bodies of water nearby to affect temperatures.

Kansas has fairly cold winters and warm summers. Usual temperatures range from about 31° F in winter to about 79° F in July.

The eastern part of the state gets about 35 inches of precipitation a year. The western part gets only about 18 inches. Most of the state's precipitation comes as spring and summer rains.

Winds blowing in from the west help keep the air clean of pollution. Kansas sometimes gets tornadoes.

Where you live, which month of the year is coldest? Which is warmest? Which is wettest?

Florida: Tropical

Florida does not have the cold winters that states further north have. It is closer to the equator than other states, so the sunlight it gets is more intense. Florida is also a peninsula, with water on three sides.

The water helps warm the state in winter and cool it in summer. Usual temperatures range from about 59° F in January to about 81° F in July.

Temperatures throughout the state seldom drop below 50° F. But sometimes, in the northern parts of the state, temperatures may drop below freezing.

Florida gets quite a bit of rain, about 53 inches a year. This happens because the intense sunlight over the area evaporates a lot of water from the nearby Gulf of Mexico. The water vapor rises in the warm air. When it reaches the cooler upper air, it forms clouds and turns to rain.

Most of the rain falls with the hurricanes that occur in late summer and fall.

Miami, Florida, is warm most of the year.

Chapter Nine 105

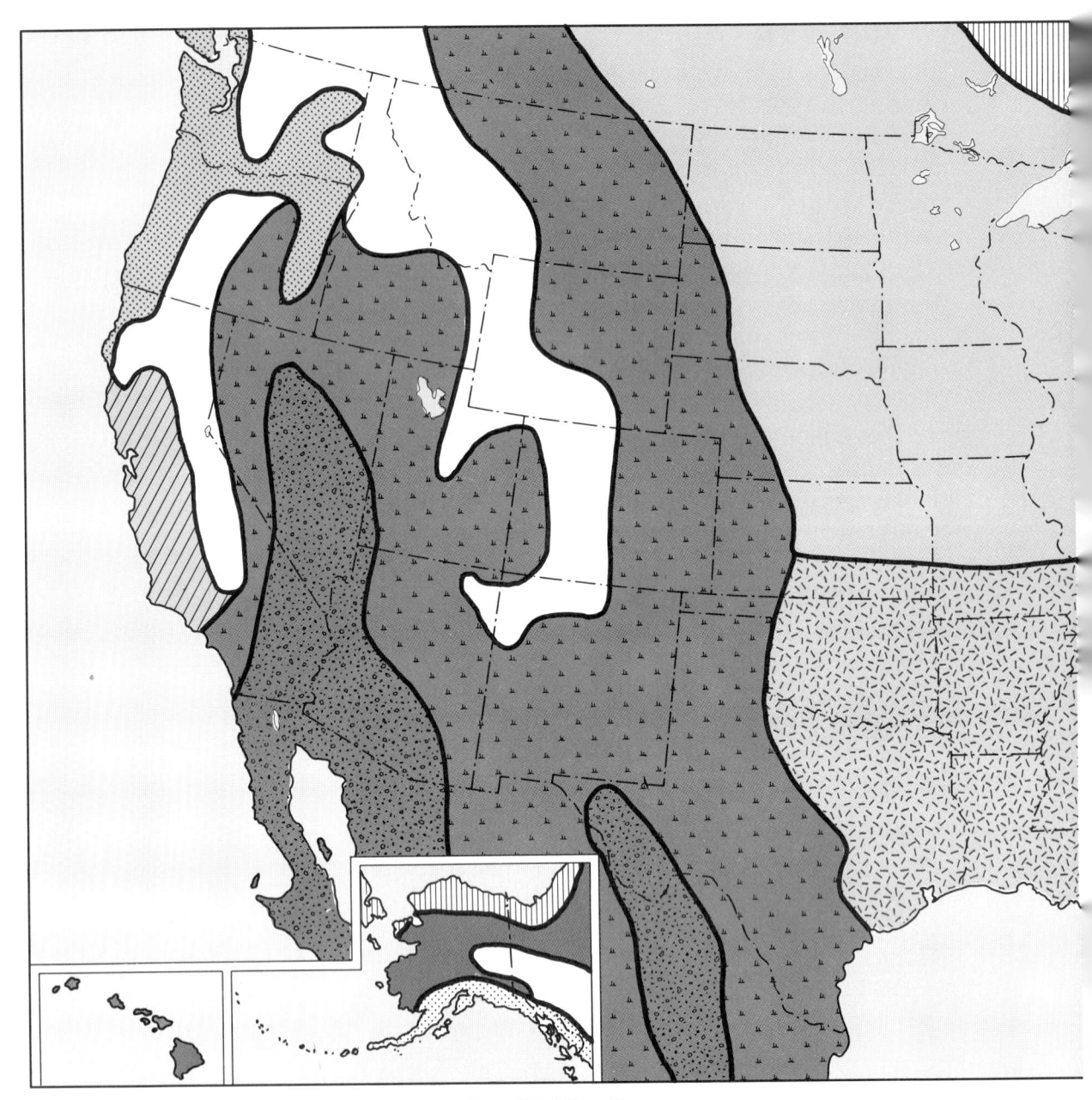

Geography Skills 9

Reading a Climate Map

UNITED STATES CLIMATE

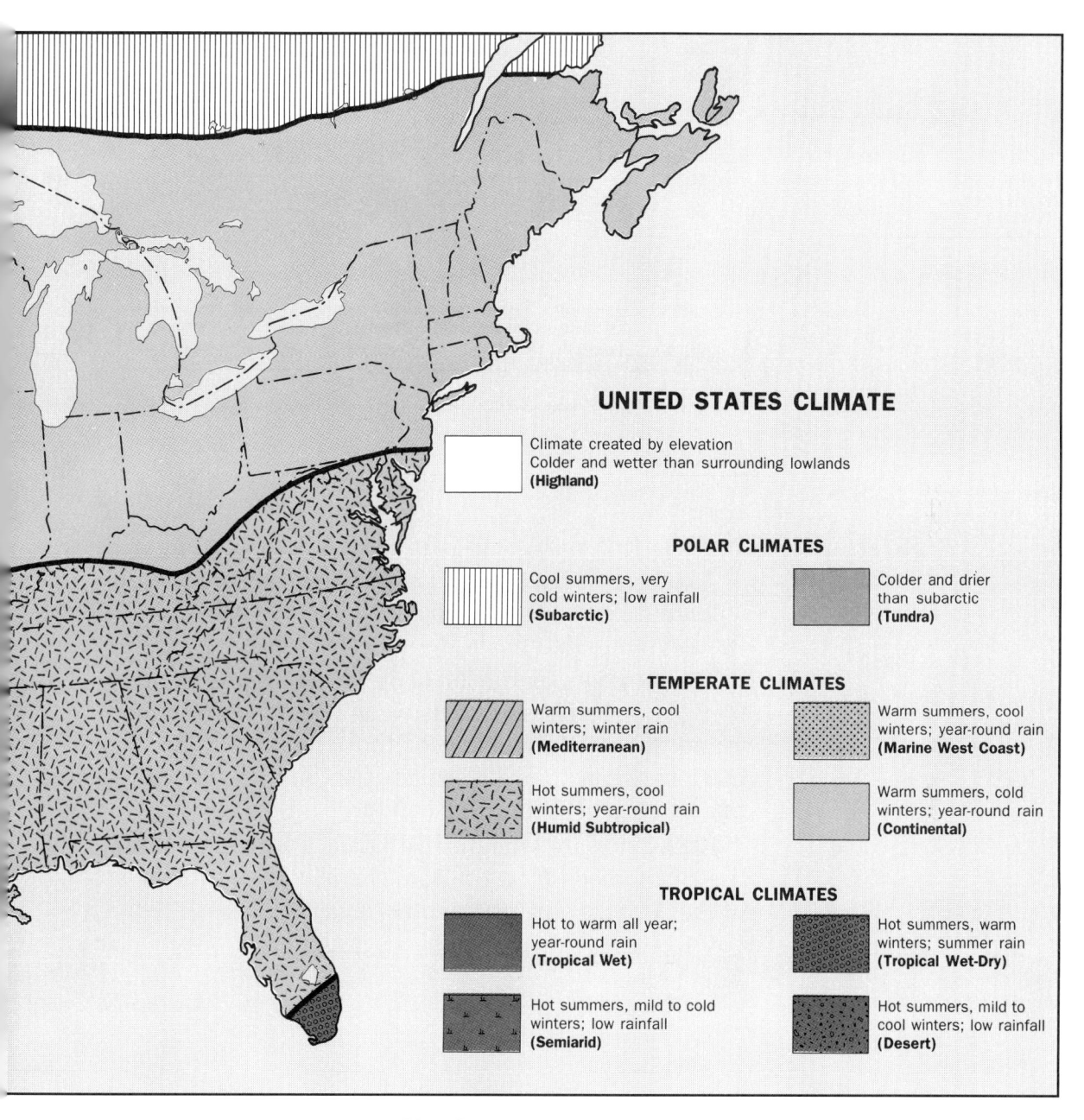

Climate created by elevation
Colder and wetter than surrounding lowlands
(Highland)

POLAR CLIMATES

Cool summers, very cold winters; low rainfall
(Subarctic)

Colder and drier than subarctic
(Tundra)

TEMPERATE CLIMATES

Warm summers, cool winters; winter rain
(Mediterranean)

Warm summers, cool winters; year-round rain
(Marine West Coast)

Hot summers, cool winters; year-round rain
(Humid Subtropical)

Warm summers, cold winters; year-round rain
(Continental)

TROPICAL CLIMATES

Hot to warm all year; year-round rain
(Tropical Wet)

Hot summers, warm winters; summer rain
(Tropical Wet-Dry)

Hot summers, mild to cold winters; low rainfall
(Semiarid)

Hot summers, mild to cool winters; low rainfall
(Desert)

Map Study
1. Look at the eastern half of the country. As you move south, do temperatures rise or fall?
2. In which half of the country, eastern or western, is climate most affected by elevation?
3. Which state is hot to warm all year and has year-round rain?

Chapter Nine

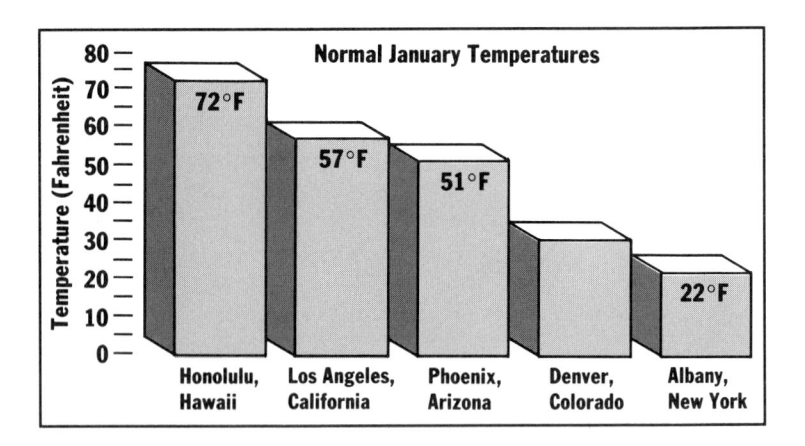

Geography Skills 10

Reading a Bar Graph

A bar graph can give you a quick way to compare amounts. The bar graph above compares normal January temperatures in five different cities.

The numbers on the left show temperatures from 0° F to 80° F. The marks between two numbers stand for numbers halfway between those numbers. The mark between 10 and 20 stands for 15. What does the mark between 50 and 60 stand for?

Each bar shows the normal January temperature in the city named below the bar. The number at the top of the bar tells what that temperature is.

What is the normal January temperature in Los Angeles?

If the number is not printed at the top of the bar, you can still tell what the number should be. Use a ruler or piece of paper to help you. Place the ruler so that its bottom edge runs from the top of the bar to the numbers on the left—like this:

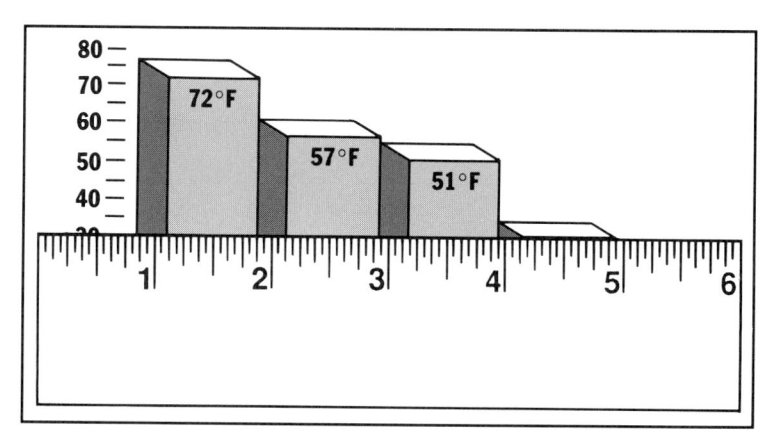

Graph Study
1. What is the normal January temperature in Denver?
2. What is the normal January temperature in Albany?
3. Which of the five cities is warmest in January?
4. Which two cities have normal January temperatures that are below freezing?

Chapter Review

Summary

1. The climate of a place is its usual yearly weather.

2. Earth's three main temperature regions are the polar, the temperate, and the tropical regions.

3. Five things may affect the climate of a place:

    - how intensely the sun's rays shine on it;
    - how close it is to a large body of water;
    - the temperature of any nearby ocean currents;
    - how high it is above sea level;
    - where the winds that pass overhead come from.

4. The water cycle starts with the sun's evaporating water from Earth's surface. Rising water vapor forms clouds. Water from the clouds returns to Earth as rain, snow, sleet, or hail.

5. The climates in different parts of the United States can be quite different.

Thinking and Writing

Answer these questions in complete sentences on a separate sheet of paper.

1. Explain the difference between weather and climate.
2. Explain the difference between sleet and hail.
3. What is different about the places where hurricanes start and the places where tornadoes start?
4. How does the climate of eastern Kansas differ from the climate of western Kansas? During which times of the year would you be most likely to notice this difference?
5. On which side of a coastal mountain range would you be likely to find the most rain?
6. Describe temperature differences in the three main temperature regions.

Questions to Discuss

1. What is the climate like where you live? Talk about temperature, precipitation, and winds. Give reasons why the climate is the way it is.
2. How does climate affect: your clothing; the kind of building you live in; your outdoor activities?

Special Project

Learn and report about two states that have very different climates. You might compare Alaska and Hawaii, Florida and Maine, or Minnesota and Arizona. List the reasons these places have such different climates. Report to the class.

Geography Skills 11

Dividing the United States into Regions

To help you learn about United States geography, in this book the country is divided into six geographic regions. There are between five and 12 states in each region. All the states in a region have some things in common.

Look at the map on the right. What are the names of the six regions? Which region is your state part of? What are the names of the other states in your region?

In upcoming chapters you will learn something new about each of the regions, such as:
- the kind of climate it has;
- the kind of farming and business it has;
- what the people who live there do.

Right now, use this map to learn which regions have access to major bodies of water. You have access to a place when you can get to it easily.

Map Study
1. Which region has access to the Pacific Ocean?
2. Which two regions have access to the Atlantic Ocean?
3. Which two regions have access to the Gulf of Mexico?
4. Which two regions have access to the Great Lakes?
5. Which three regions have access to the Mississippi River?

Now compare the map on the right with the landform map on pages 68 and 69.

6. Which four regions have many mountains?
7. Which two regions are mostly plains?

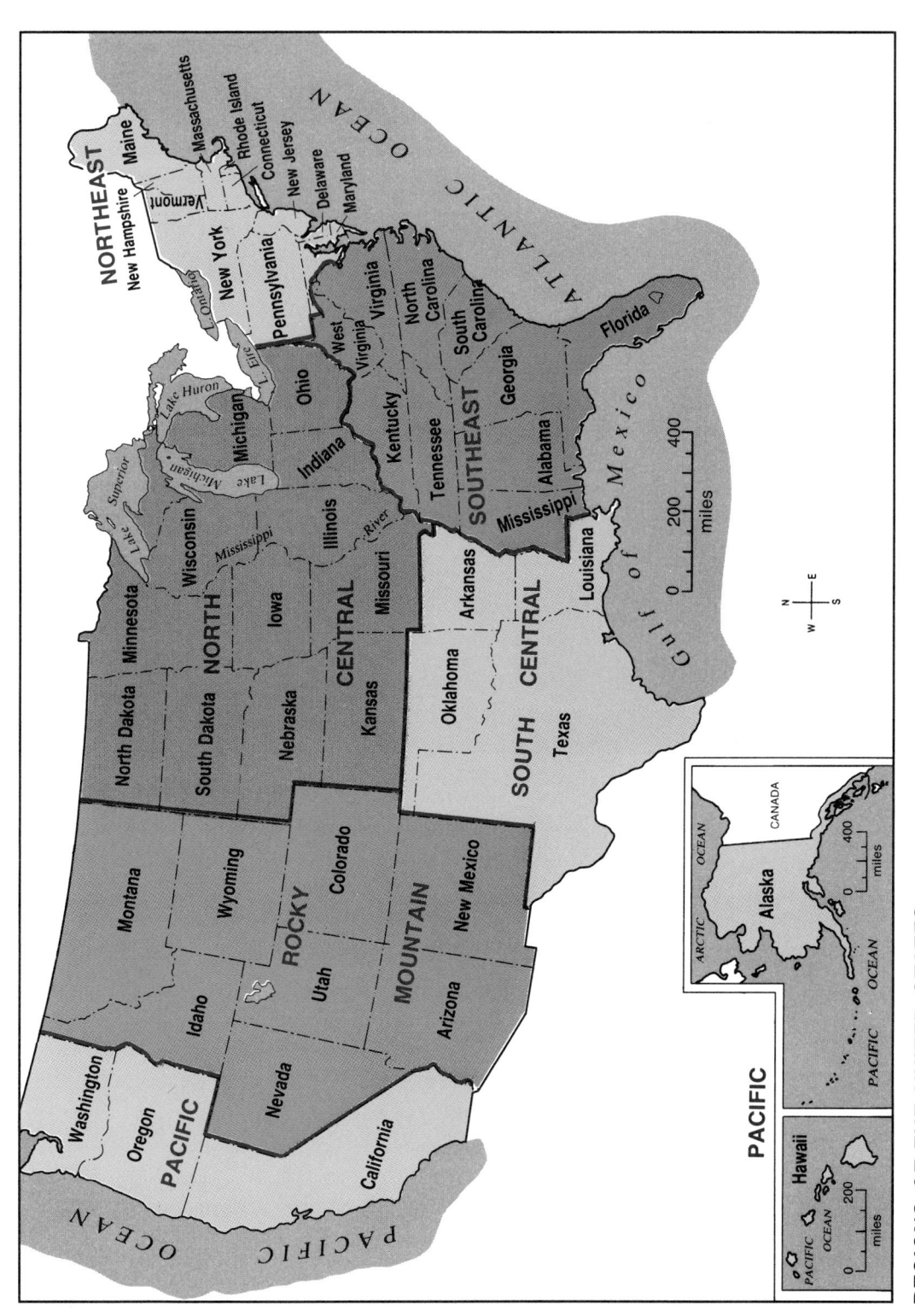

REGIONS OF THE UNITED STATES

Chapter 10
Climate of the United States

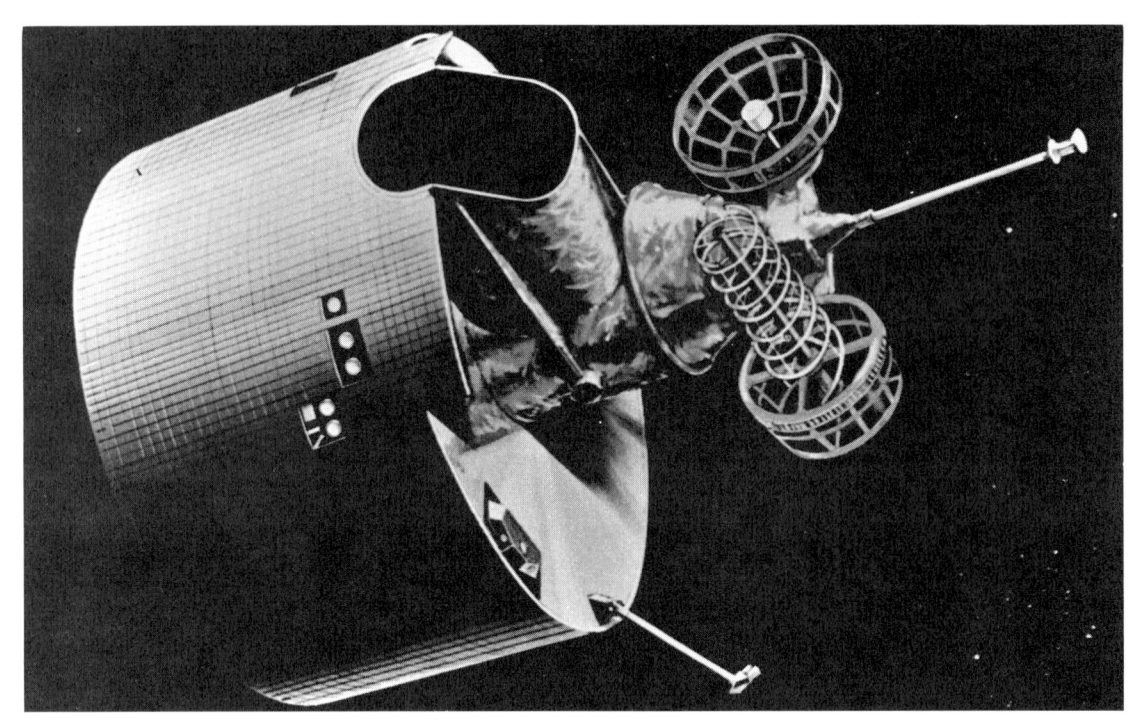

Satellites, airplanes, weather balloons, and ships are all used to collect weather and climate information. This is a weather satellite.

Chapter Learning Objectives
1. Tell how the climate differs in the different parts of the Pacific Region.
2. Tell how the climate differs from north to south and from highland to lowland areas in the Rocky Mountain Region.
3. Describe temperature ranges and precipitation amounts in the North Central Region.
4. Describe the Northeast's changing seasons and its varying amounts of precipitation.
5. Tell how the climate differs in the different parts of the South Central Region.
6. Describe temperature ranges and precipitation amounts in the Southeast.

Words To Know

blizzard a blinding, windy snowstorm
thunder a sound caused when air suddenly heats and expands
humid full of moisture

No geographic region has just one climate. There are weather differences in different parts of every region. The differences may be large, as they are in the Pacific Region. Or they may be small, as they are in the Southeast.

As you have learned, differences in climate depend mainly on:
- elevation,
- distance from the equator,
- and distance from a large body of water.

In this chapter, you will read about the climate in each of the six geographic regions. Knowing about climate will help you to understand the later lessons in this book. For example, you will better understand why certain kinds of crops are grown in one region but not in another. Or why many people move from one region to another.

Before you begin reading about each region, turn to the region map on page 113. Then look at the climate map on pages 106–107. This will give you a general idea of the region's climate before you start reading about it here.

Pacific Region

Hawaii. Since it is so close to the equator, Hawaii is warm enough for swimming and sunbathing all year round. Cooling breezes from the Pacific Ocean keep it from getting very hot. Average temperatures range from a low of 73° F in January to a high of 81° F in September.

The moist ocean breezes help make Hawaii one of the wettest places on Earth. One mountain on the island of Kauai gets about 450 inches of rain per year!

Alaska. Alaska has three climate areas. Northern Alaska is very cold and dry. The valleys of central Alaska are slightly warmer and wetter. But the southern coast of Alaska is much warmer and wetter than the other two areas. This difference is due to the warm Japan Current that flows close by. Winds that pass over the current bring warmth and moisture.

Turn to the map on page 82 to trace the path of the Japan Current.

Pacific Coast States. The Japan Current also affects the coastal areas of Washington, Oregon, and northern California. They get more rainfall and milder temperatures than areas further inland.

Most of the rest of California has a dry climate. The average yearly rainfall is under 20 inches in most places. The greatest amount of rain comes in winter.

Average inland temperatures in southern California range from the 40s in winter to the 80s in summer. Coastal and mountain areas are cooler, with snow at the higher elevations.

Rocky Mountain Region

In July, there is still plenty of snow on the peaks of many of the Rocky Mountains. But lowland deserts in the southern part of the region are blistering hot.

In the deserts, there is a big drop in temperature after the sun goes down. You may feel hot in just a T-shirt during the day. But that same night you'll feel cold without a warm jacket.

Western States Rainfall

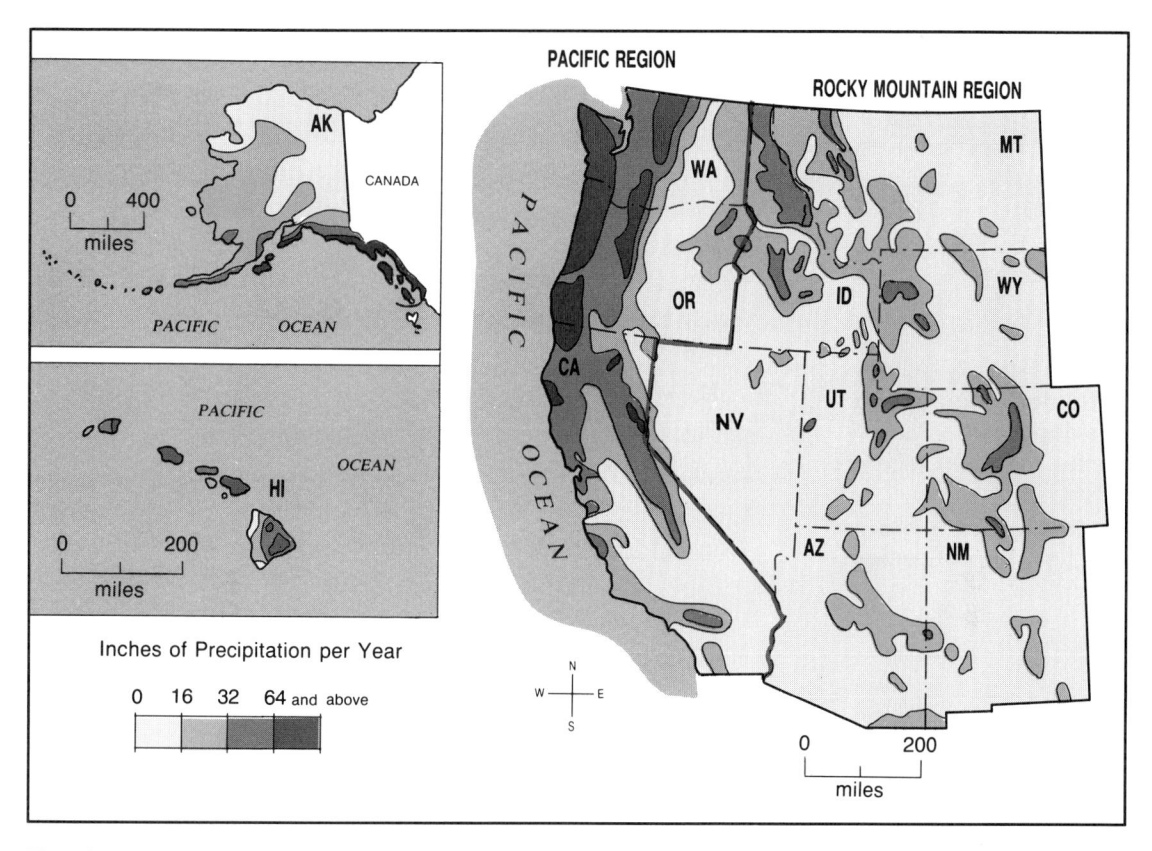

Map Study The map above shows the average, or usual, amount of precipitation in the Pacific and Rocky Mountain Regions.
1. Which is wetter—the Pacific or the Rocky Mountain Region?
2. Which states have areas that get more than 64 inches of precipitation a year?
3. Why do you think the dry areas are so dry? (Hint: Remember what happens when wind-driven clouds are blocked by mountains.)

The region gets lots of snow in winter. This is especially true in the north and at higher elevations. But even the wettest parts of the region get only about 19 inches of precipitation per year.

Snow sometimes comes in **blizzards**. A blizzard is a blinding snowstorm with high winds.

Chapter Ten **117**

North Central Region

Climate differences in the North Central Region are not as great as those in the Pacific and Rocky Mountain Regions. Yet there are big differences between summer and winter temperatures. For example, temperatures in northern Minnesota may range from a low of -34° F in winter to over 100° F in summer. Average temperatures range from 20° F in January to 83° F in July.

Blizzards are common in northern parts of the region. Further south the winters are milder.

Areas near the Great Lakes have warmer temperatures in winter than other parts of the North Central Region. In summer, they have cooler temperatures.

Average yearly precipitation ranges from 15 to 47 inches. This includes rain, snow, sleet, and hail. It is driest in the western part of the region and wettest in the Ohio River Valley. Northern parts of the region get the most snow. It can come as early as November and stay on the ground through April.

Northeast Region

Mountains and the Atlantic Ocean greatly affect the climate of the Northeast Region. The coldest spots are in the mountain areas. The warmest are along the coast.

The region has four seasons that are almost equal in length. Cold winter days give way to a warm spring. Hot summers follow, and then come the crisp, cool days of fall.

In fall, the leaves of many of this region's trees turn red, gold, and orange. This rich display of color is greatest in New England.

New England is the northern part of the Northeast Region. It includes Maine, New Hampshire, Vermont, Massachusetts, Connecticut, and Rhode Island.

Blizzards are defined as having winds of 35 miles per hour or more. "Severe blizzards" are those whose winds are higher than 45 miles per hour.

AVERAGE MONTHLY PRECIPITATION

■ Bismarck, ND ■ Philadelphia, PA

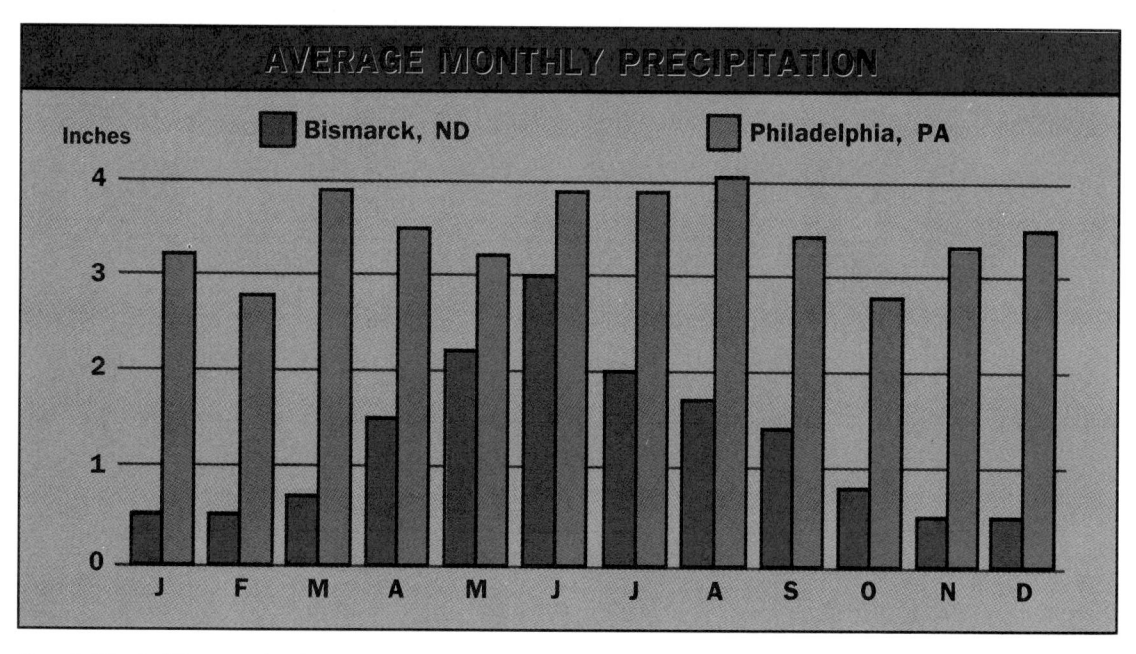

Graph Study The graph above compares average monthly precipitation in Bismarck, North Dakota, and Philadelphia, Pennsylvania.
1. Which city gets the least precipitation throughout the year?
2. In which month does each city get the most precipitation?
3. In which city does the amount of precipitation differ most from one time of year to another?
4. What may be the reasons one city gets more precipitation than the other? (Hint: Check the location of each city on the map of the United States on pages 292-293.)

The Northeast gets some precipitation every month. In the north, much of the precipitation comes in the form of sleet and snow. Parts of Maine get up to 100 inches of snow. Buffalo, New York, averages about 80 inches. Blizzards are fairly common in the north.

In contrast, southern New Jersey, Delaware, and Maryland get only about 20 inches of snow a year. Precipitation also comes in the form of spring showers and summer **thunder** storms.

A tornado is a twisting wind storm. Northern Hemisphere winds move in a counterclockwise direction. Southern Hemisphere winds move in a clockwise direction.

South Central Region

The South Central Region has four kinds of climate:

- Louisiana and the coast of Texas are affected by the warm waters of the Gulf of Mexico. They have warm, **humid** summers and mild winters. Humid weather makes the air damp and sticky. Winter temperatures sometimes fall below freezing, but snow is rare.
- Western Texas is mostly cool and dry.
- Central Texas and most of Oklahoma are warm and dry.
- Arkansas is mostly warm and rainy.

From March to June, the South Central Region gets many tornadoes. A tornado will usually come late in the afternoon or evening of a very hot, humid day. First a cone-shaped cloud made of water vapor and dust forms over the land. Then the cloud becomes a twisting windstorm. The top of an average tornado is 250 yards wide. It is narrower at the bottom. The winds in a tornado may reach speeds of 300 miles per hour. Where it touches ground, a tornado can destroy everything in its path.

Southeast Region

Most of the Southeast enjoys mild weather most of the year. But the weather is not the same everywhere. In some places, temperatures rarely fall below 60° F. In others, temperatures sometimes go below freezing.

The warmest areas are on the southern coastal plains and on the lowlands west of the Appalachians. The coolest areas, as you might guess, are in the mountains.

Most of the region's precipitation comes in the form of rain. The northern areas and higher mountains do get some snow. Rainfall averages from 40 to 70 inches per year. The heaviest rainfall comes along the coasts. Most of the rain falls during summer afternoon thunderstorms.

Summer and fall also bring terrible hurricanes. These storms can be 300 miles wide. Their winds move at a speed of 75 to 140 miles per hour.

The hurricanes usually form over the Atlantic Ocean east of the Caribbean Sea. Then they move west and northeast into the Caribbean and the Gulf of Mexico. Hurricanes often hit the shores of Florida and the Gulf Coast states. They can do great damage.

Parts of the Southeast also have tornadoes.

On the lower right side of the map on page 289, find the area where hurricanes form and strike.

Chapter Review

Summary

1. The Pacific Region includes:
   - the warm, wet islands of Hawaii;
   - the cold, dry lands of northern Alaska;
   - the slightly warmer, wetter valleys of central Alaska;
   - the mild, wet coastlands from southern Alaska to northern California;
   - the warm, dry valleys of southern California;
   - the highlands and mountains of Alaska, Hawaii, and the Pacific Coast states.

2. The Rocky Mountain Region has snowcapped mountains as well as very hot deserts. Daytime and nighttime temperatures vary greatly in these deserts. Precipitation in the region ranges from less than 10 inches in the deserts to about 19 inches elsewhere. Blizzards hit the northern areas.

3. Most of the North Central Region has a wide range of temperatures from winter to summer. Here precipitation ranges from about 15 to 47 inches and includes rain, snow, sleet, and hail. The snow sometimes comes in blizzards.

4. The Northeast has four almost equally divided seasons. The area usually gets some kind of precipitation every month. Sometimes in winter there are blizzards. The northern part of this region has the lowest temperatures and the greatest amount of snowfall.

5. The South Central Region has four climate areas:
   - Louisiana and the coast of Texas are usually warm and humid and have mild winters.
   - Western Texas is cool and dry.
   - Central Texas and most of Oklahoma are warm and dry.
   - Arkansas is warm and rainy.

   The region is often hit by tornadoes.

6. The Southeast Region is mostly warm and wet. Some 40 to 70 inches of rain falls there. The coolest areas are in the hills and mountains. The warmest are on the coastal plains. Temperatures rarely go below freezing in the southern part of the region. Summer and fall bring hurricanes. The region also has tornadoes.

Thinking and Writing

Answer these questions in complete sentences on a separate piece of paper.

1. How does the climate of the southern coast of Alaska differ from the climate of northern Alaska?
2. How do daytime and nighttime temperatures differ in the deserts of the Rocky Mountain Region?
3. How does the range of temperatures in the North Central Region differ from the range in Hawaii?
4. How does the temperature vary in the Northeast during winter, spring, summer, and fall?
5. Why do Louisiana and the coast of Texas have warm, humid summers and mild winters?
6. How does the amount of precipitation in the Rocky Mountain Region differ from the amount in the Southeast?

Questions to Discuss

1. Which region or state do you think has the best climate for living and working? Why do you think that?
2. What do you think people should do to be prepared for blizzards, tornadoes, or hurricanes?

Special Project

Ask your librarian for help in finding information about the worst blizzards, tornadoes, or hurricanes. Take notes. Report back to the class. You might play the role of a reporter describing the storm on radio or TV.

Chapter 11
Vegetation and Soil

A broadleaf forest

Chapter Learning Objectives
1. Identify five main types of vegetation.
2. Identify four kinds of forest vegetation.
3. Compare needleleaf and broadleaf trees.
4. Describe grassland vegetation.
5. Describe tundra vegetation.
6. Describe desert vegetation.
7. Tell why different places on the same mountain can have different kinds of vegetation.
8. Explain the importance of soil.
9. Use a map key to read a vegetation map.

Words To Know

vegetation the kinds of plants that grow in a place
tundra a cold, treeless land where only tiny plants can grow in summer
needleleaf a kind of tree that has leaves shaped like needles
broadleaf a kind of tree with wide leaves rather than needle-shaped leaves
steppe a grassland found in cool dry climates
prairie a treeless area with tall grass
savanna a grassland found in warm climates that have both wet and dry seasons
humus dead plant and animal matter that provides plants with nutrients
nutrient a substance in soil that gives plants what they need to grow
fertilizer a substance added to soil to provide nutrients

Vegetation Types

Some plants need a lot of warmth and water. Others need much less. So climate affects the **vegetation**, or kinds of plants, that grow in a place.

The main types of vegetation are forest, grassland, **tundra,** desert, and highland. To learn about them, let's visit some different states.

Vegetation: **Needleleaf Forest**
State: **Maine**

The forests of northern Maine have mostly **needleleaf** trees. Needleleaf trees have long thin pointed leaves that look like needles. These trees stay green all year.

Needleleaf trees grow mostly in climate regions that have cool to cold winters. They are often found on high cool mountains. But they also grow in warmer places. They can grow well in poor soils.

Vegetation: **Mixed Forests**
State: **West Virginia**

Both needleleaf and **broadleaf** trees grow in West Virginia. Different broadleaf trees have flat leaves of different sizes. In places with warm summers and cold winters, broadleaf trees lose their leaves in fall when the weather gets cool. They grow new leaves in spring when the weather warms up again.

Broadleaf Trees:
ash, beech, birch, elm, oak, maple, poplar, sycamore, willow

Broadleaf tree

Needleleaf tree

Needleleaf Trees:
pine, cedar, cypress, fir, juniper, larch, redwood, spruce, yew

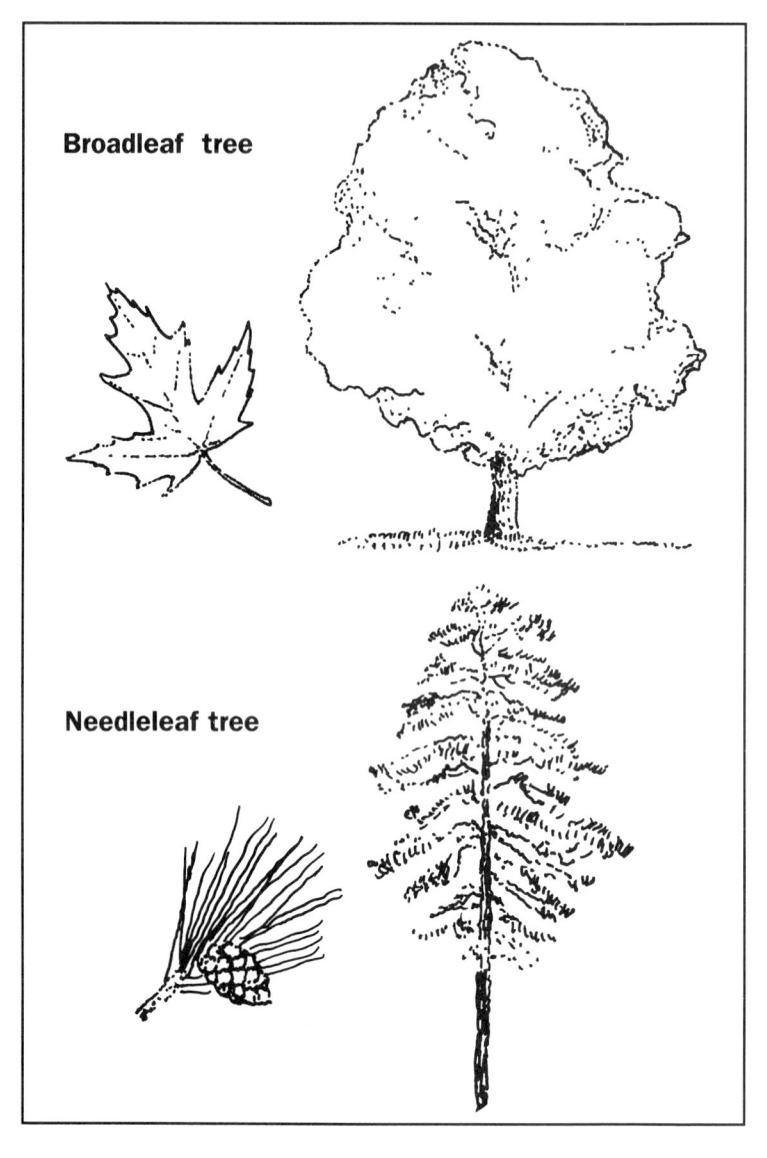

Vegetation: **Tropical Broadleaf Forests**
State: **Hawaii**

In parts of Hawaii that are warm and wet most of the year, there are thick tropical broadleaf forests. The trees there stay green all year.

Vegetation: **Scrub Forests**
State: **California**

Southern California is too dry for forests of large trees. But it does get enough rain for scrub forests to grow.

Scrub forests have short scrub trees with thick bark and waxy leaves. These trees do well in climates that are warm and dry for most of the year.

Vegetation: **Desert**
State: **Arizona**

If you drive through Arizona, you will see mainly thorny scrubs and cacti. Their hard outer parts help them store water. That's important for desert plants. Deserts get ten or fewer inches of rain a year. Only plants that need little water can grow there.

Vegetation: **Highland**
State: **Idaho**

Different kinds of vegetation can be found on the same mountain. On the side that gets enough rain, broadleaf trees grow at the lower elevations. Halfway up, there may be mixed forests. At the higher, cooler elevations there may be only needleleaf trees.

If the other side of the mountain gets little rain, it will have no forests at all. It will have only desert vegetation. And at very high elevations, the climate is too cold and dry for any trees to grow.

Vegetation: **Grasslands**
States: **Nebraska, Iowa, and Florida**

Parts of Nebraska and Iowa are covered by grasslands with few, if any, trees. Most of Nebraska's grasslands are called **steppes**. Steppes have short grass. Most of Iowa's grasslands are called **prairies**. Prairies have tall grass. Steppes and prairies are found where the climate is cool to cold and mostly dry.

Parts of southern Florida have grasslands called **savannas**. Along with the grass, savannas have some

Prairie planted in wheat

widely spaced trees and shrubs. They are found in warm climates that have both wet and dry seasons.

Vegetation: **Tundra**
State: **Alaska**

The cold, dry, almost bare land of the north coast of Alaska is a tundra. Very little grows there other than low bushes and small plants. During the short summer, tiny flowers bloom.

Places that are warm and wet have the most vegetation. Places that are cold and dry have the least vegetation.

Soil

Soil is deeper in some places than in others. It ranges from a few inches to many feet deep. But not all land is covered with soil. Some land is bare rock. And some land is covered with sand.

Most plants grow in soil. Soil comes from weathered, or worn down, rock. Rock gets worn down by the action of rain, ice, running water, and chemicals.

Soil contains more than weathered rock. It contains tiny living things too small for us to see without a microscope. And it contains the remains of plants and animals that have died.

The dead plant and animal matter is called **humus**. Humus gives plants some of the **nutrients** they need. They get other nutrients from other parts of the soil. Nutrients are the things plants need to grow.

Soil soaks up rainwater and stores it for plants to use.

Plants that do not need much water grow best in sandy soil. Sandy soil is loose. Water passes through it quickly.

Plants that need lots of water grow best in soil that has a lot of clay in it. Clay soil, which gets sticky when wet, holds water longer than sandy soil does.

Farmland Soil

Farmers plant crops that grow best in their climates and on the kinds of soil they have on their farms. Sandy soils are good for root crops like carrots and potatoes. Clay soils are good for wheat and other grains.

If the soil does not have enough nutrients in it, many farmers use **fertilizers.** Fertilizers add nutrients to the soil.

Different kinds of vegetation grow in different kinds and amounts of soil. Plants and trees take in water and nutrients through their root systems. Usually, the larger a tree is, the larger its root system will be.

Chapter Eleven **131**

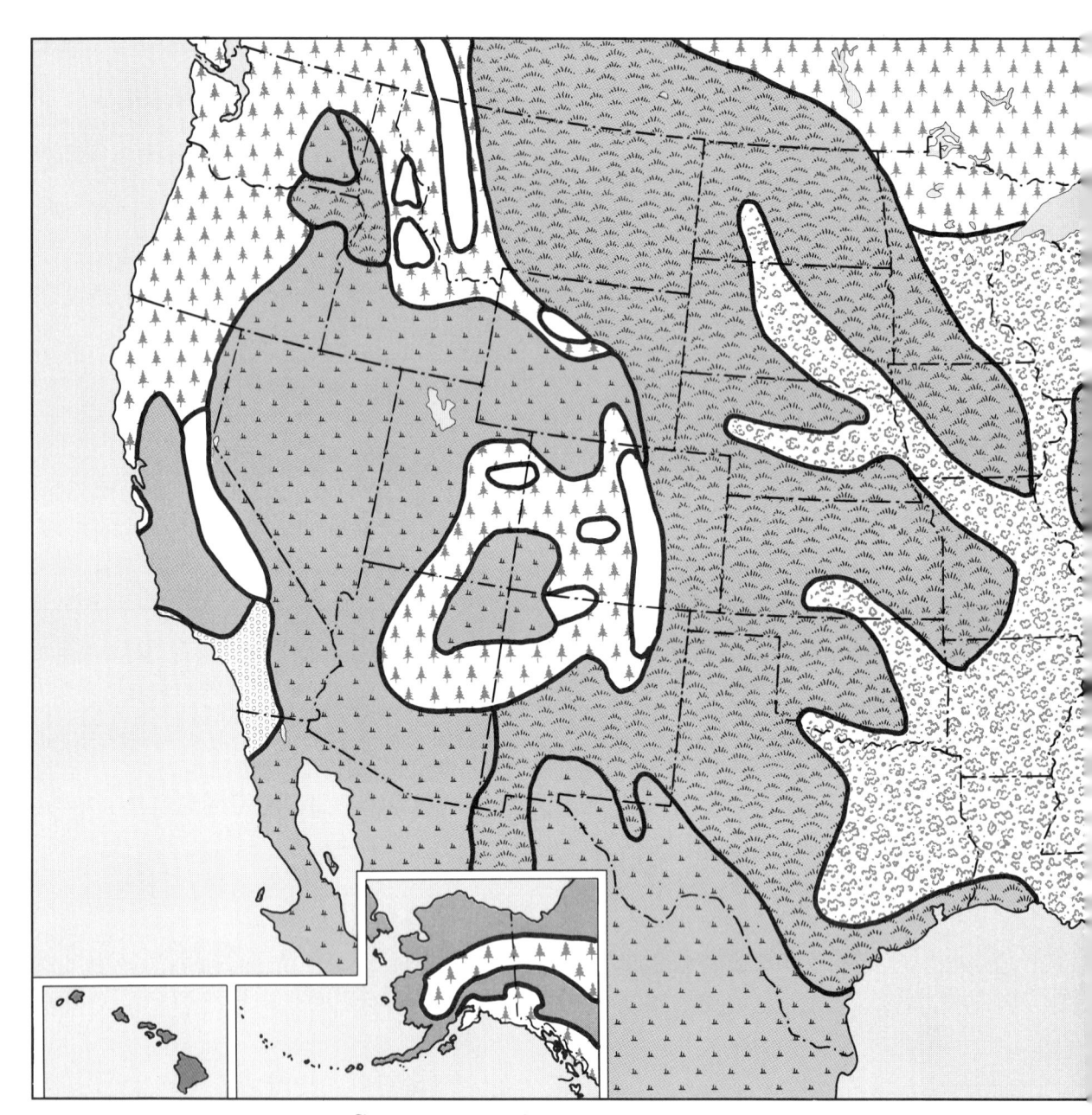

Geography Skills 12

Reading a Vegetation Map

132 Chapter Eleven

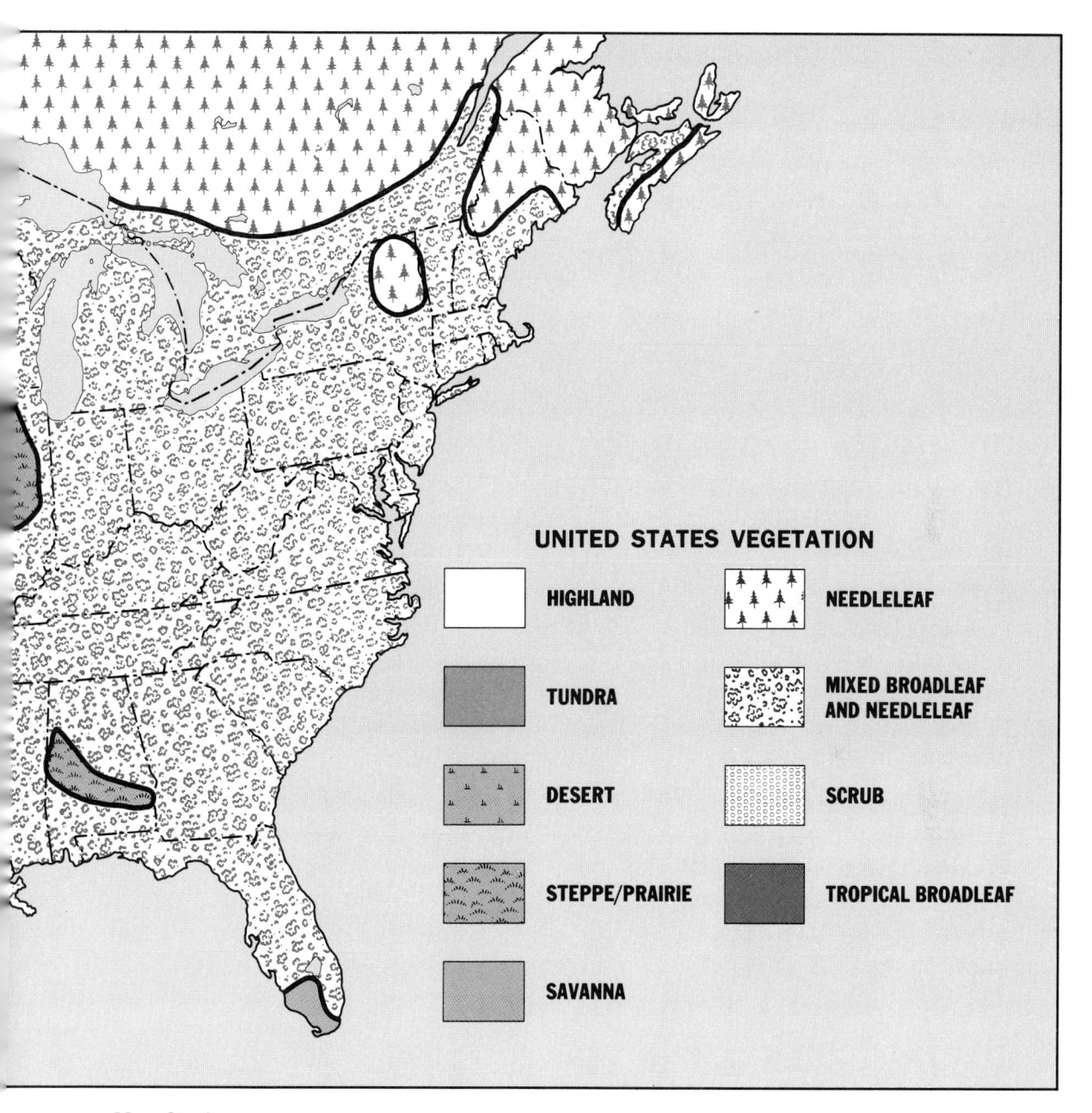

UNITED STATES VEGETATION

- HIGHLAND
- TUNDRA
- DESERT
- STEPPE/PRAIRIE
- SAVANNA
- NEEDLELEAF
- MIXED BROADLEAF AND NEEDLELEAF
- SCRUB
- TROPICAL BROADLEAF

Map Study
1. Which kind of vegetation does most of the eastern half of the United States have?
2. Which three kinds of vegetation does most of the western half of the United States have?
3. What kind of vegetation does your state have?

Chapter Eleven 133

Chapter Review

Summary

1. The main types of vegetation are: forest, grassland, tundra, desert, and highland.

2. There are four kinds of forest vegetation: needleleaf, broadleaf, tropical broadleaf, and scrub.

3. Needleleaf trees grow where it is cool or cold in the winter. They stay green all year.

4. In warm climates, broadleaf trees stay green all year. In cooler climates, they lose their leaves in fall and get new ones in spring.

5. Steppes are grasslands with short grass and no trees. Prairies have few trees and tall grass. Both steppes and prairies are found in cooler, drier climates.

6. Savannas are grasslands that have some widely spaced trees and shrubs. They are found where it is warm all year and there is a short rainy season.

7. Only low bushes and tiny plants grow on tundras, where the winters are long and bitterly cold.

8. Deserts may have cacti, thorny shrubs, and other plants that need very little water.

9. The vegetation on a mountain changes with the elevation and the amount of precipitation.

10. Soil gives plants the nutrients and water they need.

Thinking and Writing

Answer these questions in complete sentences on a separate sheet of paper.

1. How does the amount of precipitation change as we move south along the coast of California?
2. What is similar about cedar, cypress, and fir trees?
3. How is the climate that supports scrub forests similar to the climate that supports cacti?
4. How do steppes differ from prairies? In what way are they similar?
5. How do plants that grow well in sandy soil differ from plants that grow well in clay soil?
6. How are humus and fertilizer alike?

Questions to Discuss

1. Describe the following kinds of vegetation. Tell how climate affects each one.
    - forest
    - grassland
    - desert
    - tundra
    - highland
2. Which of the five main types of vegetation are found where you live?

Special Projects

1. Cut out pictures of different kinds of vegetation from old magazines. Paste them on paper. Tell what kind of vegetation each picture shows.
2. Collect soil samples from different parts of your town. Plant bean seeds in each sample. See which soils the beans grow best in.

Chapter 12
U.S. Agriculture

Cattle are raised on grazing lands. Then they are sent to feeding lots where they are fattened up on corn.

Chapter Learning Objectives
1. Name at least two important crops raised in each of the six geographic regions.
2. Tell which states are the leading producers of corn, wheat, cotton, and potatoes.
3. Tell which states are the leading producers of beef cattle, sheep, hogs, chickens, and milk products.
4. Explain why certain crops and animals are raised where they are.
5. Name the regions that depend heavily on irrigation for farming.

Words To Know

agriculture the growing of crops and raising of animals
grain any grass plant grown for its seeds
dairy milk and milk products
poultry animals such as chickens, ducks, and turkeys that are raised for their meat or eggs
fertile able to produce; good for growing crops
bushel a measurement that equals about 32 quarts
citrus fruits that include oranges, grapefruits, lemons, and limes
graze to allow cattle to feed on open grassland
cereals grains that can be used as food; also, a kind of food made from these grains
soybean the seed of the soybean plant; it can be used as food or as a source of cooking oil
cranberry a red berry from eastern Massachusetts
alfalfa a plant grown as food for horses and cattle
bale a large bundle; one bale of cotton weighs about 480 pounds

Do you know where peanuts are grown? How about pineapples? Where do you think most of the beef for making hamburgers comes from? In this unit, you will learn where these and other foods are grown. You will learn about **agriculture** in the United States.

The United States is one of the world's leading producers of food. It has a wide variety of soils and climates. Therefore, a wide variety of fruits, vegetables, and **grains** can be grown here. The climate, soil, and landforms in a region determine what can be grown in that region. The length of the growing season is also important.

As you read about each region, look for what is special about it as a farming area. Look for the main products of the region. See which states are leading producers of certain foods. Some of the information about leading producers is contained in graphs. Questions next to each graph will help you remember the information and work with it.

Pacific Region

Hawaii. This state has volcanic soil and year-round warmth. It is ideal for growing pineapple and sugar cane. Coffee beans are grown on the cooler slopes of some mountains. Raising beef cattle is a big business on the islands of Maui and Hawaii.

Alaska. This state has a short growing season and limited farmland. Alaska must get most of its food from the mainland. But there are some small **dairy**, **poultry**, and vegetable farms. They're found in the valleys near Fairbanks and Anchorage.

Washington and Oregon. Both states have mild climates, good soil, and plentiful supplies of water.

Washington is the nation's leading producer of apples. Pears and other fruits are also grown there. Oregon's Willamette Valley is famous for vegetables and strawberries. Flower growing is also a big business in Oregon.

Wheat is grown on the dry eastern plateau of Washington. Wheat needs less water than most fruits and vegetables.

California. California has a warm climate and **fertile** valleys. It is America's leading producer of fruits and vegetables. It is the only state that has the climate needed to grow figs, dates, olives, and almonds.

In the north, grapes are an important crop. In the south, oranges and other **citrus** fruits are grown.

California leads the nation in egg production. It is also the nation's second largest producer of beef cattle and sheep.

Because southern California is very dry, it depends on irrigation for growing crops. Water for irrigation comes from nearby rivers and from northern California rivers. Southern California also gets water from the Sierra Nevada Mountains.

LEADING U.S. POTATO PRODUCERS

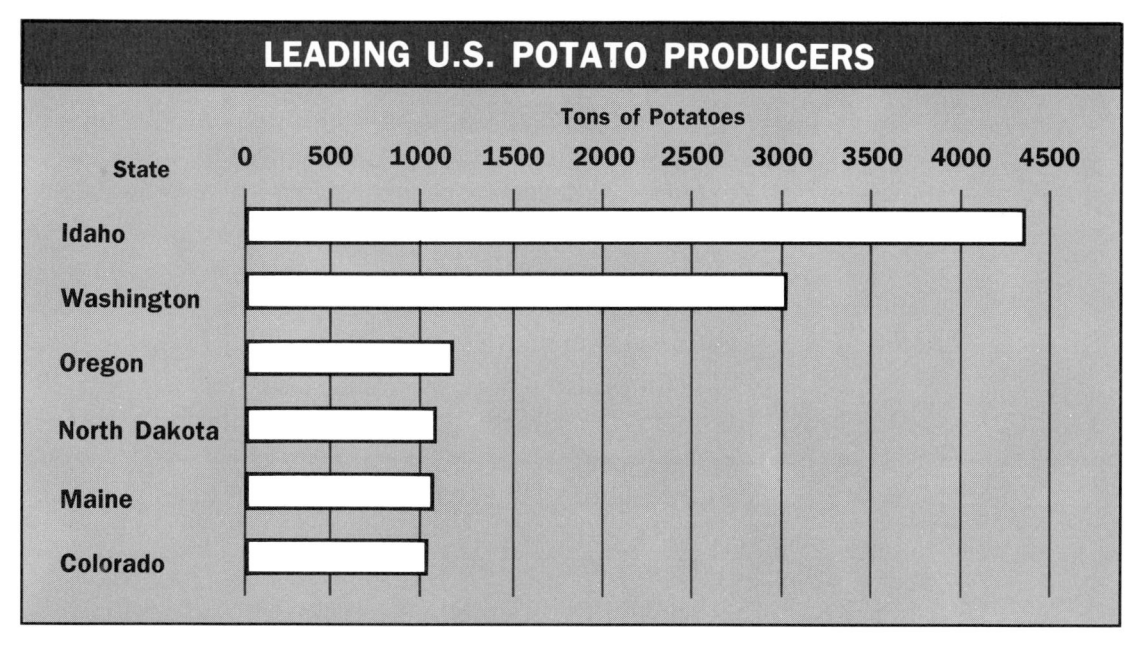

State	Tons of Potatoes (approx.)
Idaho	4300
Washington	3400
Oregon	800
North Dakota	700
Maine	700
Colorado	700

Graph Study The graph above shows the number of tons of potatoes produced in six states during one recent year.
1. About how many tons of potatoes were grown in Idaho?
2. Which state was the second highest producer?

Rocky Mountain Region

Have you eaten any baked or french fried potatoes lately? There's a good chance those potatoes came from irrigated farms along the Snake River in Idaho. Idaho is the number-one potato producer in the United States.

On the plains of eastern Colorado and northeastern Montana there are large wheat farms. On the dry grasslands east and west of the Rocky Mountains, sheep and cattle are **grazed**. Wyoming and Montana have some of the largest ranches in the United States. Cattle herders there often use jeeps and helicopters, instead of horses, to round up cattle.

Cotton is grown on irrigated lands in Arizona and New Mexico. Fruits and vegetables are grown on irrigated lands in Arizona and Utah.

North Central Region

The western part of the North Central Region has rich soils, flat plains, and limited precipitation. The area is well suited for growing wheat and other **cereals**. Cereals are grains that can be used as food.

The seeds of grain plants are often ground into flour. The flour is then used to make bread, pasta, and other products. Such foods as oatmeal and bran flakes are also made from grains.

Further east, where precipitation is greater, corn is the major crop. Both sweet corn and feed corn are raised. People eat sweet corn. Feed corn is given to cattle and hogs. These animals are also major products of the region. Iowa is the nation's leading producer of both corn and hogs.

Most of the region's cattle come from other regions. They are shipped to the corn growing areas to be fattened up. They are sold to meat companies.

What did you eat today that may have come from the North Central Region?

Other major crops grown in the region are **soybeans**, rye, barley, hay, and potatoes. Soybeans are used to feed animals. They also have many other uses. Have you ever eaten tofu or soy sauce? Both are made from soybeans.

Wisconsin and parts of Montana and Michigan have cool summers and hilly land. This makes them better suited for dairy farms than for growing crops. Wisconsin is the nation's leading producer of milk.

Northeast Region

The New England states have cool summers. Most of the land is covered with a thin, rocky layer of soil. It is not suited for growing large crops. Instead, there are small dairy, poultry, and vegetable farms.

In the river valleys, though, some large crops are grown. These valleys have deep, rich soil. Maine is famous for its potatoes. Tobacco is grown on the flat, fertile lands of the Connecticut River Valley.

LEADING U.S. WHEAT PRODUCERS

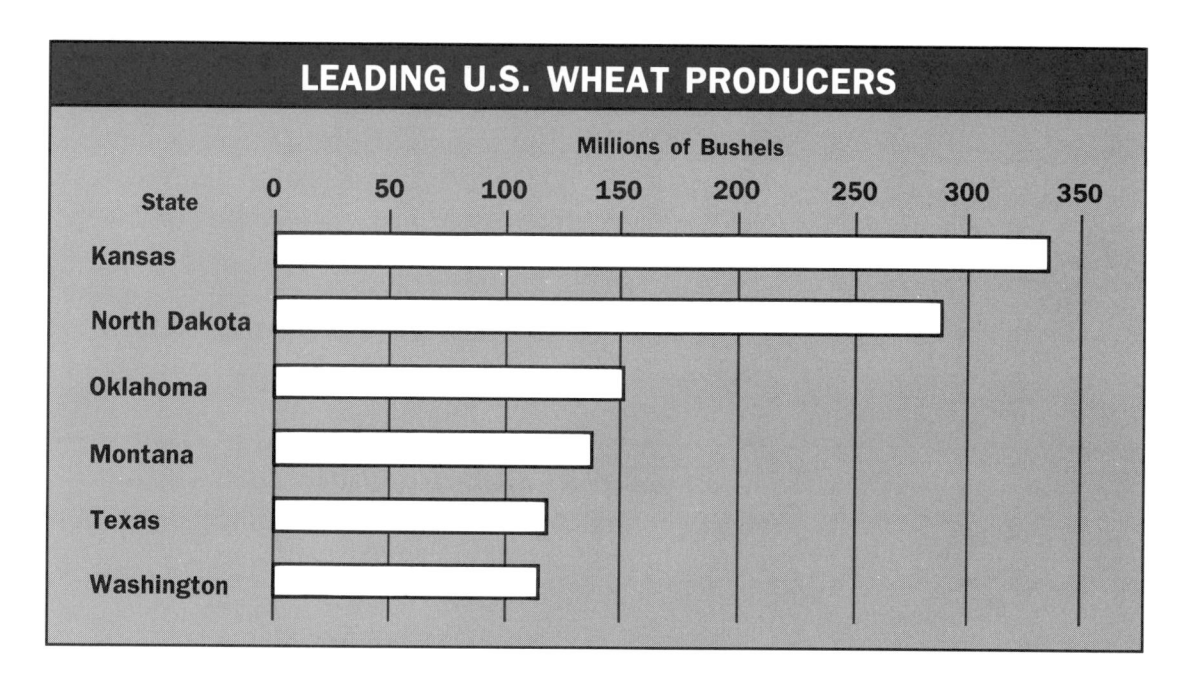

State	Millions of Bushels
Kansas	~330
North Dakota	~290
Oklahoma	~150
Montana	~140
Texas	~120
Washington	~110

Graph Study The graph above shows how many millions of **bushels** of wheat were produced in six states during one recent year.
1. About how many bushels of wheat were produced in Kansas?
2. About how much did all six states produce?

Most maple syrup consumed in the United States comes from the sap of Vermont's maple trees. Cranberry sauce is made from cranberries. In the United States, this fruit is grown only in eastern Massachusetts.

Further south in the Northeast Region, the climate is slightly warmer. There is more flat and gently rolling land in this area. New York and Pennsylvania have many dairy farms. New York also grows large amounts of apples and grapes.

Poultry is raised in all the states. Delaware raises the most chickens. Delaware also grows large crops of sweet corn, potatoes, and strawberries. Maryland grows large crops of barley, wheat, and soybeans. Southeastern New Jersey has small vegetable farms.

Chapter Twelve 141

South Central Region

Most of the South Central Region has flat or gently rolling land. But the amount of precipitation and the richness of the soil differs greatly within the region.

In much of Arkansas, Louisiana, and the coastal plains of Texas the soil is rich. Also, the rainfall is plentiful. The area is well suited for raising rice, sugar cane, cotton, citrus fruits, and sweet potatoes. In addition, Arkansas is the nation's leading producer of chickens.

Areas along the Rio Grande and near the Gulf Coast have a long growing season. And they have either good rainfall or water for irrigation. These areas produce large crops of citrus fruits and vegetables.

The eastern parts of Texas and Oklahoma get enough rainfall to grow corn, **alfalfa**, barley, and oats. Alfalfa is a kind of hay used to feed animals.

Where else is irrigation important for farming?

The western parts of Texas and Oklahoma get far less rain. But there is enough rain to grow wheat in central and western Oklahoma. Irrigation is used in Texas and Oklahoma to grow feed grains and cotton.

Vast grazing lands cover much of central and western Texas. Cattle are also raised in other parts of the state. Texas is the country's number-one producer of both beef cattle and sheep.

Southeast Region

Fertile soil and warm, moist weather make most of the Southeast's lowlands excellent for farming.

Virginia, Kentucky, and North Carolina are the country's leading tobacco producing states. Rice, soybeans, and some cotton are grown there as well.

Virginia's sandy coastal plain is good for raising potatoes, tomatoes, and strawberries.

LEADING U.S. COTTON PRODUCERS

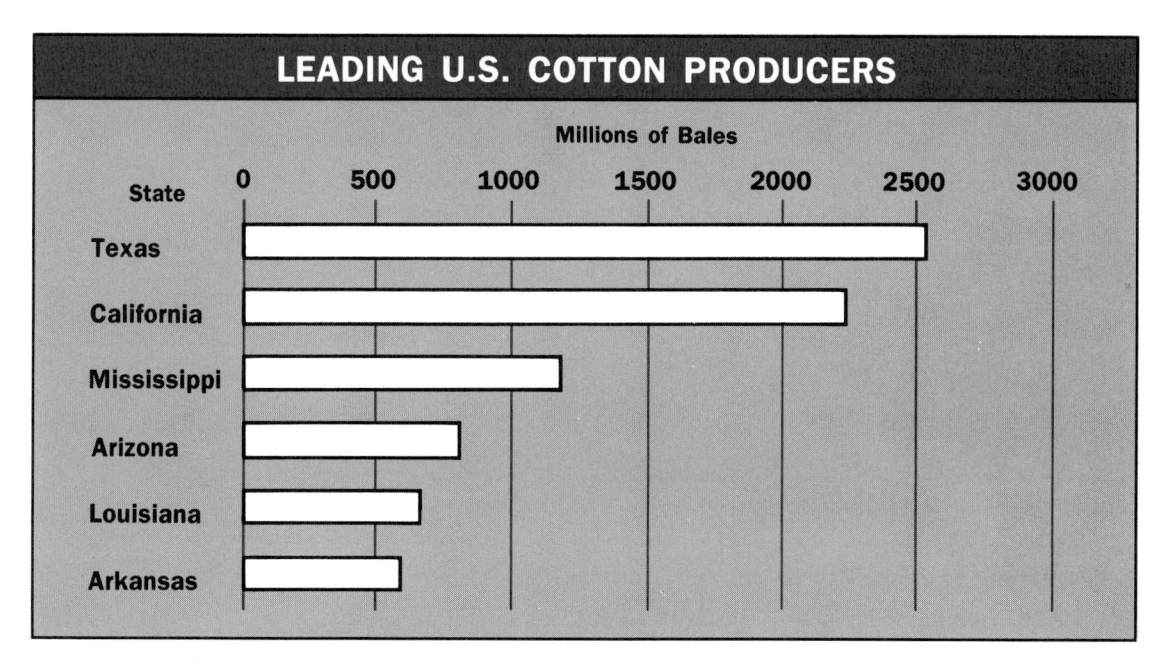

State	Millions of Bales
Texas	~2500
California	~2300
Mississippi	~1100
Arizona	~700
Louisiana	~500
Arkansas	~450

Graph Study The graph above shows how many millions of bales of cotton were produced in six states during one recent year.
1. About how many bales of cotton were grown in Texas?
2. Which of these six states produced the least?

Most of the country's peaches come from the Southeast coastal plains. South Carolina is the country's number-one peach producer.

From Virginia south to Georgia and Alabama, peanuts are a major crop. Georgia leads the United States in peanut production.

Florida is the country's number-one producer of citrus fruits. It also raises large numbers of beef cattle. Mississippi, Alabama, and Tennessee produce large cotton crops.

Chapter Review

Summary

1. Some of the important crops in each of the six geographic regions are:

    Pacific pineapples, apples, pears, dates, figs, grapes, citrus fruits, vegetables

    Rocky Mountain potatoes, wheat, cotton, fruits, vegetables

    North Central corn, wheat, soybeans, rye, barley

    Northeast potatoes, tobacco, cranberries, apples, sweet corn, barley, vegetables

    South Central citrus fruits, rice, sugar cane, cotton, sweet potatoes, wheat and other grains

    Southeast tobacco, peanuts, peaches, citrus fruits, cotton, rice, soybeans

2. The leading producers of the following crops are:

    corn . . . . . Iowa
    potatoes . . . . . Idaho
    wheat . . . . . Kansas
    cotton . . . . . Texas

3. The leading producers of the following animal products are:

    beef cattle . . . . . Texas
    sheep . . . . . Texas
    hogs . . . . . Iowa
    chickens . . . . . Arkansas
    milk . . . . . Wisconsin

4. Some reasons certain crops and animals are raised in certain places are:

    Pacific Region. Southern California is the only place with the right climate for growing figs, dates, and almonds.

    North Central Region. This region has fertile soil, but its growing season and precipitation are too limited for many crops. However, the region is well suited for growing wheat, corn, and other grains.

    Rocky Mountain and South Central Regions. Much of the land in these two regions is either too rugged or dry for farming. That's why a good deal of land is used for grazing sheep and cattle.

    South Central Region. The Gulf Coast's warm weather and wet lands make it suitable for growing rice and sugar cane.

5. States with areas that depend heavily on irrigation are: California, Arizona, New Mexico, Oklahoma, Texas, and Idaho.

Thinking and Writing

Answer these questions in complete sentences on a separate sheet of paper.

1. How would the climate of a wheat-producing area differ from the climate of a citrus-producing area?
2. How does sweet corn differ from feed corn?
3. How are farmers in dry Arizona able to produce fruits and vegetables?
4. How is agriculture in the Rocky Mountain Region similar to agriculture in the South Central Region? How is it different?
5. Why might cattle raised in Texas be sent to Iowa before being sold to meat companies?
6. Why isn't the land in New England as good for farming as the land in the rest of the Northeast?

Questions to Discuss

1. What determines which kind of foods can be grown in a region?
2. Why does Alaska "import" most of its food from other states? What effect do you think this has on the cost of food in Alaska?

Special Projects

1. Make a drawing of your favorite meal or sandwich. Write down which region or regions each food in the drawing might have come from.
2. Talk to a food store manager. Find out which fruits and vegetables in the store come from nearby farms. Report back to the class.

Chapters 9–12

REVIEW

Answer these questions on a separate sheet of paper.

A. Key Words

blizzard
citrus
climate
elevation
grains
fertile
humid
nutrients
precipitation
tundra

Choose the word from the list on the left that best completes each sentence below.

1. Southern California's ____ is usually warm and dry.
2. Mount McKinley's ____ is 20,320 feet.
3. A ____ is a blinding snow storm.
4. Weather that is ____ can make you feel damp and sticky.
5. Deserts get very little ____ .
6. Grapefruits, oranges, and lemons are ____ fruits.
7. Plants grow best in ____ soil.
8. Soil provides plants with the ____ they need.
9. Grass plants whose seeds can be ground into flour are ____ .
10. Only tiny plants and low bushes grow on a ____ .

B. Key Facts

Choose the word or words that best complete each sentence.

11. As elevation rises, temperature ____ .
    a. rises   b. doesn't change   c. drops
12. Winter temperatures along a coast are usually ____ .
    a. warmer than inland areas   b. colder than inland areas   c. the same as inland areas
13. Clouds form when rising water vapor ____ .
    a. cools   b. heats up   c. freezes
14. The southern parts of the United States mainland are usually ____ .
    a. cool to cold   b. warm to cool   c. warm to hot

15. The driest parts of the U.S. mainland are in ____ .

   a. Arizona, New Mexico, and southern California
   b. Maine, New Hampshire, and Vermont
   c. Florida, Georgia, and Alabama

16. In the North Central Region, the difference between winter and summer temperatures is ____ .

   a. small   b. great

17. Warm places with plenty of rainfall have mostly ____ .

   a. scrub forests   b. needleleaf forests
   c. broadleaf forests

18. Large parts of southern Arizona and New Mexico are covered with ____ .

   a. forests   b. grass   c. cacti

19. Most of the nation's sheep and cattle are raised ____ .

   a. west of the Mississippi River   b. east of the Mississippi River   c. north of the Ohio River

20. Most of the nation's wheat and corn come from the ____ .

   a. South Central region   b. Pacific region
   c. North Central region

C. Main Ideas

Answer the questions below.

21. Name the steps in the water cycle. Start with evaporation and end with the return of water to the sea.
22. Tell why the amount of rainfall on one side of a mountain may be different from that on the other side.
23. Tell what soil is made of.

Chapter 13
Earth's Renewable Resources

Farming in the late 20th Century

Chapter Learning Objectives

1. Explain what a resource is.
2. Define and give examples of renewable resources.
3. Identify the sun as our chief source of heat, light, and other forms of energy.
4. Tell how air serves as a resource.
5. Describe the uses to which water is put.
6. Tell how humans make use of animals.
7. Describe plants as a resource.
8. Tell how forests and the soil are used as resources.

Words To Know

resource something we need or can use

energy the power to do work

What Is a Resource?

Suppose we had no air to breathe or water to drink. What would happen to us?

We would soon die. Air and water are two of Earth's many **resources.** Resources include everything we get from Earth that we need or can use. We call something a resource if we are able to make use of it. Sometimes this means having the tools and skills to do that.

Think of rich soil full of nutrients. If no one uses the soil, it is not a resource. But suppose a farmer grows crops in the soil. Then the soil becomes a resource.

Suppose the farmer uses an animal to help with the work. Then the animal is also a resource.

To make use of the soil and the animal, the farmer needs certain tools and skills. What tools and skills do you think a farmer might need?

Farming in Florida in the early 20th Century

Chapter Thirteen **149**

A cave man chipping flint.

What tools do you use at home? What tools do you use at school?

Our Needs Change

Sometimes we replace one resource with another. Long ago, before people had metal tools, flint was an important resource. Flint is a rock found on Earth's surface. It is easy to chip and shape. People made flint arrowheads, knives, and digging tools.

Then people found out how to make harder, stronger arrowheads and tools from metal. They learned how to get metal from the ground. They learned how to shape it. When they no longer needed flint, they no longer thought of it as an important resource.

At one time, whale oil was an important resource. People burned it in lamps to have light at night. Sailors with special boats and tools hunted for whales all over the world. But when kerosene lamps came into use, whale oil became a much less important resource. Kerosene is made from oil that comes from the ground.

Today, we use electricity to light our lamps. Coal, oil, and water power are the main resources we use to produce the electricity.

Renewable Resources

Some resources are renewable. That is, they can be replaced if they are used. Let's see how we use some of our renewable resources.

Energy from the Sun

The sun gives us heat. The heat warms us and helps plants grow. The sun gives us light. Plants need both warmth and light to grow.

Plants store **energy** from the sun. Energy is power. When you eat foods made from plants, energy enters your body. It gives you the power to walk, run, and do all the things you do.

The energy stored in oil and coal also came from the sun. You will learn more about this in Chapter 14.

Air

Living things need certain gases to stay alive. Plants take in carbon dioxide from the air. They give back oxygen. Animals breathe in the oxygen. They breathe out carbon dioxide. The air is like a bank. It holds the gases until they are needed.

Water vapor in the air keeps us from burning up in the daytime and freezing at night. It is also part of the cycle that brings us fresh water.

Farming makes use of many of Earth's resources.

Water

Living things cannot go for long without water. Animals need water to digest food, stay cool, and get rid of wastes. Plants need water to grow.

We use water at home for cooking and cleaning. Farmers use water to raise their crops and keep their animals alive. Some factories use large amounts of water.

Water is also important for travel. Boats carry millions of people up and down rivers and across lakes and oceans. Ships carry millions of tons of goods on Earth's waterways.

Water is used in some places to make electricity. This is done by building a dam across a river to hold back the water. Then some of the water is allowed to flow over the blades of large wheels. The turning wheels drive generators. The generators produce electricity. The electricity is carried over wires to where it will be used.

The human body is 65% water.

Water passing through this dam helps make electricity.

Life depends on water.

How Much Water Do We Use?

1. The average person in the United States uses 168 gallons of water per day.
2. In the average home, 107,000 gallons of water are used per year.
3. It takes about six gallons of water to flush a toilet.
4. It takes 25 to 50 gallons of water to take a shower.
5. If you leave the water running while brushing your teeth, you'll use about two gallons of water.
6. If you leave the water running while shaving, you'll use 10 to 15 gallons of water.
7. It takes 20 gallons of water to wash a sinkful of dishes.
8. It takes 10 to 12 gallons of water to run a dishwasher.

Animals

Think of how important animals are to us.

Do you eat eggs or meat? These foods come from animals.

Do you drink milk? Milk comes from cows. Butter, cream, and cheese are made from milk.

Do you have a sweater, scarf, or anything else made of wool? Wool comes from the hair of sheep.

Do you wear leather shoes or own a leather wallet? Leather comes from the skins of animals.

In some parts of the world, people still hunt to get what they need from animals. But today, most of these needs are met by animals raised on farms and ranches.

In many parts of the world, animals are used to do work. Horses, oxen, and water buffalo are used to pull plows and turn the heavy wheels that make flour from grain. Elephants move heavy logs. Animals also carry people and goods from one place to another.

How much of the food that you eat comes from animals? How much of it comes from plants?

This woman is a member of a wool gathering cooperative in Guatemala.

Planting rice

Fish is an important food for many people. Most of the fish and seafood we eat comes from rivers and oceans. But today, fish are also being raised in large ponds on fish farms.

Plants

Plants are our chief source of food. We eat fruits and vegetables. We eat grains like rice, wheat, and corn. And we eat foods made from grains, such as bread and noodles. We may eat meat from cows, sheep, chickens, and pigs. But all those animals are plant eaters. Without plants, farmers couldn't raise animals.

Some of our clothing comes from plants. Is any of your clothing made of cotton? Cotton comes from the cotton plant. In warm climates, people may wear straw hats or other clothing made from plants. In some places, people make baskets from parts of plants.

Plants are renewable resources because new plants can be grown to replace those that are used.

Cotton, wool, and silk are called "natural fibers." Polyester and other cloths made of chemicals are called "synthetic fibers."

Chapter Thirteen **155**

Forests

How far would you have to travel to get to the nearest forest?

Look around you. How many things do you see that are made of wood? Wood is used to build houses and furniture. It is used to make pencils and rulers. It is ground up to make paper. In many parts of the world, people heat and cook with wood.

Do you have rubber tires on your bike or car? Some rubber comes from the sap of rubber trees.

A tree being tapped for rubber.

156　Chapter Thirteen

Some medicines also come from trees.

Forests are very important to us for other reasons. They are home to thousands of kinds of birds and animals. And they are enjoyable places for people to camp, hike, fish, or hunt.

Forests help keep soil from washing or blowing away. They also fill the air with oxygen and water vapor. As you read earlier, animals need oxygen to breathe. And water vapor is part of the water cycle.

Soil

Soil is one of our most important resources. Trees and other plants grow in it. Most of the world's food comes from plants grown in soil.

Only certain parts of the world have soil that is good for farming. The best farmland is found in valleys and deltas, where rivers have left deep layers of soil. Soil that has just the right mix of nutrients makes the best farmland.

All the resources we have talked about so far are renewable. Some take very little time to replace, such as sunlight, air, and water. Trees take much longer. And it may take hundreds or thousands of years to replace soil that has washed or blown away.

A grove of rubber trees

Chapter Review

Summary

1. Resources are things we get from Earth that we need or can use.
2. Renewable resources are resources that can be replaced after they are used.
3. The sun is our chief source of heat, light, and other forms of energy.
4. Air supplies animals with oxygen and plants with carbon dioxide.
5. Water is used for drinking, cooking, cleaning, and watering crops. It is also used in some factories, and to make electricity.
6. Animals supply us with both food and clothing.
7. Plants are used for food and to make clothing.
8. Forests may be enjoyed as places to camp, hike, fish, or hunt. Forests supply us with wood, rubber, and other products. They also hold soil in place and fill the air with oxygen and water vapor.
9. Soil is a very important resource; most of our food is grown in it.

Thinking and Writing

Answer these questions in complete sentences on a separate sheet of paper.

1. Look at the photographs on pages 148 and 149. Which resource is the same in both pictures?
2. Which of the renewable resources mentioned in this chapter is everyone always using?
3. Plants and animals are both living things. And both are resources. In terms of how they use gases in the atmosphere, how are they different from each other?
4. Look at the photograph on page 151. Which of the resources mentioned in this chapter are being used?
5. In what way do ranchers depend on plant life?
6. As resources, how are water and soil alike? How are they different?

Question to Discuss

Choose one of the resources listed below. Tell how your life would change if that resource suddenly disappeared.

- sunlight
- air
- water
- animals
- plants
- forests
- soil

Special Project

Form teams. Find the answers to these questions. Report your answers to the class.

Where does your school's electricity come from? How is it produced? How does it get to your school?

Chapter Thirteen

Chapter 14
Earth's Nonrenewable Resources

Workers use platforms like this to reach oil buried below the ocean floor.

Chapter Learning Objectives

1. Describe the formation and some of the uses of coal and oil.
2. Describe some of the uses of iron, copper, aluminum, lead, silver, and gold. Tell how they are obtained.
3. Explain why mineral resources are not renewable.
4. Describe problems associated with the burning of coal and oil, logging and mining, and the dumping of waste water.
5. Describe some of the steps being taken to address these problems.
6. Use a map to explain the distribution of world iron and copper supplies.
7. Use a pie graph to explain the distribution of world oil reserves.

Words To Know

crude oil oil from under the ground before it is made into a product, such as gasoline

fuel any material that is burned to provide energy

pollute to make unhealthy, as in *polluting the air and water*

smog dirty air made of fog, smoke, and chemicals

acid a chemical substance that wears away other substances

Some natural resources took thousands and even millions of years to form. Once they are used up, they cannot be replaced. We use many of these nonrenewable resources in some way everyday.

In this unit, you will read about nonrenewable resources. And you will learn about some of the resource problems we are facing.

Nonrenewable Resources

Oil

There has been oil below Earth's surface for millions of years. How did it get there?

Scientists believe the oil was made from the remains of tiny sea plants and animals. When the plants and animals died, they sank to the ocean floor. Layer upon layer of these dead plants and animals were built up. Then they were buried under sediment that came from rivers flowing into the ocean.

The weight of the water and sediment pressed down on the dead matter for millions of years. Scientists say this caused it to turn into oil and natural gas. Later, some of the places that had oil were pushed up above the water. They became dry land. Today, there is oil below both dry land and the ocean's floor.

Special drills are used to get at the oil. The drills are long enough and strong enough to cut through rock.

When the oil is reached, pipes and pumps are used to bring it up to the surface.

What do you use that's made of plastic?

What comes out of the ground is a thick black liquid called **crude oil**. Crude oil is used to make heating oil, motor oil, gasoline, plastic, and many other products. It has become one of our most important resources.

Coal

Coal is a black rock that burns slowly and gives off a lot of heat. It is used as a **fuel** in factories where steel and other metal products are made.

Coal is also used in some power plants that make electricity. The coal is burned to heat water. The water becomes steam. The steam turns the wheels that drive generators.

Scientists believe it took millions of years for coal to be formed. They say that temperatures were much warmer on Earth millions of years ago. Much of Earth's surface was covered then with muddy land called swamps. Large tropical plants grew in these muddy swamps.

When the plants died, they fell into the swamps. In time, the swamps became covered with soil and rock. The soil and rock pressed down on the plant matter for millions of years. It became coal.

Notice that both coal and oil are made mostly from dead plants. While they were living, those plants stored up energy from the sun. So the energy we get from coal and oil really comes from the sun!

Coal is buried below Earth's surface. Workers dig mines to get at the coal.

An open pit mine

In some places, the miners dig a shaft, or long deep hole, down to where the coal is. Then they dig tunnels branching out from the shaft.

But most of today's big coal mines are strip mines. Huge machines first strip away the trees and soil. They uncover the coal. Then other huge machines dig it up.

The Metals

Coal and oil are minerals that formed from living things. Other minerals were formed in other ways. But they, too, took millions of years to form. And they, too, have to be brought out of Earth's crust.

Shaft mines are used to bring up some of these minerals. Strip mines and open pit mines are used to get at others. Open pit mines are like huge holes in the ground big enough for trucks to drive down into.

Steel mill

Minerals are often found mixed together in rock. Many minerals are metals. Rock that contains metal is called ore. Miners dig out the ore. Then they remove the metal from it.

Iron, copper, lead, and aluminum are all metals. So are silver and gold. Can you name at least one thing that is made from each of these metals?

Iron is used to make iron fences and other things. But its most important use is in the making of steel. Iron is mixed with other minerals to produce steel. Steel is very strong and lasts for a long time. It is used to build cars, ships, trains, bridges, and large buildings. Some pots, pans, knives, forks, and spoons are also made from steel.

Copper is an important metal. Have you talked on the phone lately? Your voice went out over copper wires. Are there any lights on right now where you are? The electricity is coming in on copper wires. Copper is also used to make water pipes.

Lead is a very heavy metal. Divers use lead weights to help keep them down under water. Lead is also used to make fishing weights and the small weights that balance car wheels. Lead has other uses as well.

Aluminum is a very light but strong metal. It comes from an ore called bauxite. Aluminum is used to make pots and pans, soft drink cans, bicycle wheels, auto parts, and other things.

Silver and gold are used to make jewelry. These minerals also have many other uses. Silver is used in photography. Gold is used for some dental work. Do you own anything made with silver or gold?

All the minerals we have talked about are nonrenewable. When they are used up, there will be no more of them.

What do you use that's made of aluminum?

Finished steel beams

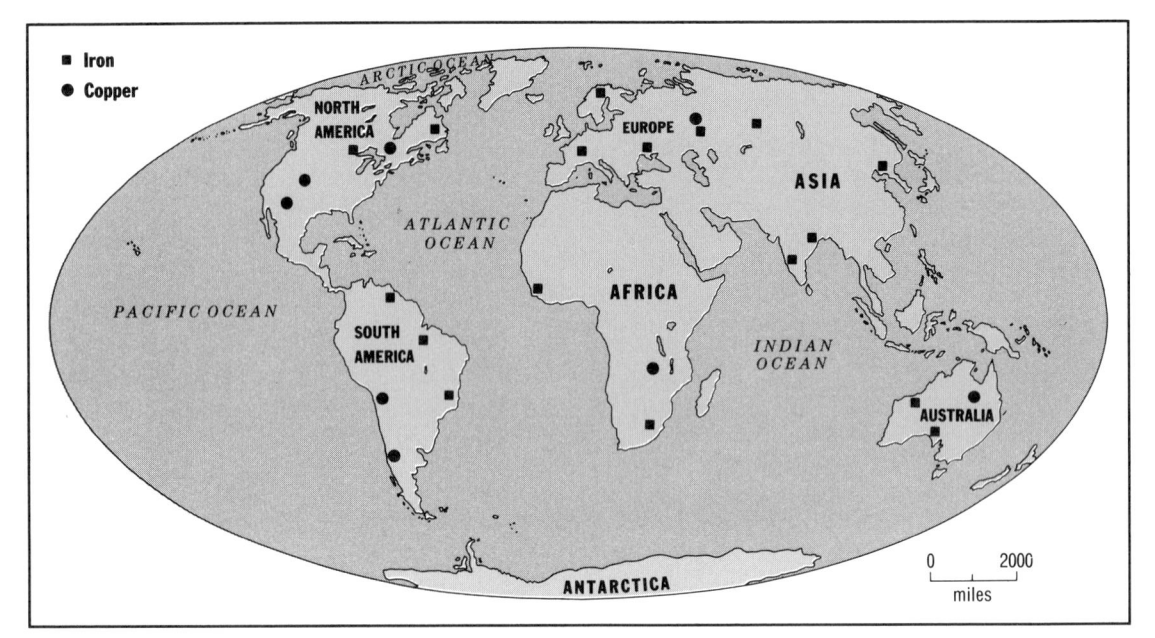

Map Study The map above shows where most of the world's iron and copper are found. Use the map to answer these questions.

World Iron and Copper Supplies

1. Are there more iron mines or copper mines in the world?
2. Does the United States have any copper?
3. Which continent has the most iron mines?
4. Suppose a country does not have any iron or copper of its own. How do you think it might get these?

Geography Skills 13

Reading a Pie Graph

A pie graph is useful for showing how a whole thing is divided into parts. For example, the pie graph on the right shows how much of Earth's surface is water and how much is land.

You can tell which there is more of by the size of each part of the graph. The graph shows that only one-third of Earth's surface is land. All the rest is water.

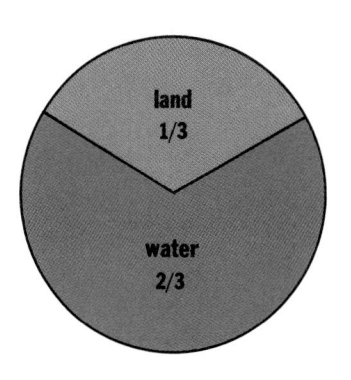

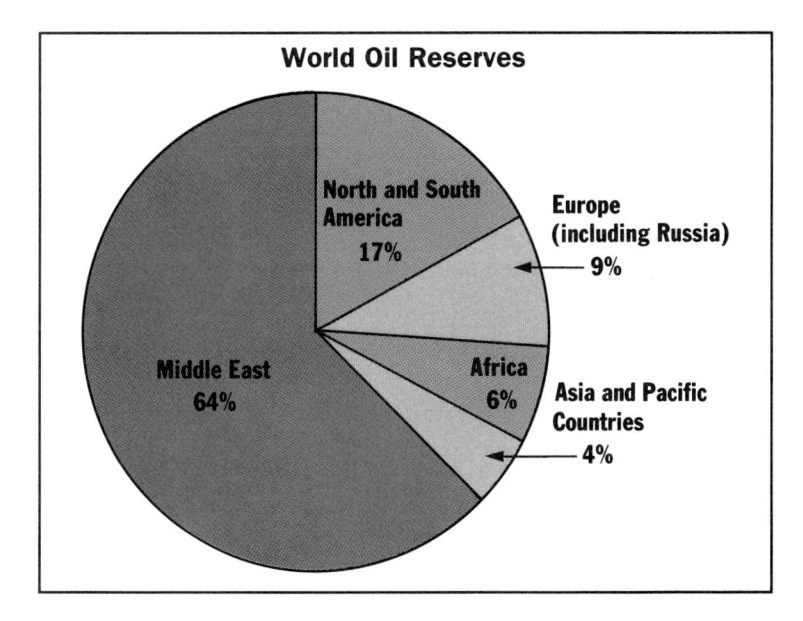

World Oil Reserves

- Middle East 64%
- North and South America 17%
- Europe (including Russia) 9%
- Africa 6%
- Asia and Pacific Countries 4%

Graph Study This pie graph shows how the world's oil reserves are distributed. "Oil reserves" refer to oil that is still in the ground. Look at the graph. Read the names of the different parts of the world that are listed on the graph. Then answer these questions:
1. Which part of the world has the most oil reserves?
2. Which part of the world has the least oil reserves?
3. Does the Middle East have more or less oil than all the rest of the world?

Problems

Today we are using huge amounts of some non-renewable resources. We may soon run out of them. We are in danger of ruining some of our renewable resources, too. We are also **polluting** the planet we live on. Let's take a look at some of these problems.

Smoke coming out of factory smokestacks may contain harmful chemicals.

Polluting the Air and Water

Coal and oil are wonderful sources of energy. But when they burn, they add chemicals to the air. Some of the chemicals are harmful to living things and can cause illness and death.

Sometimes the chemicals mix with other things in the air and make **smog.** Smog hangs over cities in a thick dark cloud. It can cause your eyes to water and can make breathing difficult.

168   Chapter Fourteen

Sometimes chemicals in the air mix with rainwater. The water turns the chemicals into **acids.** Acid rain harms the plants it falls on. If it falls on or runs into streams, rivers, or lakes, it can kill fish. Acid rain can be strong enough to dissolve rock.

Water can be polluted in another way. Many factories use tons of water every day. Then, they may dump the used water into rivers and lakes. This water may contain harmful chemicals that can kill plants and fish. Birds and other animals that eat the plants and fish may die also.

How clean is your nearest river?

We, too, can get sick from eating things that live in polluted water. And we can get sick if we swim in it. We cannot drink polluted water or use it for watering crops.

Oil Spills

Much of the world's oil lies under water. Wells are sunk down from oil-drilling platforms to where the oil is. Sometimes these wells leak, and then the oil spills out, killing fish and other sea life.

Spills are also caused by huge ships, called tankers, that carry oil around the world. Sometimes these tankers leak or even break apart. Then tons of oil spill out into the ocean. The oil kills sea life. It may also wash up onto beaches. Sea birds get coated with the oil. They cannot fly, and they may not be able to breathe. Many die.

Mining and Forestry Problems

You read earlier about strip and open pit mines. They are the cheapest and fastest way to get at minerals buried in the ground. But strip mining strips away trees and soil. And open pit mining leaves huge ugly holes in the ground.

Cutting down forests causes problems, too. Can you guess what some of the problems are?

Chapter Fourteen **169**

Trees soak up water. When they are gone, rainwater washes away the soil. Wind can blow it away, too. Trees give off water vapor. When forests are cut down, the climate of a place can change. There may be less rain. And where there is less plant life, there is likely to be less animal life.

Dealing with the Problems

Many people are working to save our resources. Here are some of the things they are doing.

Pollution Controls

Governments have made laws to control air pollution. Automobiles can release only certain amounts of harmful chemicals into the air. The same is true of factories.

Laws have also been made to control water pollution. Factories are not allowed to dump certain wastes into rivers and lakes. They must remove harmful chemicals from water before they dump it.

Many polluted rivers and lakes are being cleaned up. But it will take years to make them safe again.

Using New Sources of Energy

Windmills are being used to make electricity. And some people are trapping heat from the sun with solar panels. You may have seen these panels on rooftops where you live. The energy they collect can help heat a building or make hot water.

Saving and Recycling Resources

People are trying to cut down on the amounts of coal, oil, and other resources they use. They shut off unneeded lights to cut down on the electricity they use. That saves coal and oil because these resources are burned to produce electricity.

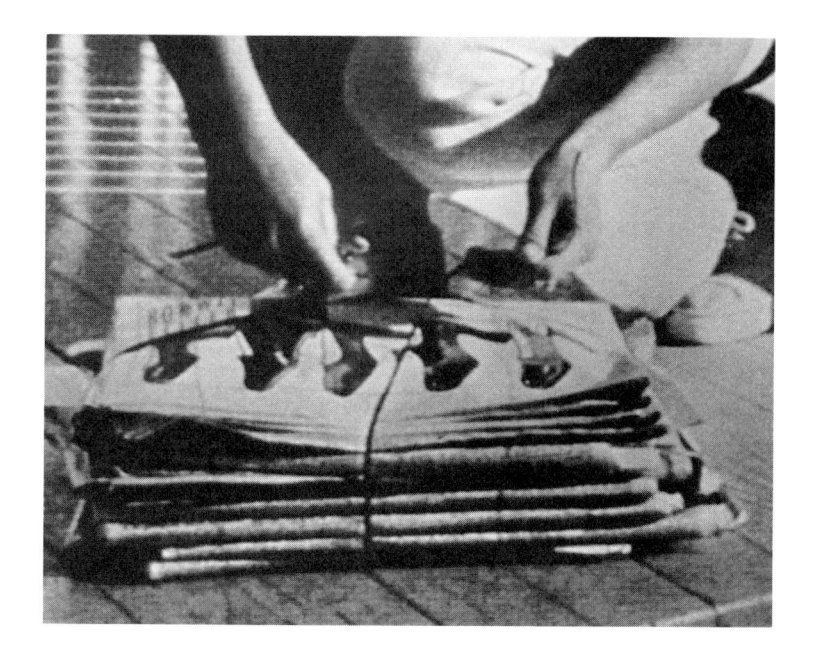

Aluminum cans, plastic and glass bottles, and newspapers can all be easily recycled.

Driving to school or work in carpools is another way to help save oil.

Do you turn in aluminum cans and glass jars and bottles to recycling centers? The metal and glass can be melted down and used again.

Newspapers can be recycled. Some community groups recycle newspapers to raise money.

Old cars and other machines made of metal are also recycled. The metal is melted down and new things are made with it.

In the United States, more paper is thrown away every day than any other product.

Replacing Soil and Trees

Some mining companies now take steps to repair the places they have mined. They fill in open pits. They replace the soil and plant new grass and trees.

Some logging companies also plant new trees after they have cut down part of a forest.

These are some of the things that people are doing to help save our resources.

Can you think of anything you can do to help?

Chapter Fourteen **171**

Chapter Review

Summary

1. Scientists believe that oil was formed from dead sea life. We get heating oil, motor oil, gasoline, plastic, and other products from crude oil.

2. Scientists believe coal was formed from layers of dead plants. Coal is used to produce steel and electricity.

3. Metals such as iron and copper are minerals that come from rocks called ores. Iron is used to make steel. Copper is used to make wire and pipe.

4. Coal, oil, and other mineral resources are nonrenewable. That is, they cannot be replaced. When they are used up, there will be no more of them.

5. Some resource problems we face are pollution, oil spills, and the loss of forests and soil.

6. To help solve the problems, we are:
   - limiting the amounts of harmful chemicals that automobiles and factories release into the air;
   - putting controls on the dumping of waste water;
   - using windmills to produce electricity and solar panels to produce heat;
   - shutting off unneeded lights;
   - carpooling;
   - recycling metal, glass, and paper products;
   - replacing and replanting soil in some mining areas;
   - replanting some forests after trees are cut down.

Thinking and Writing

Answer these questions in complete sentences on a separate sheet of paper.

1. What is the difference between a renewable and a nonrenewable resource?
2. Suppose the world suddenly ran out of oil. How would this affect your life? Tell two ways.
3. What is the difference between a shaft mine and an open pit mine?
4. Tell three ways in which iron and copper are like coal and oil.
5. How might greater use of solar energy lead to a cleaner atmosphere?
6. How might greater use of public transportation lead to cleaner oceans?

Questions to Discuss

1. What are some nonrenewable resources that you use every day? How do you use them?
2. Does your community have a recycling center? If so, what does it collect?

Special Projects

Form teams. Try to find the answers to the questions below. Report your answers to the class.

1. What kind of air and water pollution problems do you have in your area?
2. Do you live near a recycling center? If so, what does it collect and what happens to the things it collects?

Chapter 15
How We Use the Land

Housing development in Daly City, California

Chapter Learning Objectives
1. Explain the seven major ways people use land.
2. Use a map to tell the major uses of land in different parts of the United States.
3. Explain why the amount of farmland in the United States is shrinking.
4. Explain the role of the federal government in land ownership.
5. Explain how local governments try to control land use by planning for change and growth.

Words To Know

quarry a large pit where stone is removed from the side of a hill or mountain
refuge a safe place
orchard an area of land planted with fruit trees

acre a unit of measure; an acre of land is about the size of a football field

There is a limited amount of usable land on Earth. As you have learned, much of the land is covered with high, rugged mountains. Few people can live there. And large portions of Earth's plains are too cold or too dry for people to live on. So usable land is one of our most important resources.

Throughout history, people have had to decide how to use the land. Long ago, most Native Americans lived by hunting and gathering. They left the land as they found it. Other Native Americans used only small patches of land for growing crops.

When settlers came from Europe, they cut down miles and miles of forests to make room for farms and towns.

Later, people built roads and highways. They also built dams across rivers, flooding nearby valleys. Today, we are replacing many farmlands and wooded areas with buildings, roads, and parking lots.

Are we making the best use of the land that we can? That's an important question in many places.

Seven Major Uses of Land in the United States

The following seven ways of using the land appear in the order of how much land each one makes use of. Agriculture uses the greatest amount of land. Towns and cities take up the smallest amount.

Agriculture

In the United States, more land is used for farming and ranching than for any other purpose.

Forests

The federal government is located in Washington D.C. It is in charge of the whole country.

Forests cover great amounts of land. Some are privately owned. Some are owned by the federal government and by state governments.

Most of the trees in private forests are cut down and used for building and other purposes.

Governments also allow logging in some parts of federal and state forests.

Recreation and Wildlife Protection

In the countryside, large amounts of land are used for such activities as hiking, camping, and skiing. Large areas are also set aside for wildlife **refuges**. In a wildlife refuge, animals are protected from hunters. Some of the land in towns and cities is used for parks, golf courses, playgrounds, and playing fields.

Mining

Oil fields, mines, and **quarries** take up some of the land. A quarry is a place where blocks of stone are cut from the side of a hill or mountain. Sometimes mines and quarries are found in areas that are also used for forestry, farming, and ranching.

U.S. LAND USE

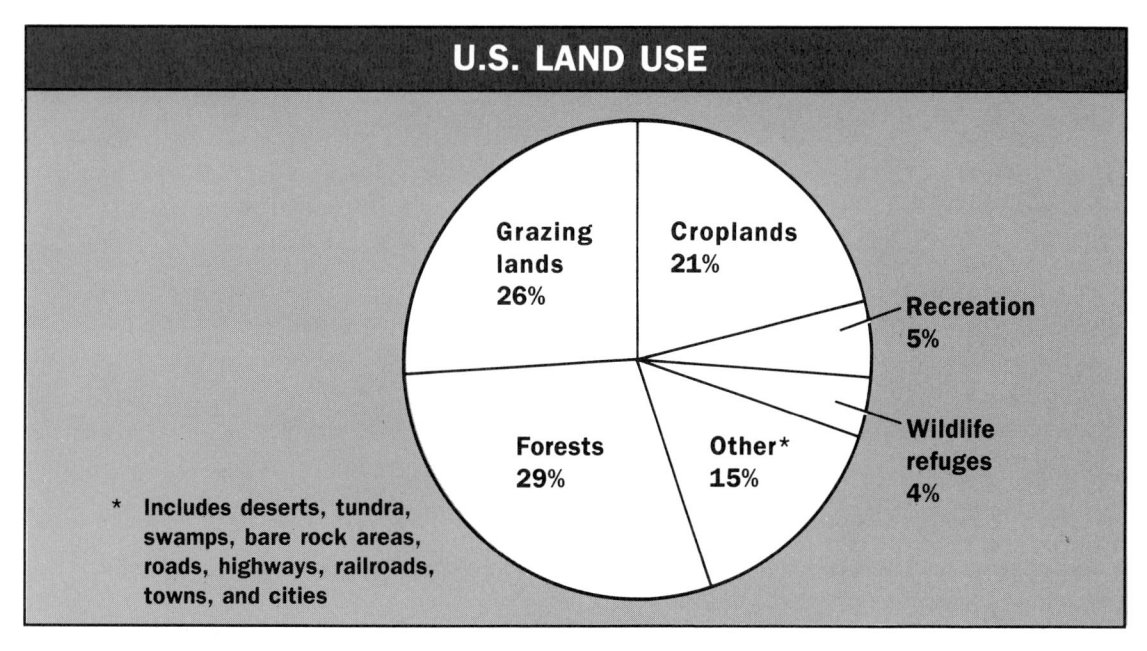

- Grazing lands 26%
- Croplands 21%
- Recreation 5%
- Wildlife refuges 4%
- Other* 15%
- Forests 29%

* Includes deserts, tundra, swamps, bare rock areas, roads, highways, railroads, towns, and cities

Graph Study
1. What percentage of U.S. land is covered by forests?
2. What percentage of U.S. land is used for grazing?
3. What percentage of U.S. land is used for recreation?

Water Bodies

Cities and farmlands use very large amounts of water. Usually the water is stored in lakes. The lakes are often formed by flooding a valley. The valley may have once been used for farming or ranching.

Highways, Railroads, and Airports

Roads and highways already take up great amounts of land, and more are being built every year. Railroads also make use of much of the land. And more and more land is now being used to build airports.

Cities and Towns

There are dozens of large cities, hundreds of smaller cities, and thousands of towns in the United States. Still, they cover only about 2% of the land.

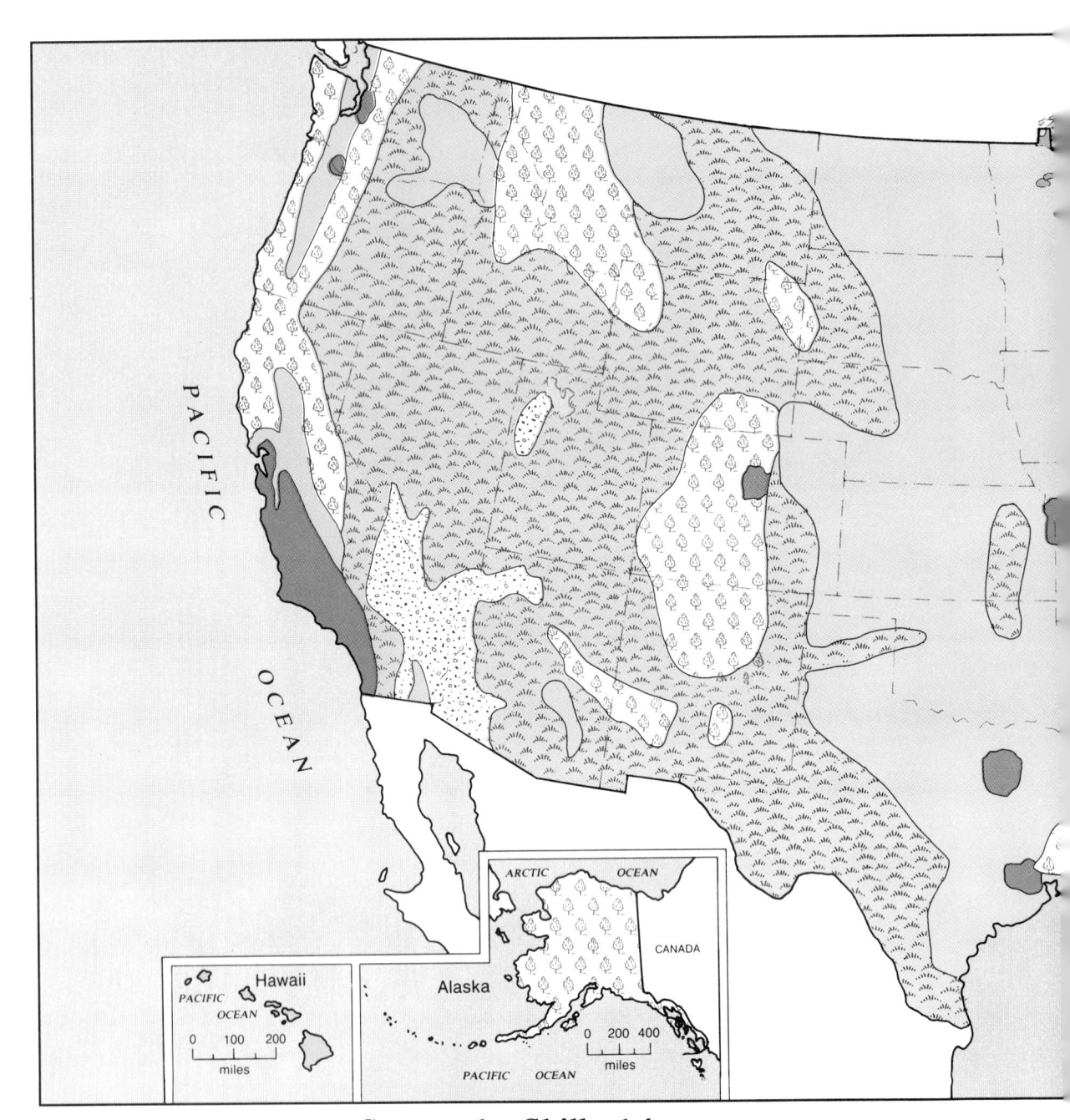

Geography Skills 14

Reading a Land-Use Map

178 Chapter Fifteen

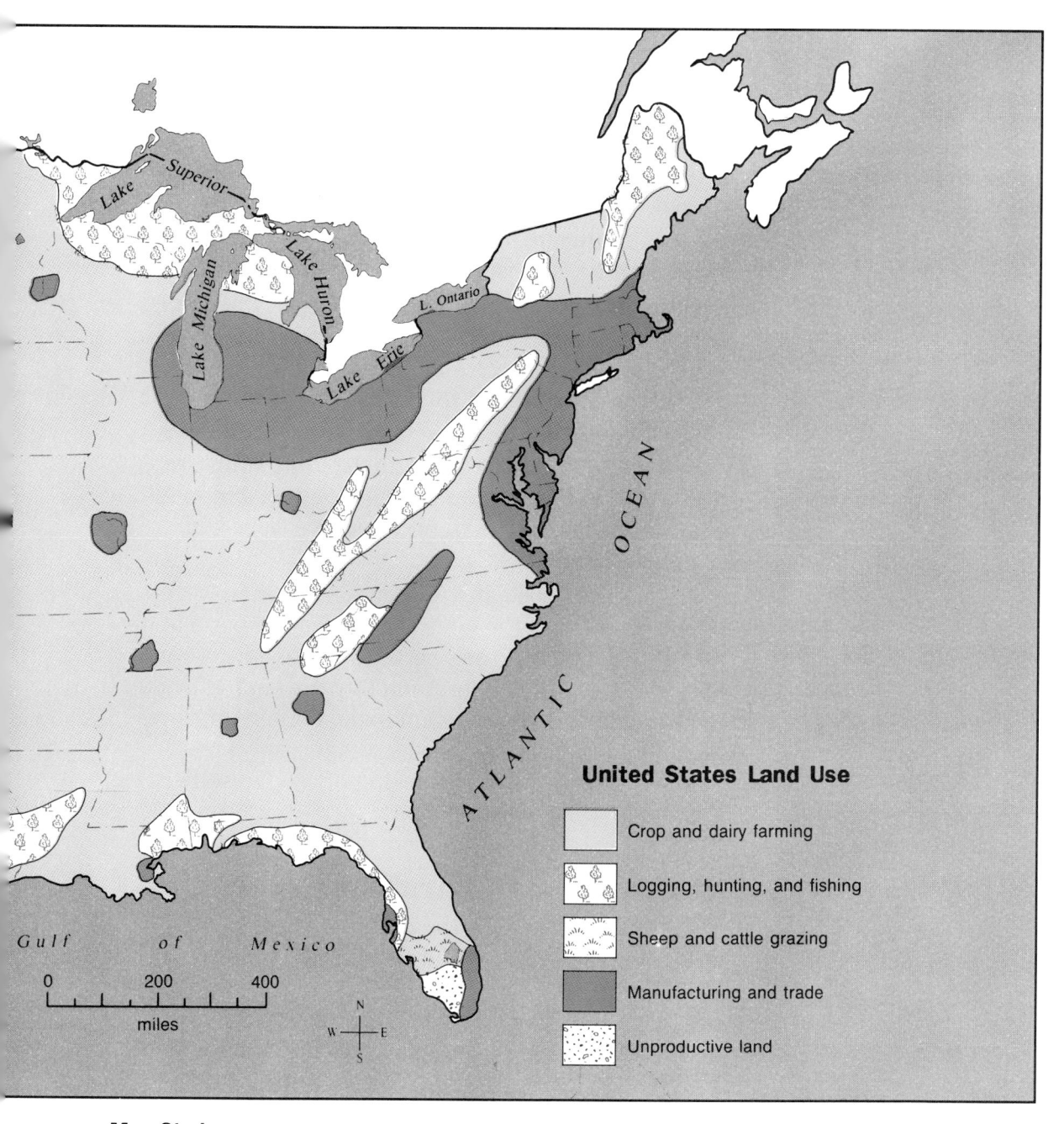

United States Land Use

- Crop and dairy farming
- Logging, hunting, and fishing
- Sheep and cattle grazing
- Manufacturing and trade
- Unproductive land

Map Study
1. What is most of the land in the eastern two-thirds of the United States used for?
2. What is most of the land around the Great Lakes used for?

Chapter Fifteen **179**

Land owned by the federal government is owned by all the people in the United States.

If your town has a public park, it is owned by all the people in your town.

Public Lands in the United States

The federal government owns about one-third of all the land in the United States. Most of this land is in the Rocky Mountain and Pacific regions. The state with the largest amount of federally owned land is Alaska.

Most of the public land in the West is used for forests, parks, and wildlife refuges.

Large areas of federal land throughout the United States are used for military bases. And many acres of land are used for government buildings and national cemeteries.

Some of the public forest lands are rented out to private logging companies. Other public lands are rented out to mining companies. Logging and mining companies pay for the right to remove trees and minerals from the land.

During the 1800s, the government wanted to get people to settle in the central and western parts of the country. It offered to sell parts of the land for a very low price. Before people could buy the land, they had to live on it for five years and make certain improvements. In recent times Alaska was the only state where low-priced land was being offered to settlers by the federal government.

Shrinking U.S. Farmlands

In the United States, the number of farms and the amount of land used for farming is decreasing. Homes, factories, and shopping centers are replacing growing fields, grazing lands, and **orchards**. An orchard is an area of land planted with fruit trees. Three main forces have led to this change.

First, farming has become a big business in the United States. Many small family farms have trouble competing with large company-owned farms. So many farmers have turned to other kinds of work.

NUMBER OF U.S. FARMS

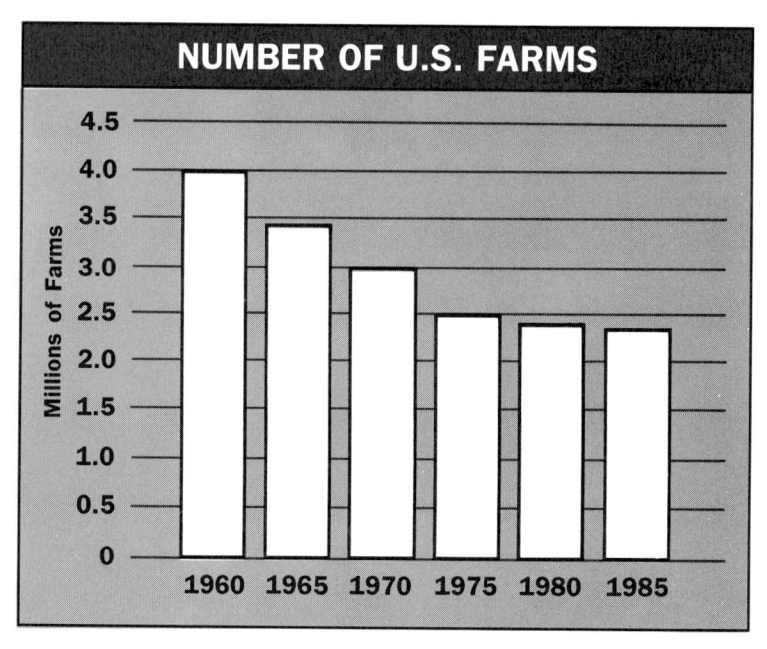

Graph Study
1. How many millions of farms were there in the United States in 1960?
2. About how many million less were there in 1985?
3. In which 10-year period did the number of farms decrease the most—1960 to 1970 or 1975 to 1985?

Second, improved machines and ways of farming have helped farmers produce more food per **acre**. An acre is about the size of a football field. The farmers can now get as much food as before on fewer acres. So some farmers have sold part of their land for other uses.

Third, many American towns and cities are growing. They need more land for homes, businesses, streets, and other things. This demand for land has raised the value of nearby farmland. Often, a farming family can make more money by selling their land than by farming it. Many farmers are doing just that.

Chapter Fifteen **181**

Government Control of Land Use

Most of the land in the United States is owned privately. But that does not mean private owners can do anything they want with the land.

Federal, state, and local governments all have a say in how people may use their land. The governments try to prevent pollution, erosion, and overcrowding. They try to protect wildlife. Builders must get permission before they build on or change the land.

City and County Planners

To help control the growth of their towns and cities, most local governments hire planners. The planners figure out how to make the best use of local land. They decide if an area should be used for homes, businesses, or factories. They decide which lands should be kept open for parks and playgrounds.

The planners also figure out where new schools, hospitals, fire stations, and other public places will be needed. They figure out where new roads should be built.

Why shouldn't airports be built near crowded housing areas?

Planners try to make sure airports aren't built near crowded housing areas. They try to make sure new housing areas will have access to roads, jobs, schools, and stores. They try to make sure that factory wastes won't damage water supplies.

Master Plan

Planners work with community leaders and others to come up with a master plan. The plan uses drawings, models, and maps. It shows the way the community looks today and the way it could look in the future.

Scale models help planners decide what should be built where.

Once the master plan has been approved, it becomes law. All new building projects have to keep with the plan. People who want to build homes can build them only in areas approved for homes. People who want to build factories can build them only in areas approved for factories. Land set aside for parks may not be used for anything else.

Chapter Review

Summary

1. Much of Earth's land is not suitable for people to live on or use. It may be too high and rugged, too hot and dry, or too cold. In the United States, more land is used for farming and ranching than for anything else. Towns and cities take up the smallest amount of land. Other uses to which the land is put are forests, recreation, mineral and water resources, and highways, railroads, and airports.

2. Most of the western third of the United States is forest and grazing land. Most of the central and eastern part is farmland. The largest amount of land used for manufacturing and trade is in the northeast and in the area near the Great Lakes.

3. In the United States, much farmland is being sold. The land is being used to build new homes, factories, and businesses. Smaller farms have also become parts of larger company-owned farms.

4. The federal government owns about a third of the land in the United States. Most of the federally owned land is in Alaska and the Rocky Mountain Region. Most federal land is used for forests, parks, wildlife refuges, and military bases.

5. Most land in the United States is privately owned. But federal, state, and local governments have a say in how the land may be used. Planners help local governments make decisions about how to make the best use of local lands.

Thinking and Writing

Answer these questions in complete sentences on a separate sheet of paper.

1. What effect did early European settlements have on the amount of forests in the United States?
2. Tell one effect a growing demand for water can have on the amount of farmland in a place.
3. Why do you think the federal government sets some land aside for wildlife refuges?
4. If a lumber company wants to cut more trees, what might it be able to do besides buy a forest?
5. Why do you think the federal government sold land at a low price in Alaska?
6. What do people raising cattle need that people growing apple trees don't need?

Questions to Discuss

1. Why is it important that towns and cities plan their growth rather than just let things happen?
2. Do you think we should be concerned about the shrinking amount of farmland in the United States? Why or why not?

Special Project

Walk around your neighborhood. See how much of the land is used for homes, businesses, factories, public services and so on. Write or tape record a report about land use in your neighborhood. You might take photographs also.

Chapters 13–15

REVIEW

Answer these questions on a separate sheet of paper.

A. Key Words

acre
electricity
energy
orchards
crude oil
pollutes
quarry
refuges
resources
smog

Number your paper from 1 to 10. Then read each sentence below. Find the word in the list on the left that best completes each sentence. Write that word next to the proper number on your paper.

1. Both animals and machines need ____ in order to move.
2. Earth's crust provides us with many useful ____ .
3. The burning of coal and oil ____ the air.
4. Smoke, chemicals, and fog mix and form ____ .
5. Some lights, heaters, and machines run on ____ .
6. An ____ of land is about the size of a football field.
7. Gasoline is made from ____ .
8. Fruit trees are grown in ____ .
9. Workers remove rock and stone from a ____ .
10. Wild animals are protected in wildlife ____ .

B. Key Facts

Number your paper from 11 to 20. Next to each number, write the word or words in parentheses that best complete each sentence below.

11. Plants store energy from the (moon / sun).
12. Water power is used to produce (generators / electricity).
13. Forests fill the air with water vapor and (oxygen / carbon dioxide).
14. Coal was formed from plants that died millions of years ago in (deserts / swamps).
15. Oil was formed from tiny (sea / river) plants and animals that died millions of years ago.
16. Coal, oil, and metals such as iron are examples of (renewable / nonrenewable) resources.
17. We (can / can not) get sick from swimming in polluted water.
18. In the United States, more land is used for (recreation / agriculture) than for any other purpose.
19. The amount of farmland in the United States is (increasing / decreasing).
20. The federal government owns large amounts of land in the Rocky Mountain region and in (Indiana / Alaska).

C. Main Ideas

Answer any five questions below. Number your paper with the same numbers as the questions you choose.

21. Tell how any two of the following resources help us:

    sun, air, water, animals, plants, forests, soil.
22. Tell how coal or oil was formed.
23. Tell the difference between shaft mines, strip mines, and open pit mines.
24. Give two reasons why metals such as steel and aluminum are important resources.
25. Name two problems caused by any of the following:

    pollution, mining, oil spills, logging.
26. Name two things that some people are doing about any two of the problems listed above.
27. Give one reason why the amount of farmland in the United States is changing.
28. Name one way in which planners help cities plan for growth.

Unit 3
Industry, Transportation, and Population

Chapter 16
Making, Buying, and Selling Things

Chapter 17
Moving Goods, People, and Ideas

Chapter 18
U.S. Resource Industries

Chapter 19
Other U.S. Industries

Chapter 20
Earth Has Billions of People

Chapter 21
People Live in Culture Groups

Chapter 22
People of the United States

Chapter 16
Making, Buying, and Selling Things

Pennsylvania steel furnaces, 1905

Chapter Learning Objectives
1. Describe the growth of America's first factories.
2. Describe the growth of the U.S. steel industry.
3. Describe recent changes in U.S. industry.
4. Explain why countries import and export goods.
5. Explain why some countries are less developed than others.
6. Use a table to study incomes in eight countries.
7. Explain the kinds of help that some developing countries have received.

Words To Know

raw materials the things from which a product is made, such as leather, rubber, and glue in shoes

industry a group of companies that make similar products or that offer similar services

manufacture to make a product by hand or machine

export to sell goods to other countries

import to buy goods from other countries

per capita for each person

Do you own a bike, watch, or radio? Each of these things is made in a factory. A factory is a building where products are made with the help of machines.

Industry

The First U.S. Factories

In 1845 Americans began building factories in the northeastern United States, where there are many rivers and waterfalls. The moving water was used to turn large waterwheels. The waterwheels then drove the moving parts of machines.

The Northeast also had two big port cities, Boston and New York. Raw materials could be brought in by ship and finished goods shipped out.

Raw materials are the things that go into making a product. For example, leather, rubber, and glue are raw materials for making shoes.

Which port city do you live closest to?

Steel and Auto Industries

Later in the 1800s, America's steel industry grew up near the Great Lakes. An industry is a group of companies that make similar products or that offer similar services.

Chapter Sixteen **191**

The steel industry started in the Great Lakes region for three main reasons:
- Large amounts of iron ore were found in Minnesota and Michigan. Iron is melted with other metals to make steel.
- The iron ore could be shipped cheaply by boat on the Great Lakes.
- Large amounts of coal were found in the Appalachian mountain states. Coal was needed to produce the heat that melts the iron and other metals.

Steel mills were soon making steel in Chicago, Cleveland, Pittsburgh, and other nearby cities within reach of the iron mines and coal fields.

Later, a new industry began in the Great Lakes area. Steel from nearby mills was used to manufacture, or make, cars and trucks.

Industries Change

Not long ago, many companies that used steel began buying it from other countries, where it was cheaper. Many steel mills and coal mines closed in the United States. Thousands of workers lost their jobs. Now the United States steel industry is growing again.

In recent years, new centers of industry have grown in other parts of the country. Big shipping ports and large amounts of oil and natural gas attracted businesses to California and Texas. Lower pay for workers and other lower costs attracted many businesses to the South.

Another big change has been the growth of service industries. Service is something that is done for someone. Cooks, nurses, sales clerks, and firefighters all provide services. In the United States, there are now more service workers than workers who produce goods.

The people who write text books provide service. The people who print text books produce goods.

192 Chapter Sixteen

Ships like these carry millions of tons of goods from one country to another.

Trading Between Countries

Most of the world's nonfood products are made in only a small number of countries. Some of the biggest producers are the United States, Japan, Canada, and the countries of western Europe. How do people in other countries get the things they need or want?

Countries trade with one another. Or rather, business people in one country trade with business people in other countries. Some countries have a lot of oil, copper, or other resources. But they may not have enough money to build factories of their own. These countries export their resources to countries that will buy them. And they import the things they want from countries that make them. To **export** goods is to sell them to other countries. To **import** goods is to buy them from other countries.

Chapter Sixteen 193

Three Examples

Nigeria is a country that has a lot of oil. But it does not have many factories. Nigeria exports oil and imports manufactured goods.

Japan has few resources. But it has a large highly trained population and a good deal of money. Japan imports oil and raw materials from other countries. It turns raw materials into cars, computers, radios, TV sets, and other goods.

Some of these products stay in Japan and are bought there. The rest are exported to other countries.

The United States imports cars, clothing, and other products even though it also makes these things. The main reason is that these things often can be made more cheaply in other countries. Companies in many other countries have lower costs than companies in the United States. Also, these goods may sometimes be better made in other countries.

Check the labels on the things you own to see where they come from.

Take a look at the clothing you are wearing. Your shoes may come from Brazil. Your shirt or blouse may come from Taiwan or Hong Kong. Your watch may come from Japan.

Food

Countries export foods they can sell in other countries. They import foods they do not grow enough of at home.

What foods have you eaten that came from other countries?

Some countries grow food mainly for export instead of for meeting their people's food needs. That is, they grow crops such as coffee or bananas that will bring high prices in other countries.

Some foods are imported because they are cheaper in other countries. In many cases, though, imported foods cost more.

Special Project

Use an encyclopedia to find out which countries these foods come from:
- bananas • black pepper • coconuts
- cocoa • coffee • jalapeño peppers
- olives • vanilla beans

A village in Nigeria

When people have jobs they have money to spend.

Rich Countries and Poor Countries

The countries of the world have not all developed, or built up, their industries at the same speed. The United States, Japan, Canada, and the countries of western Europe have developed much faster than most other countries. They are the richer countries of the world.

A few countries are developing quickly. But many countries have few industries or resources. And some of them are very poor.

The Developed Countries

Most of the developed countries began building up their industries more than a hundred years ago. They had a head start on the other countries.

Industry brings wealth or money to a country. Because of their industries, developed countries have more jobs for their people. When people have jobs, they have money to spend.

If the people earn more than they need for food, clothing, and shelter, then they can buy other things. They can buy radios, TV sets, and other products. That, in turn, may lead to the building of more factories to make all the things people want to buy.

Developing Countries

Some countries have few industries because they were once ruled by other countries that removed their resources and wealth. Later, when the countries became free, they lacked money and skilled workers to build up their own industries.

Some of the developing countries have resources they can sell to the developed countries. Most of the money earned by the poorer developing countries is spent on food, farm machinery, and medicine. Wealthier developing countries can also buy cars, radios, TV sets, and other products people like to have.

Some developing countries have gained great wealth because they have oil and can sell it to developed countries.

Farming in Developing Countries

Some developing countries, such as Chad, have few, if any, resources to sell. They may have few, if any, industries. Often there aren't many jobs. People live mainly from the food they can grow themselves.

Only 2% of the land in Chad can be plowed. But 81% of Chad's labor force works in agriculture.

Most of the farmers in these countries are too poor to buy the land and machinery needed to grow more food. They can only produce enough for their own families. If there is a famine, the people often go hungry.

In some of the countries that grow crops for export, such as Guatemala, a few people or companies own most of the farmland. Farm workers earn very little and have little or no land to grow their own food.

One developing country that has made improvements in farming is Zimbabwe. It is now better able to feed people without having to import food. This leaves more money to develop industries.

Per Capita Income	
United Arab Emirate	$16,100
United States	$14,565
Canada	$11,778
Japan	$9,452
Taiwan	$2,871
Guatemala	$1,300
Nigeria	$660
Chad	$90

Your librarian can help you find the per capita income for your own state.

Table Study This table shows how much money the people in some countries earned in 1985. **Per capita** means *for each person*. These are the average amounts for all the people in these countries.
1. Which of these countries had the highest per capita income?
2. Which country had the lowest per capita income?
3. By how many dollars did income in these two countries differ?
4. About how many times greater than Chad's per capita income was Japan's?

Helping the Developing Countries

Developed countries have helped developing countries. They've given or loaned money and tools. They've sent food in times of famine. Many teachers, doctors, nurses, and other trained workers go to developing countries. They've been able to help many people improve their lives. But sometimes ideas that come from one region or one culture don't work well in another. Then people must keep looking for new ways that work.

Will the poor countries ever catch up with the rich countries, or even come close? Only time will tell.

How do you think a rich country can best help a poor country?

The woman on the left is an English teacher visiting Botswana, Africa, from the United States. The woman on the right is showing her a traditional method of sifting flour.

Chapter Review

Summary

1. In modern factories, workers turn out products by machine instead of by hand.

2. The first factories in the United States were in the Northeast. The Northeast had two big ports and the water power needed to run machines.

3. America's steel industry began near the Great Lakes, close to large amounts of iron and coal.

4. The auto industry started and grew in Detroit, Michigan, close to a ready supply of steel.

5. The amounts and kinds of goods and services a country produces change over time. Businesses develop in places that support their growth. In the United States, there are more service workers than workers who produce goods.

6. Countries trade with one another. They export certain goods. That is, they sell goods to countries that need or want them. And they import certain goods. They buy goods that they need or want.

7. Only a small number of the world's countries have developed large industries. Others are just beginning to develop their industries. Most of the developing countries are poor.

8. Less developed countries often lack money, resources, industries, and skilled workers.

9. Rich countries sometimes help poor countries by sending them money, food, tools, and skilled workers.

Thinking and Writing

Answer these questions in complete sentences on a separate sheet of paper.

1. An automobile and a painting can both be thought of as products. In terms of how and where they are produced, what is the difference between the two?
2. How are raw materials related to finished goods?
3. Explain the difference between imported goods and exported goods.
4. Give two reasons why a large, well developed country might import goods it can produce itself.
5. How are Germany and France like the United States and Japan?
6. What does this chapter call the countries that have money, resources, and skilled workers?

Questions to Discuss

1. What are some of the reasons industries start where they do?
2. Why might some countries be richer than others?
3. Do you think the rich, developed countries of the world should help the others? Why or why not?

Special Project

Find out what kind of factories are in your town, city, or state. What products do they make? Are they part of an industry that is growing, staying about the same size, or becoming smaller?

Chapter 17
Moving Goods, People, and Ideas

Cities are centers for communications and trade. They are points through which people, goods, and ideas move.

Chapter Learning Objectives
1. Describe the development of road transportation.
2. Use a map to study highway systems.
3. Contrast the advantages and disadvantages of truck, railroad, water, and air transportation.
4. Describe the functions of pipelines and cable links.
5. Describe how the following inventions affected communications: telegraph, telephone, radio, television, computers.

Words To Know

transport to carry
interstate highway a highway that runs from one state to another

cargo the goods carried on a ship or plane

Transportation

Think back to the days of the early hunters and gatherers. At that time, people had only one way to get themselves and their belongings from place to place. They walked wherever they were going. They carried their belongings on their heads or backs.

A giant step forward in moving people and goods came with the invention of the wheel. Once people had wheels, they could build carts and wagons.

Animals were also used to help people **transport** themselves and their belongings. To transport means to carry. Animals pulling carts and wagons could transport large heavy loads over long distances.

> ### Think About It
> How do *you* transport your belongings from one place to another? How do the goods you use most often get to you? Trace the route of any one object you use back to its source. For instance, where do you think this sheet of paper may have come from? What happened to it before it reached you?

The Growth of Road Systems

When people walked back and forth between villages, they made paths and trails. When they started using carts and wagons, they widened the paths and trails into roadways. As villages became towns and towns became cities, roadways were paved.

Moving goods in the African country of Niger.

In the poorer countries of the world, many villages are still connected only by paths, trails, or dirt roads. There, most of the people still travel by foot or on animals. They still use carts and wagons to carry their goods. Or they carry things on their backs or heads.

The richer countries of the world are crisscrossed by paved roads. In the United States, people can now drive on 42,500 miles of **interstate highways.** These highways connect the country's major cities and towns.

Each state also has many other streets, roads, and highways.

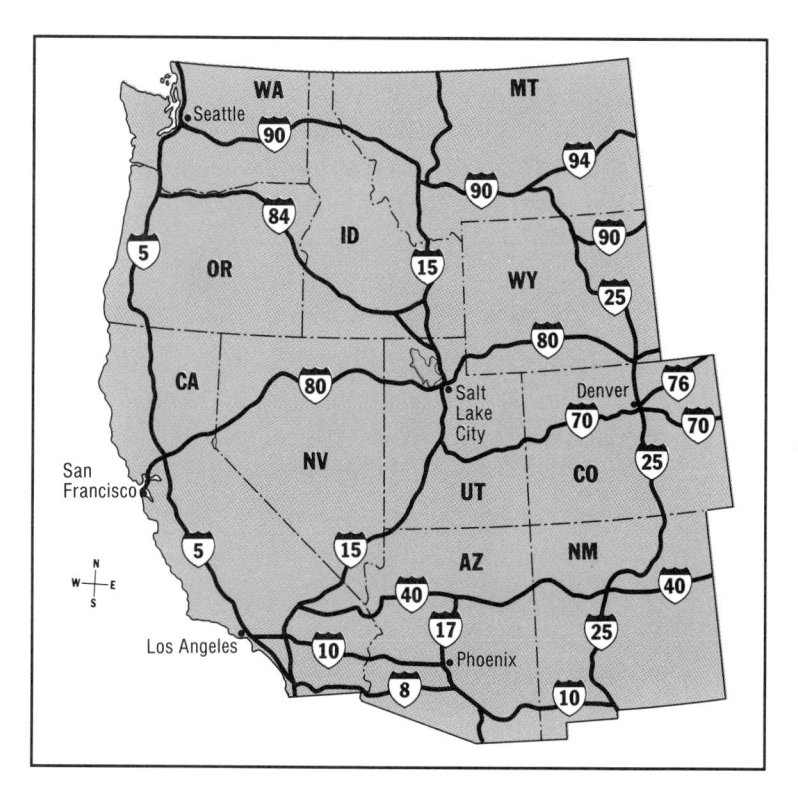

Map Study The map above shows part of the U.S. interstate highway system. Each highway has a number. Use the map to answer the questions below:
1. Which highway will take you all the way from Los Angeles, California, to Seattle, Washington?
2. Which highways will take you from Los Angeles to Salt Lake City, Utah?
3. Which interstate highway will take you from Los Angeles to Phoenix, Arizona?

Trucks

Trucks are the fastest growing form of transportation in the United States. They carry loads that weigh many thousands of pounds. They can go anywhere there are roads for them to travel on.

Many trucks have cooling systems. This allows them to carry foods that need to be kept cold.

One kind of truck has a separate tractor and trailer. The tractor does the pulling. The trailer carries the load. A driver can deliver the trailer and leave it to be unloaded. Then he or she can pick up another trailer.

Sometimes the trailers are put on trains for long trips. A train can carry dozens of loaded trailers. At the end of the trip, the trailers are taken off the train. Tractors then pull the loaded trailers to where they are going.

Trucks give door-to-door service. But they add to the air pollution problem. For some kinds of shipping, they are not as cheap as trains or boats.

The containers in this yard are waiting to be loaded onto trailer trucks.

Railroads

The first railroads were built over 150 years ago, well before cars and trucks were invented. They gave people a way to travel more safely and quickly. They gave companies a way of sending heavy loads over mountains that wagons couldn't cross. A trip that once took weeks by wagon took only days by train.

Many of this country's towns grew up beside railroad tracks. Big cities grew where trains from different places all came together at a port.

Few of us take long train trips these days. We drive cars or take airplanes instead. But in and around some of America's big cities, millions of people ride trains to work and school. That helps save oil and cuts down on air pollution. Trains also carry millions of pounds of food, resources, raw materials, and finished products every day.

Trains are cheaper than trucks for sending large shipments over long distances. But they can only go where there are tracks.

Many people take trains to and from work or school. How can this cut down on air pollution?

The first passenger railroad in the United States was the Baltimore & Ohio. Track was first laid for this line on July 4, 1828. How long ago was that?

Chapter Seventeen   **207**

Water Transportation

People learned long ago that they could travel and transport goods over water. At first, they used rafts and small boats. Later, they built bigger boats and ships that could cross oceans.

In the 1700s, a sailing trip across the Atlantic Ocean took about 2 1/2 months. By 1900, ships with steam engines took only seven days. Today, some ships can make the trip in five days.

Canals Help Shipping

In Chapter 8, you read about the canals of the Great Lakes and the Saint Lawrence Seaway. You learned how the canals help ships travel from lake to lake and out to sea.

In Europe, canals connect many of the large rivers. This makes it possible for shippers to send goods hundreds of miles by inland waterways. Canals are also important in England and in China.

One of the most important canals for world shipping is the Panama Canal. It connects the Atlantic and Pacific Oceans. Ships pass through the canal instead of going all the way around South America. This saves 8,000 miles on a trip from Atlantic to Pacific ports.

Transporting goods over water is usually the cheapest way to move them long distances. But it is also the slowest. And **cargo** can only be sent where ships and boats can go.

The building of the Panama Canal, 1913

Air Travel

Air travel is only about 100 years old. The early planes were tiny and flew only short distances. But later, planes got bigger, faster, and safer.

In the 1950s, planes began to use jet engines. Most of today's jetliners fly at speeds between 500 and 600 miles an hour. Some jetliners fly at 1,500 miles an hour.

Passenger planes carry people and mail. They may also carry small amounts of cargo. Cargo planes carry only cargo.

The fastest way to ship things is by plane. But it is also the most expensive way. And shipments can only be sent to where there are airports. From there, they travel by truck to where they are going.

In 1889 Nellie Bly set a record by sailing around the world in 72 days, six hours, and 11 minutes. In 1961, a spacecraft piloted by Yuri Gargarin circled the globe in one hour and 48 minutes.

Cargo that is shipped by plane is carried to and from airports by truck.

Where does the water that runs through the pipes in your house come from? Where does it go when it leaves your house?

Pipelines and Cable Links

Much of what we need does not come to us by truck, train, ship, or plane. For example, how does water get to your house?

Most homes, factories, and businesses get their water through pipelines. Other pipelines carry wastes away from those places.

Pipelines also carry oil and natural gas. The Alaskan Pipeline is 800 miles long. It carries oil from Prudhoe Bay to the port of Valdez.

Cables are another kind of carrier. Some cables carry electrical power from place to place. Other cables carry telephone messages. TV programs are also sent out over cables.

Communication

Have you talked on the telephone, watched TV, or listened to the radio lately? All of these allow the sending of messages that can be received at almost the same moment they are sent.

210   Chapter Seventeen

Long ago, messages were sent by drums. The drummer used a code. Each set of drumbeats meant something. Drums are still used in some places to send messages back and forth.

Telegraph

The beginning of a new age in sending messages came in 1844. That's when telegraph machines were first used. Like the drum, a telegraph machine sends messages in code. But the messages go out over wires.

Telephone

The trouble with the telegraph was that it could only send coded messages, not the sound of someone speaking. In 1876 Alexander Graham Bell invented the telephone. Today, we can call and talk to people in almost any country in the world.

Alexander Graham Bell with an early version of his telephone.

Radio

Telephones, too, had a problem. They had to be hooked up to each other with telephone lines.

In 1921 Guglielmo Marconi found a way of sending telegraph signals without using wires. This led to the invention of the radio. Today, even in places that do not have telephones, people can get messages by radio.

Compare this table to the per capita income table in Chapter 16. How does the information on this table relate to the information there?

Country	Population	Number of radios per person
United Arab Emirate	1,455,000	1.30
United States	247,498,000	1.94
Canada	25,334,000	1.12
Japan	123,231,000	1.76
Taiwan	20,283,000	1.64
Guatemala	9,412,000	1.53
Nigeria	115,152,000	1.13
Chad	5,714,000	1.02

Television

The first television show was in 1936. In the 1950s, television became popular. Today, it gives us a chance to see the world without leaving our homes.

We see sports events from all over the world. We see floods, storms, and even war. Often, we see these things as they are happening.

Television also helps us learn about the foods, clothing, music, and ways of life in other countries. At the same time, people in other countries are learning about us.

Computers

Another way to send and receive messages quickly is with computers. The amount of information that travels back and forth on computers is growing every day. New ways are continually being found to put these machines to work.

Used widely, all these forms of communication can help the people of the world become neighbors rather than strangers.

Computers are changing the ways in which we communicate with each other.

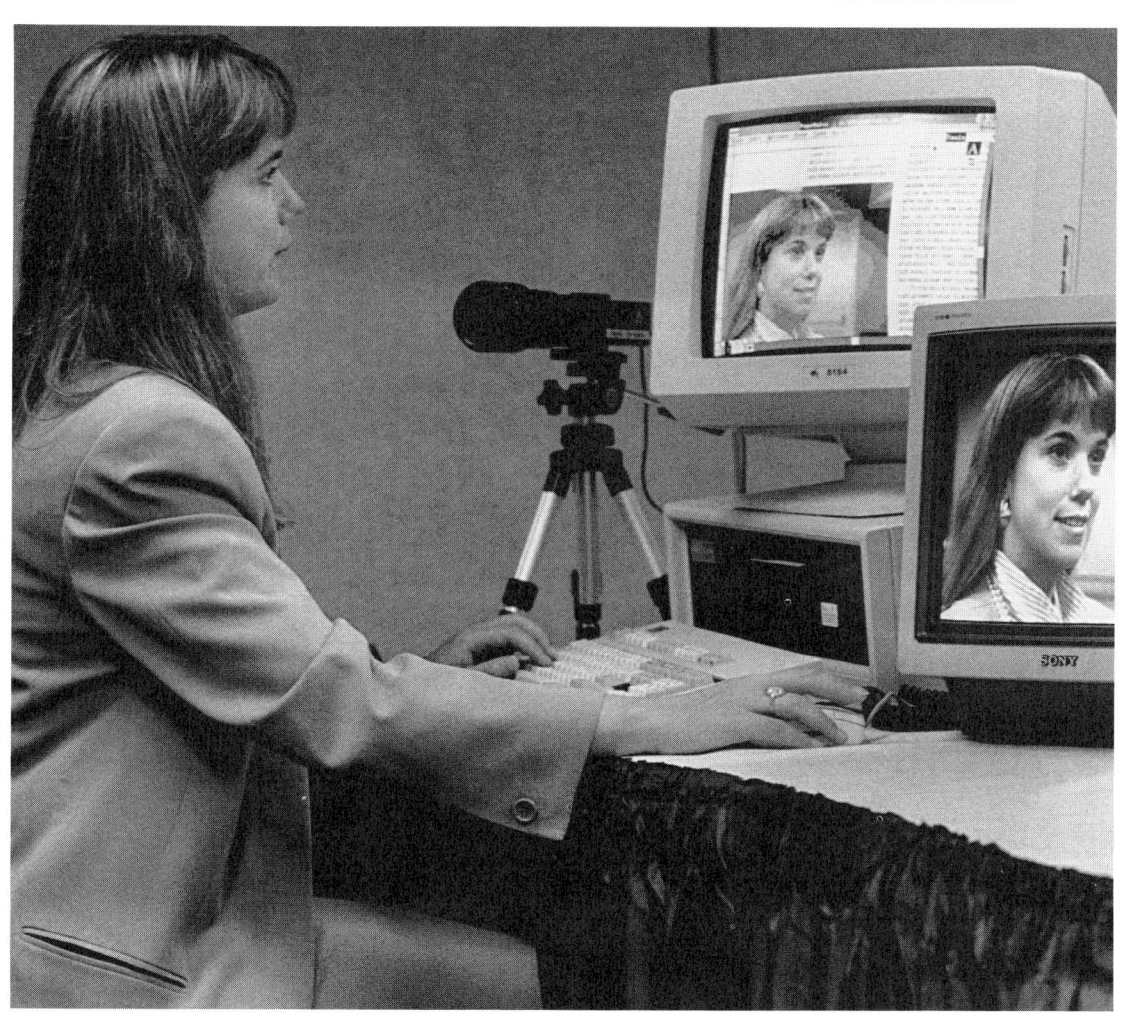

Chapter Review

Summary

1. In poor countries people still travel on foot and move goods with animals, carts, and wagons.

2. The richer countries of the world have many good roads. In the United States, the interstate highway system connects most big cities and towns.

3. Trucks give door-to-door service but add to pollution problems. Truck transport is usually more costly than rail or water transport.

4. Train transport is often cheaper than truck, but trains can only go where there are tracks.

5. Water transport is the cheapest but also the slowest way to move goods. It is limited to where ships can go.

6. Air travel is the fastest but also the most expensive way to move goods. It is limited to where there are airports.

7. Pipelines carry such things as water, oil, natural gas, and wastes. Cables carry electricity, telephone messages, and TV programs.

8. Many inventions have made it possible to receive messages at almost the same time they are sent.

Thinking and Writing

Answer these questions in complete sentences on a separate sheet of paper.

1. What had to be invented a long time before cars and trucks could be invented?
2. Often, the transportation systems in poor countries are not well developed. Which mineral resource do they probably use less of than the rich countries do?
3. What can trucks do that railroads, ships, and planes can't do?
4. In terms of what they carry, how are passenger and cargo planes alike? How are they different?
5. Look at the photo on page 210. How did the box being loaded onto the plane probably get to the airport?
6. What is the single biggest difference between a television news report and a radio news report?

Questions to Discuss

1. How would your life be different if cars, trucks, and busses had never been invented?
2. How would your life be different if the radio, television, and telephone had never been invented?
3. What new ways do you think people might find for traveling and for sending goods and messages?

Special Project

Find out all you can about the transportation in your area. How do people who live near you travel? How do companies ship goods?

Chapter 18
U.S. Resource Industries

Fishing is an important industry in all regions in the United States that have access to the sea.

Chapter Learning Objectives

1. Tell which four regions have important fishing industries.
2. Give at least one example of the fish and shellfish caught in each region.
3. Tell which two regions are the leading producers of lumber.
4. Give at least two examples of the kinds of lumber produced in each region.
5. Name the three states that are the nation's leading producers of coal.
6. Name the three states that are the nation's leading producers of oil.

Words To Know

fossils remains of plants and animals that lived thousands or millions of years ago

pulpwood a mash made from ground-up logs; it is used to make paper

gravel small pieces of rock

cement a mixture of several minerals that can hold sand and pebbles or crushed stone together

boron a kind of metal used to harden steel; it is also used in making glass

molybdenum a metal used to strengthen blends of other metals

potassium a mineral used in the making of fertilizers and liquid soaps

uranium a mineral used as fuel in some power plants

shale a kind of rock that is formed mostly from hardened clay

menhaden a kind of fish used mainly in animal feed and fertilizer

sulphur a pale yellow mineral used to make matches and other products

phosphate a mineral used in fertilizers

The United States is a nation rich in natural resources. One of those resources is its fertile soil. The United States also has an abundance of fish, forests, minerals, and **fossil** fuels. Fossil fuels include coal, oil, and natural gas.

Many companies develop these resources for sale. About 10% of the income of some regions comes from the sale of its natural resources. This amounts to billions of dollars every year.

As you read the chapter ahead, think of yourself as a buyer for a large company. Perhaps you buy fish for a chain of restaurants. Perhaps you buy wood for a furniture maker. Perhaps you buy iron for a steel plant. See what each region has to offer.

The maps in this chapter will show you where coal, oil, and natural gas can be found. The graphs will tell you which regions produce the most fuels and which states produce the most lumber.

Pacific Region

Fishing

The Pacific Region is one of the largest producers of fish and fish products in the United States. Fleets of fishing boats bring in tons of crab, halibut, salmon, and tuna.

Most of the region's catch comes from the Gulf of Alaska and the Bering Sea. But great numbers of salmon are also caught in the Columbia River. In fact, it is the world's number-one source of salmon.

Forestry

About one-third of Alaska, one-half of Washington and Oregon, and two-fifths of California are covered with forests. Millions of trees from these forests are cut down every year.

Logs from large trees are sent to saw mills, where they are cut into lumber. It is used for building and for making furniture and other wood products.

Logs from smaller trees are sent to **pulpwood** mills. There they are turned into a kind of mash from which paper products can be made.

Trees cut down by Pacific logging companies include cedar, fir, hemlock, pine, redwood, and spruce. One place where most trees are *not* cut down is the Redwood National Forest in California. It contains some of the world's oldest and tallest trees.

Minerals and Fossil Fuels

California and Alaska are the Pacific Region's major producers of minerals and fuels. Both states produce large amounts of sand, **gravel**, and stone. Gravel is made up of small pieces of rock. Sand, gravel, and stone are used mainly for building roads, highways, and dams. They are also used to make

The world's largest tree is the General Sherman tree in California's Sequoia National Park. It is 36 feet wide at its base and 272 feet tall.

LEADING U.S. LUMBER PRODUCERS

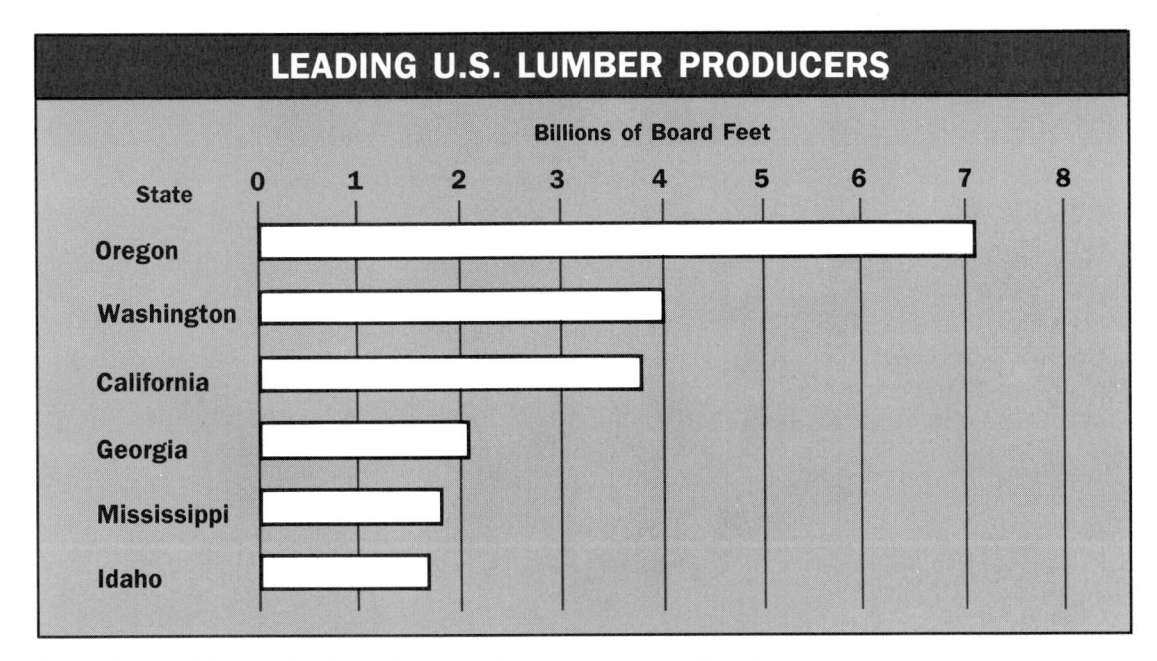

State	Billions of Board Feet
Oregon	~7
Washington	~4
California	~4
Georgia	~2
Mississippi	~1.5
Idaho	~1.5

Graph Study This graph shows how much lumber was produced in a recent year by the six leading states.
1. Which three states produced the most lumber?
2. About how much more lumber did Oregon produce than Washington?
3. How might the climate of Oregon, Washington, and northern California affect their lumber production?

strong materials for building walls, floors, and sidewalks.

California is the nation's leading producer of non-fuel minerals. It produces great amounts of **cement** and **boron**. Cement is a mixture of several minerals. It works like glue and is used to bind sand and stone. Boron is a kind of metal. It is used to harden steel and to make glass.

Alaska produces some gold. But oil has become the state's most important underground resource. Once the Alaska pipeline was completed, Alaska quickly became the nation's second largest producer of oil. California also has oil, but it is disappearing quickly.

Chapter Eighteen **219**

Rocky Mountain Region

Forestry

Much of the Rocky Mountain Region has no forests. Can you guess why?

One reason is that it is too cold for trees to grow on the tops of the highest mountains. Another is that it is too dry for trees to grow in the deserts.

But there are areas at lower elevations that do get more precipitation. Forests of evergreens, such as fir, pine, and spruce trees cover much of these areas. There are also broadleaf forests with aspen, birch, and cottonwood trees.

Idaho ranks among the top ten producers of lumber in the United States.

Minerals and Fossil Fuels

The Rocky Mountain Region is a storehouse of minerals. It has large deposits of copper, iron, lead, and zinc.

Three other important minerals mined in the region are **molybdenum, potassium,** and **uranium**. Molybdenum is used to strengthen blends of other metals. Potassium is used in the making of fertilizers and liquid soaps. Uranium is used as a fuel in some power plants in place of coal or gas.

There is also some gold and silver in the Rocky Mountain Region.

As for fossil fuels, the region has large deposits of coal. Wyoming is the second largest producer of coal in the United States.

Deposits of natural gas have been found in Wyoming and Utah. And there is oil in Wyoming, Utah, and Colorado.

Huge amounts of **shale** oil have also been found. Shale oil is oil contained in shale rock. One ton of

The highest peak in the Rocky Mountains is Mount Elbert in Colorado. It is 14,433 feet above sea level. That's 2.73 miles!

INCOME FROM MINERALS AND FOSSIL FUELS

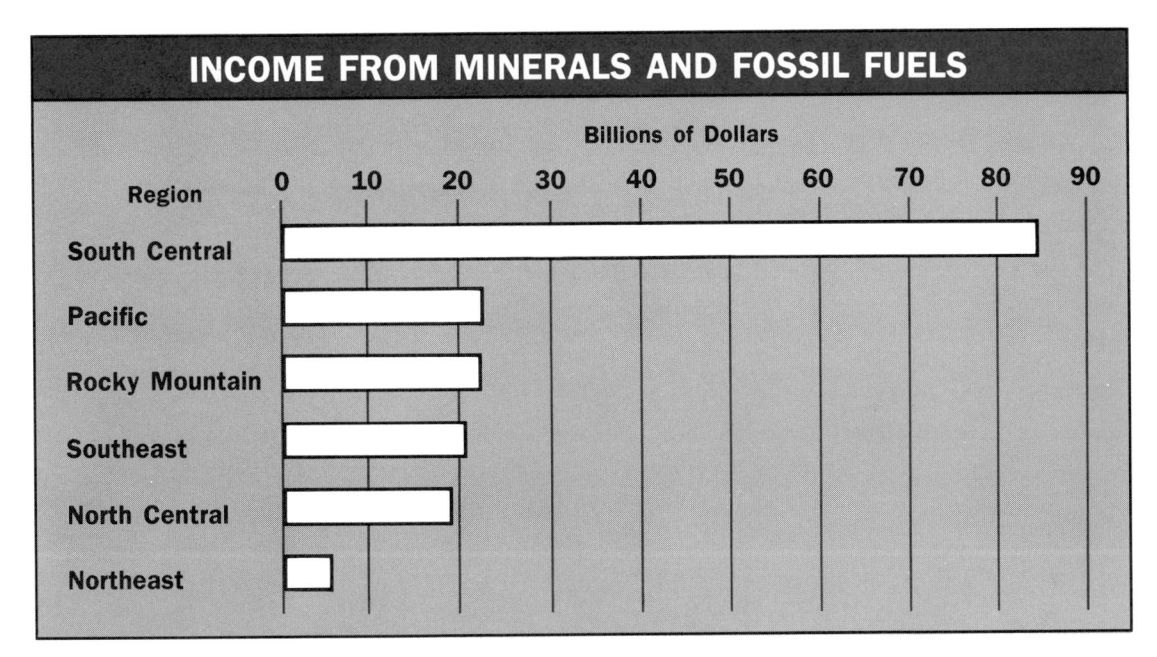

Region	Billions of Dollars
South Central	~82
Pacific	~22
Rocky Mountain	~22
Southeast	~25
North Central	~18
Northeast	~3

Graph Study This graph shows the money earned from minerals and fossil fuels during a recent year.
1. Which region earned the most money? About how many billions of dollars was this?
2. Which region earned the least? About how many billions of dollars was this?
3. Which two regions earned about the same?
4. What mineral or fossil fuel do you think the leading region may have more of than any of the others?

shale may contain from 5 to 100 gallons of oil. To be of use, though, the oil has to be removed from the shale. So far, that has been too costly. Also, removing the oil from the shale uses a lot of water. And water is one thing the area has very little of. Another problem is that waste shale blows away easily in the wind. The area would be very hard to replant once the mining was done. Still, if other energy sources aren't found, greater efforts may be made to develop shale oil.

Chapter Eighteen 221

North Central Region

Fishing

Though far from the ocean, the North Central Region does have a small fishing industry. The Great Lakes are fished mainly for alewives, carp, smelt, and whitefish.

Forestry

Much of the northern and southern parts of the region are forested. Trees cut down in the north for lumber or pulpwood include aspen, oak, maple, and pine. Trees logged in the south include beech, hickory, and walnut.

Minerals and Fossil Fuels

About half of the nation's iron ore comes from the Mesabi Range in northern Minnesota. The world's largest open-pit iron mine is located there. Iron is also found in Missouri, Michigan, and Wisconsin.

Missouri is the biggest producer of lead in the United States. Coal is found in Illinois, Indiana, and Ohio. About one-third of all the gold mined in the United States comes from South Dakota.

Cement, stone, gravel, and sand are also important mineral products of the region. Some oil and gas are found in a few of the states.

Mesabi is an American Indian word. It means "hidden giant."

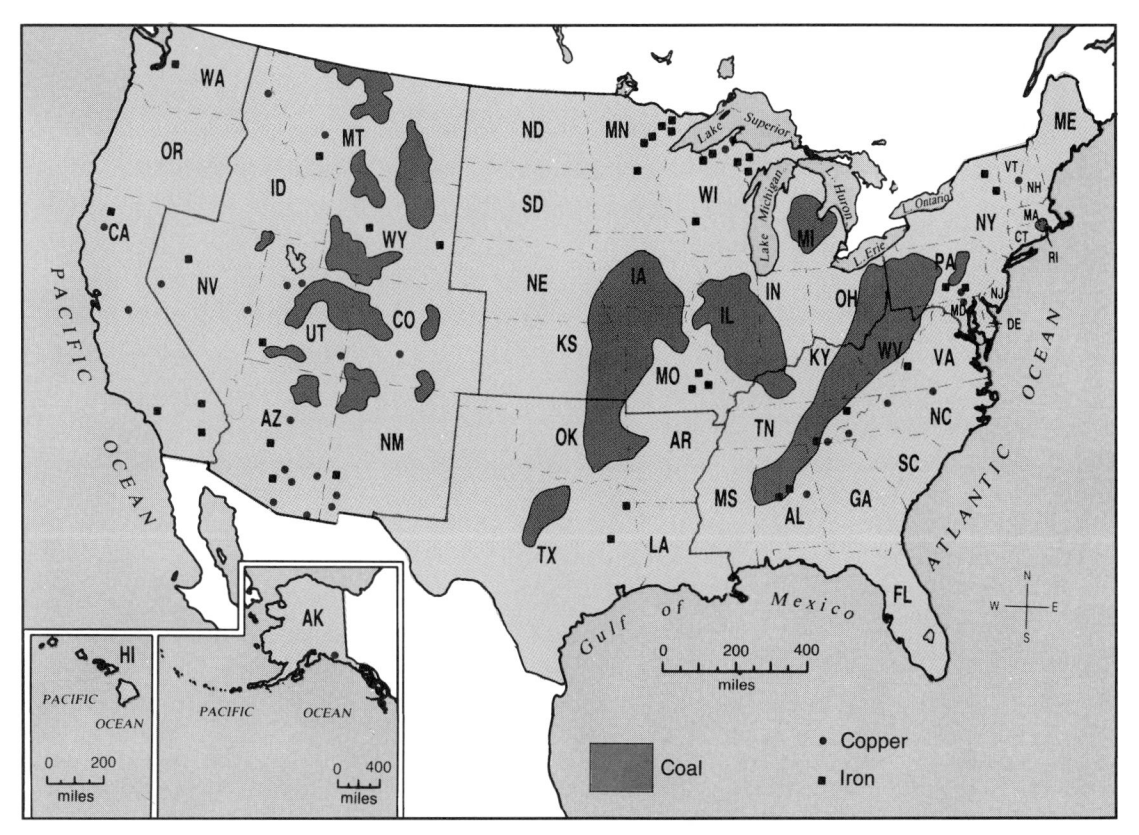

Map Study This map shows where major deposits of coal, copper, and iron are located. Only some of these deposits are being mined.

Major U.S. Deposits of Coal, Copper, and Iron

1. Which region is the only one that doesn't have coal?
2. Which state has the most copper deposits?
3. Which two states have the most iron deposits?
4. Are there major deposits of coal, copper, or iron in your state?
5. Suppose there were no iron or coal near the Great Lakes. Do you think the U.S. auto and steel industries would have started there? Why or why not?

Northeast Region

Fishing

The Northeast is a major supplier of fish and shellfish. Some of the fish are caught off the northern coast of the region. Some are caught still further north, off the coast of Newfoundland, Canada. These waters provide cod, flounder, herring, lobsters, and scallops.

The waters of the Delaware and Chesapeake Bays are also well known for shellfish. There the catch includes clams, crabs, lobsters, and oysters.

Forestry

About 80% of New England is covered with forests. Maine, Vermont, and New Hampshire are the most heavily forested. Needleleaf trees such as fir, pine, and spruce are logged there. So are broadleaf trees such as birch, oak, and maple.

The trees are used for both lumber and pulpwood. Maine is the nation's leading pulpwood producer.

Forests further south in the region are less suitable for logging than those in the north. They are used mainly for recreation.

Minerals and Fossil Fuels

Coal is the major fossil fuel of the Northwest Region. It is found mainly in western Pennsylvania. The state also has some oil and gas.

In the New England states there are many rock quarries. Blocks of granite, slate, and marble are taken from quarries in Vermont and New Hampshire. The blocks are used to form the outside walls and sometimes the floors of large buildings.

Maryland has only 31 miles of coastline on the Atlantic Ocean. But the Chesapeake Bay cuts deeply into the state. The bay has many arms and inlets. Maryland's total coastline is 3,190 miles long.

224 Chapter Eighteen

Vermont is also a leading producer of talc. Talc is ground up to make talcum powder. People use talcum powder to help keep their skin dry. Talc is also used in the making of crayons, paint, soap, and paper.

All of the states in the region produce one or more of the following: sand, gravel, and stone.

This is the Old Man of the Mountains in New Hampshire. A man's head has been naturally shaped into the granite face of Profile Mountain.

Chapter Eighteen **225**

South Central Region

Fishing

Both Texas and Louisiana have large fleets of boats that fish in the Gulf of Mexico. The fleets bring in huge catches of shrimp, oysters, crabs, flounder, menhaden, and red snapper.

Menhaden are not eaten by people, but they are very useful for other purposes. They are ground up to make food for farm animals. They are made into fertilizer. They are pressed for their oil, which is used by chemical companies. And they are also used as bait to catch other fish.

Forestry

Forests cover almost half of Arkansas and Louisiana. Arkansas ranks among the nation's top ten producers of lumber.

Both states produce wood for building materials and for paper products. Trees cut for these purposes include cypress, gum, hickory, oak, and pine.

Minerals and Fossil Fuels

Texas is the nation's leading producer of oil and gas. Louisiana ranks third, after Alaska. About one-third of the country's known supplies of oil lie under the Texas plains. Oklahoma has about 70,000 oil wells, including a few on the grounds of the state capitol building. Much of the region's oil comes from off-shore wells in the Gulf of Mexico.

Arkansas is a major source of bauxite in the United States. As you may remember, bauxite is used to make aluminum.

Texas and Louisiana are the nation's top producers of **sulphur**. Sulphur is a pale yellow mineral used to make matches, gunpowder, and insect sprays. It is also used in the making of rubber.

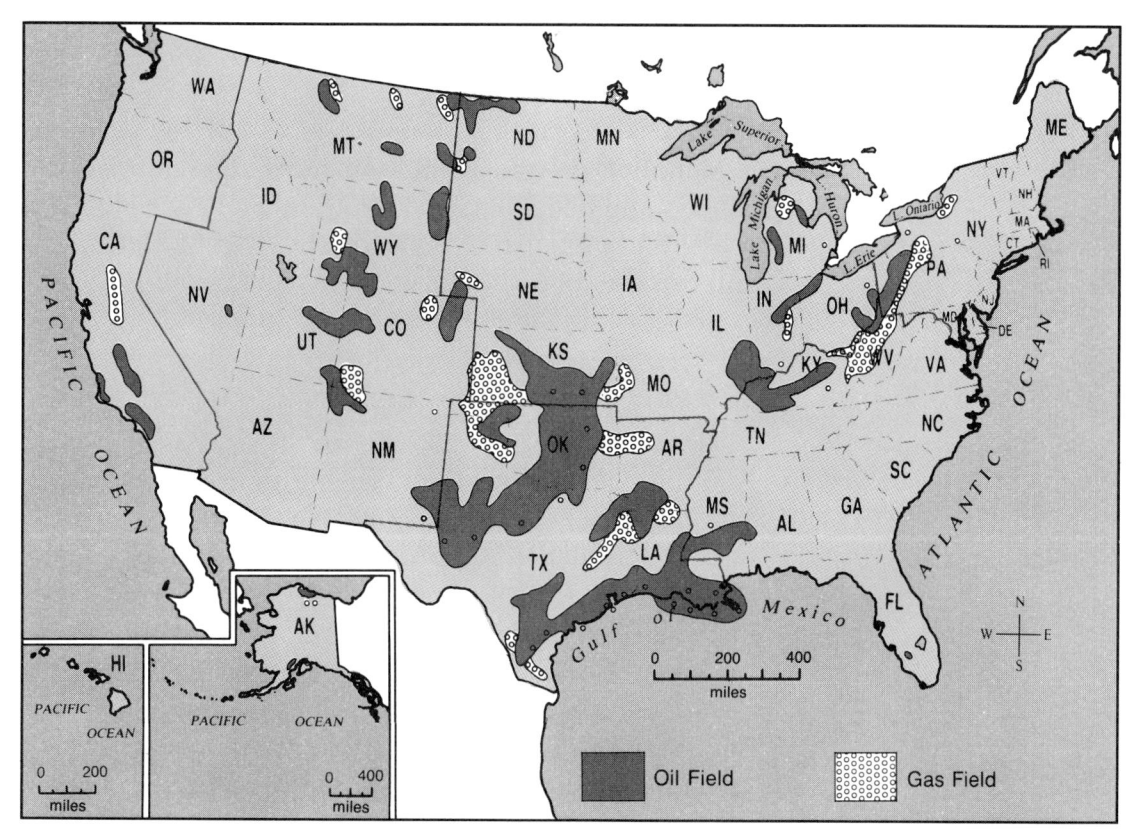

Map Study This map shows where major deposits of oil and natural gas are located. Notice that some deposits are off shore in the Gulf of Mexico.

1. Which region has the most oil and gas?
2. Which states in the Northeast and Southeast have many deposits of natural gas?
3. Does your state have major deposits of oil or natural gas?
4. Compare this map to the graph on page 221. How does the map help explain why the South Central Region had such high earnings?

Major U.S. Deposits of Oil and Natural Gas

Southeast Region

Fishing

Fishing is an important industry in the Southeast. The fishing fleets in Chesapeake Bay go after oysters, crabs, and menhaden. Those in the Atlantic Ocean and the Gulf of Mexico fish for oysters, scallops, crabs, shrimp, menhaden, and red snapper.

Forestry

Today, forests cover about a third of the land in the United States.

There are still large pine forests near coastal areas. And there are forests in the Blue Ridge and Smoky Mountains. These mountains form the southern end of the Appalachian Range.

Millions of trees in Great Smoky Mountain National Park are protected from logging. The park is located in North Carolina and Tennessee.

There are many tree farms in the Southeast. Trees that grow quickly are planted on tree farms. The trees are cut down when they become large enough to be used for lumber or pulpwood. Mississippi has more tree farms than any other state.

Trees logged in the Southeast include cedar, cypress, hickory, maple, oak, pine, and poplar.

Minerals and Fossil Fuels

The Southeast Region is a major source of sand, stone, and gravel. Alabama and Georgia are important sources of bauxite. Florida, Tennessee, and North Carolina mine large amounts of **phosphate**, which is used in fertilizers and many other products.

FISH CATCH BY REGION

Millions of Pounds

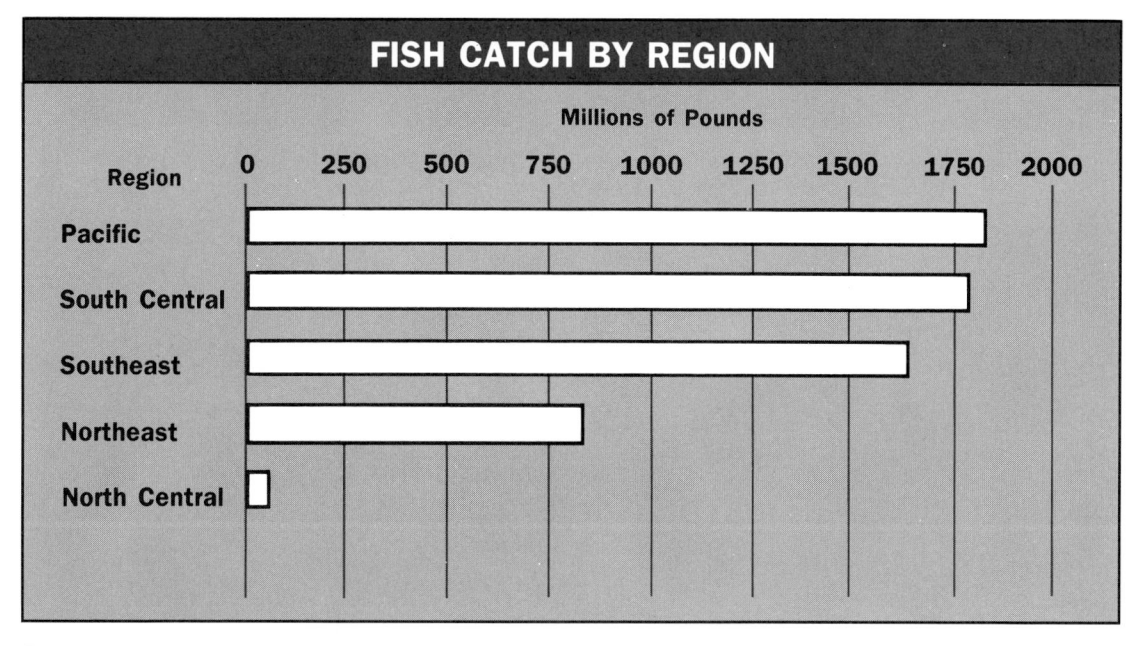

Region	Approximate Catch
Pacific	~1775
South Central	~1725
Southeast	~1550
Northeast	~725
North Central	~25

Graph Study This graph shows the amount of fish caught during a recent year in five regions.
1. Which three regions caught the most fish?
2. About how many millions of pounds of fish were caught in the South Central Region?
3. Why do you think the North Central Region's catch was so much smaller than all the others?
4. Which region isn't listed here? Why do you think it isn't?

The Southeast Region has one of the world's largest coal fields. It begins in western Pennsylvania and stretches south for 700 miles. The field runs through West Virginia, Kentucky, Tennessee, and Alabama. More than half the nation's coal comes from these states. Kentucky is the number one producer. Some oil is produced in Mississippi, Alabama, and Florida.

Today, forests cover about a third of the land in the United States.

Chapter Review

Summary

The United States is rich in natural resources. Each of its six regions has industries that develop some of the resources listed below.

1. Four of the six regions have important fishing industries. They are listed here in the order of the size of their catches. Examples of the fish and shellfish caught in each region are also given.

    Pacific *Fish:* halibut, salmon, tuna *Shellfish:* crabs

    South Central *Fish:* flounder, menhaden, red snapper *Shellfish:* crabs, oysters, shrimp

    Southeast *Fish:* menhaden, red snapper *Shellfish:* crabs, oysters, scallops, shrimp

    Northeast *Fish:* cod, flounder, herring *Shellfish:* crabs, lobsters, oysters, scallops

2. Three of the six regions have important lumber industries. They are:

    Pacific cedar, fir, pine, redwood, spruce

    South Central cypress, gum, hickory, oak, pine

    Southeast cedar, cypress, hickory, oak, pine, poplar

    The top three lumber-producing states are Oregon, Washington, and California.

    Trees logged in the other regions include the following:

    Rocky Mountain aspen, birch, cottonwood, fir, pine, spruce

    North Central aspen, beech, hickory, maple, oak, pine, walnut

    Northeast birch, fir, maple, oak, pine, spruce

3. Coal is produced in all the regions except the Pacific Region. The top three producers of coal are Kentucky, Wyoming, and West Virginia.

4. Most of the oil and gas production in the United States is centered in the South Central and Pacific Regions. The top three producers of oil are Texas, Alaska, and Louisiana.

Thinking and Writing

Answer these questions in complete sentences on a separate sheet of paper.

1. Why is the Columbia River important to fishing in the Pacific Region?
2. How does the way menhaden are used differ from the way other fish are used?
3. Why are sand, gravel, and stone important minerals?
4. Why do you think oil is so often found buried below coastal lands? (Hint: Reread page 161.)
5. What is the difference between a saw mill and a pulpwood mill?
6. Why may the Rocky Mountain Region be called a "storehouse of minerals"? Give examples to support your answer.

Questions to Discuss

1. Which of the resources discussed in this chapter are renewable? Which are not renewable?
2. Explain the statement below, and give examples to support your explanation:

    Each region depends upon all the other regions to meet its needs for minerals and fossil fuels.

Special Project

Look up your state in an encyclopedia. Find a product map. Copy the names of any fossil fuels and minerals mined in your state. Report back to your class.

Chapter 19
Other U.S. Industries

The building of computers and other electronic equipment is a growing industry in a number of regions.

Chapter Learning Objectives
1. Name three products manufactured or processed in each of six geographic regions.
2. Identify two major tourist attractions in each region.
3. Name the major business centers in the United States.
4. Locate the largest seaports in the United States.
5. Identify the two U.S. industry groups that have the largest incomes.
6. Identify the two U.S. industry groups that employ the most people.

Words To Know

tourist a person who travels for sightseeing and pleasure

public utility a company that provides telephone, electric, or gas service

electronic having to do with radios, televisions, computers, and similar products

finance the use of money

reservation an area of land set aside by the federal government for American Indians to live on

resort a place to relax and have fun in

hub the center of a wheel; also, a center for business or other activities

textile any woven cloth

retail having to do with selling directly to the public; supermarkets are retail stores

refinery a factory that turns crude oil into usable products

merchandise mart one or more large buildings with showrooms where manufacturers show their products to buyers

---

In Chapter 12, you read about agriculture in the United States. In Chapter 18, you studied the nation's resource industries. The farming, fishing, forestry, and mining industries earn billions of dollars in sales. But all their sales combined make up only 4% of the total business income in the country. This means that 96% must come from somewhere else.

Do you know which three industry groups employ the most people in the United States? The graph on page 237 will tell you. Where do you think people spend more money—in supermarkets or department stores? The table on page 243 will tell you if you're right. As you can see, a lot of the information in this chapter is contained in table or graph form. So be sure to study each of them.

Two important industries you will be reading about in this chapter are the manufacturing and **tourist** industries. Tourists are people who travel for sightseeing and pleasure. The tourist industry is made up of businesses that meet tourist's needs. It includes airlines, hotels, and tour bus companies.

Chapter Nineteen **233**

Pacific Region

Manufacturing

The major manufacturing centers of the Pacific Region are located in California and Washington. Some of the most important products manufactured there are airplanes, satellites, and parts for spacecraft. Satellites are used to send TV and telephone messages around the world. They also take pictures of Earth from out in space.

One of the most important centers of the **electronics** industry is Silicon Valley. This is a nickname for the area between San Francisco and San Jose in California. Workers there make computers and parts for other electronic products.

Have you seen a movie or TV show lately? It probably was made in the Los Angeles area. This is the main center for the nation's television and movie industry.

Food processing is a big business throughout the Pacific region. Tons of fish, fruits, and vegetables are frozen or canned there. Much of the fresh food is used to make juices, sauces, and other food products.

Tourist Industry

If you spent $1,000 a day, it would take you about 13,700 years to spend 5 billion dollars.

Tourists spend more than five billion dollars ($5,000,000,000) a year in Hawaii alone. They visit Hawaii's beautiful beaches, tropical forests, and active volcanoes.

In Alaska, tourists want to see the glaciers and wild animals, such as polar bears. They may fish, hunt, or visit an Eskimo village.

Camping, hiking, fishing, hunting, and boating are big attractions in the Pacific Coast states. Giant redwood trees and the city of San Francisco bring tourists to northern California. Warm beaches and movie studios attract visitors to Los Angeles.

SOURCE OF U.S. INCOME FROM BUSINESS & INDUSTRY

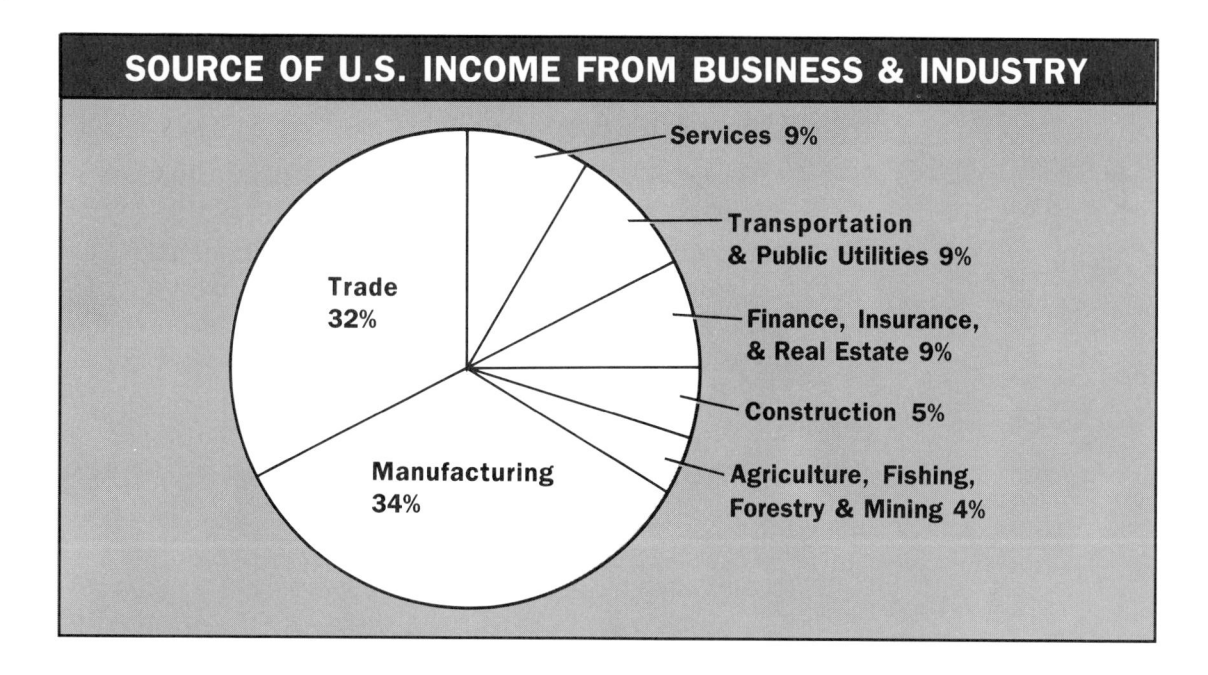

- Trade 32%
- Manufacturing 34%
- Services 9%
- Transportation & Public Utilities 9%
- Finance, Insurance, & Real Estate 9%
- Construction 5%
- Agriculture, Fishing, Forestry & Mining 4%

1. Which two industry groups provide more than 65% of U.S. business income?
2. What percent of U.S. business income comes from transportation and **public utilities?**

Note: "Trade" refers to the buying and selling of goods, both within the United States and with other countries.

Business and Transportation Centers

Los Angeles is the main center for trade and **finance** in the Pacific Region. Los Angeles and Long Beach are also important seaports. They handle more than 80 million (80,000,000) tons of cargo a year.

Seaports and airports are important to Alaska and Hawaii. Both states depend on ships and planes to bring products from the mainland. They also depend on them to carry their products *to* mainland markets.

The largest seaport and the largest airport in Hawaii are in Honolulu. Valdez is an important oil port in Alaska. Other important ports in the Pacific Region are Seattle, Portland, San Francisco, and San Diego.

One ton equals 2,000 pounds, which is about the weight of a small car.

Chapter Nineteen   235

Rocky Mountain Region

Manufacturing

The Rocky Mountain Region's manufacturing industry is the smallest in the United States. However, it is growing rapidly. This is due in part to the growth of the mining industry. Much of the manufacturing involves processing the minerals that are mined here.

But there are other kinds of manufacturing as well. Factories turn out airplanes, electronic equipment, machinery, and transportation equipment. They also produce food and wood products.

The making of sports clothing and equipment is a growing business in the region. Books and magazines are published and printed in some cities.

Denver, Colorado, and Salt Lake City, Utah, are the most important manufacturing centers.

Tourist and Retirement Industries

With all of its beautiful mountains, rivers, and streams, the Rocky Mountain Region attracts millions of tourists every year. They visit national parks, such as Yellowstone and the Grand Canyon. They visit old mining towns and Indian **reservations**. They ski at the region's many ski **resorts.**

Many people visit resorts in the warm Arizona desert. There they can play golf or tennis in the winter time.

Because of the warm climate in the desert, many older Americans retire there. To retire is to stop working at a certain age.

New service jobs are created to serve the needs of the retired people. These jobs are held by salesclerks and gardeners as well as health care and recreation workers.

U.S. EMPLOYMENT BY INDUSTRY

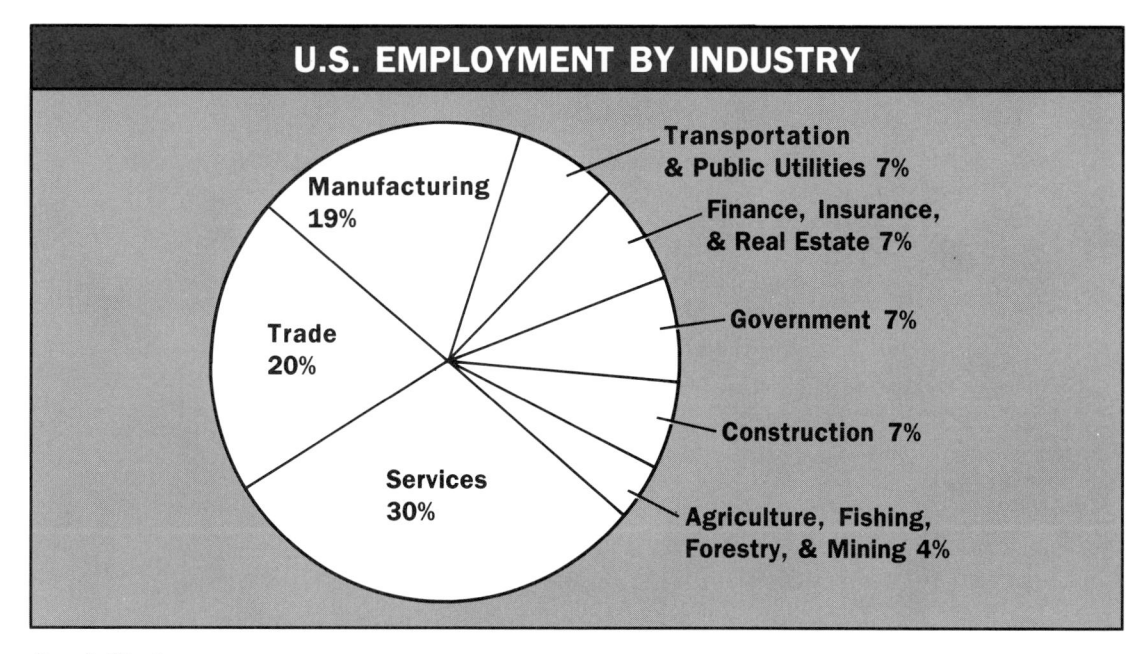

- Manufacturing 19%
- Trade 20%
- Services 30%
- Transportation & Public Utilities 7%
- Finance, Insurance, & Real Estate 7%
- Government 7%
- Construction 7%
- Agriculture, Fishing, Forestry, & Mining 4%

Graph Study
1. Which industry group employs the highest percentage of U.S. workers? What percent does it employ?
2. Which two groups combined employ half of all U.S. workers?
3. What percent of U.S. workers are employed in the agriculture, fishing, forestry, and mining industries?

Business and Transportation Centers

Denver is the major financial, trade, and transportation center for the Rocky Mountain Region. It serves the business needs of farmers, ranchers, loggers, miners, and manufacturers.

Rugged mountains and long distances between cities make fast land travel difficult. Long trains loaded with wheat, cattle, and ore must slowly snake their way through rugged mountains. There is a lot of air traffic in and out of Denver.

The federal government employs many office workers in Denver. They take care of affairs for the whole western part of the country. There is also a federal mint, where money is printed and coined.

Over 5 million people are employed by the federal government. About 2 million are in the armed forces. Others care for public lands, make and enforce federal laws, and provide other services.

Chapter Nineteen **237**

North Central Region

Manufacturing

The main manufacturing centers of the North Central Region stretch across Illinois, Indiana, and Ohio. As you learned earlier, automobiles are built in Detroit. And steel comes from cities along the southern shores of Lake Michigan and Lake Erie.

Tires and other rubber products are made in nearby Akron, Ohio. Auto glass is made in Toledo, Ohio. Steel parts for machines and heavy equipment also come from this area.

Did you have cereal or bread for breakfast? The cereal or the flour to make the bread may have come from Minneapolis, Minnesota. There, grains grown in the region are turned into cereal and flour.

What happens to all the beef cattle and hogs that are fattened up on the region's corn and soybeans? They are sent to meat packing plants where they are killed and made ready for shipment. The nation's largest meat packing plants are in Omaha, Nebraska, St. Louis, Missouri, and Kansas City, Kansas.

Tourist Industry

The windy city of Chicago has the tallest building in the world, Sears Tower. It is 110 stories high. Chicago is known for its art and history museums. And each year many concerts and plays are put on .

St. Louis is the site of the Gateway Arch. It overlooks both the city and the Mississippi River. The arch is close to 50 stories high.

Thousands of lakes in Minnesota attract people who like to boat and fish. The strange rock formations in North Dakota's Badlands are visited by many tourists. In South Dakota, visitors can see the giant carvings of the faces of four American presidents in the side of Mount Rushmore.

INCOME FROM MANUFACTURED PRODUCTS BY REGION

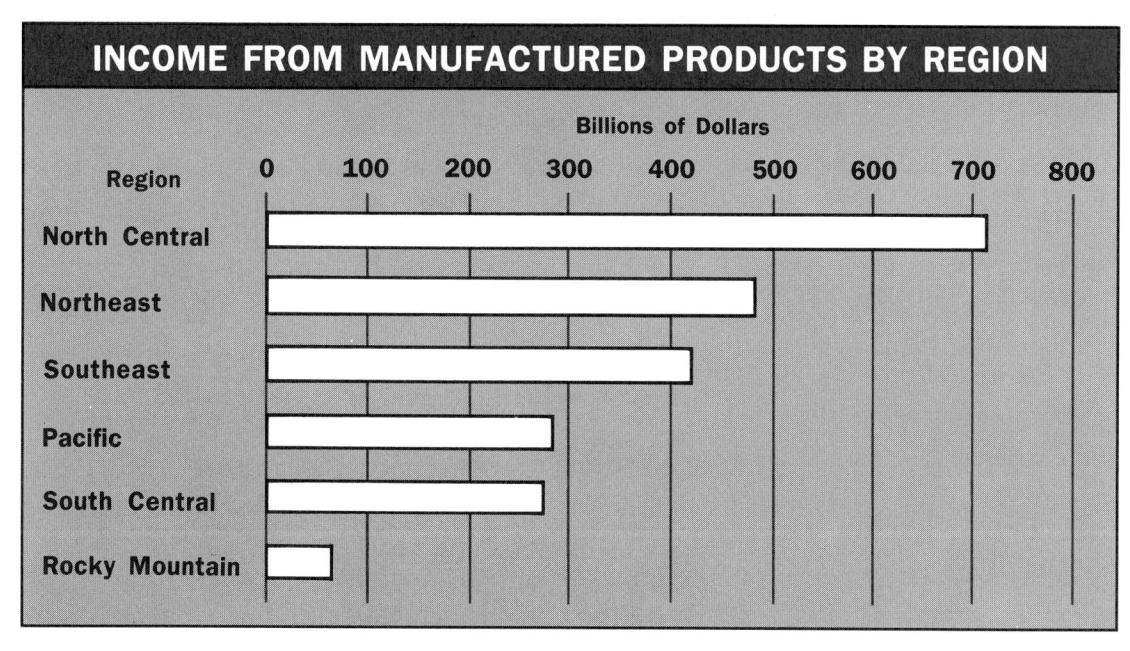

Region	Billions of Dollars
North Central	~720
Northeast	~470
Southeast	~420
Pacific	~310
South Central	~280
Rocky Mountain	~70

Graph Study
1. Which three regions receive the largest amounts of money from manufactured goods?
2. About how many times greater is the income of the South Central Region than that of the Rocky Mountain Region?
   a. 7 times   b. 3 times   c. 4 times

Business and Transportation Centers

The region's main center for finance, trade, and transportation is Chicago. Chicago's O'Hare Airport is the busiest in the nation. Chicago is also the **hub** for many of the country's major railroad lines.

Special railroad cars, trucks, ships, and barges are important to the region. Meat is transported in refrigerated trucks and railroad cars. Iron ore and grain are carried in special ships on the Great Lakes. Iron ore, coal, oil, and grain travel by barge on the Mississippi River and its tributaries.

There are many lake and river ports in the region. Three of the busiest lake ports are Duluth, Chicago, and Toledo. Two of the busiest river ports are St. Louis and Cincinnati.

Tons of Cargo Per Year

Port	Millions of Tons
Duluth, MN	29
St. Louis, MO	27
Chicago, IL	23
Toledo, OH	18
Cincinnati, OH	16

Northeast Region

Manufacturing

Much of the nation's paper and wood products come from Maine. The state also produces leather goods, such as moccasins and boots. Electronic equipment and machinery are the major products of Massachusetts. Building aircraft engines, submarines, and helicopters are the major industries of Connecticut. While most of New England's **textile** industry has moved south, wool is still woven there.

New York City is the clothing center of the United States. It produces most of the nation's books and magazines and many TV programs. Chemical production is a major industry in New Jersey. Steel and metal products are produced in Pennsylvania.

Other important products of the region include cameras, silverware, firearms, and furniture.

Tourist Industry

Many tourists visit the Northeast because it was the birthplace of the United States. They visit Plymouth, Massachusetts, where the Pilgrims lived. They visit the Boston area, where the Revolutionary War began. They visit Philadelphia, where the Constitution was written. And they visit the nation's capital, Washington, D.C.

The main business of Washington, D.C., is governing the nation. Close to 350,000 federal employees fill its offices every day.

In fall, visitors flock to Vermont and New Hampshire to see the spectacular fall colors. In winter, the many ski resorts in those states are popular. In summer, tourists crowd the beaches of Cape Cod, Massachusetts, and the New Jersey shore.

At any time of the year, New York City attracts visitors from around the world. They go there to see its tall buildings, big stores, and fine museums and parks. They attend concerts, plays, and shows.

INCOME FROM TOURISM BY REGION

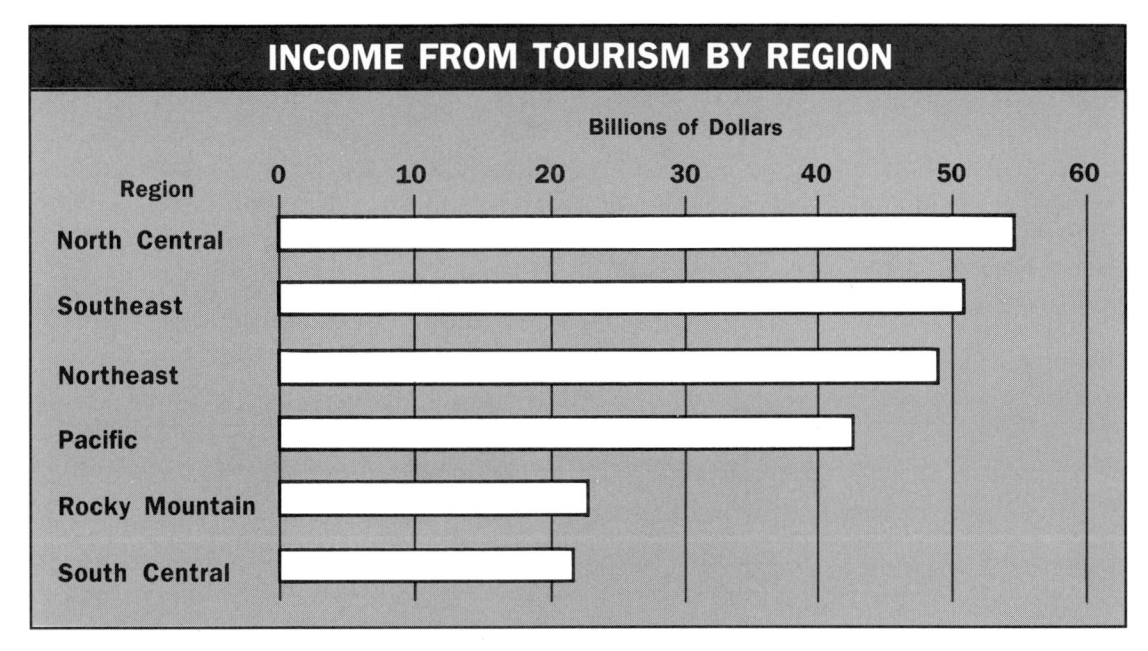

Billions of Dollars

Region	
North Central	~55
Southeast	~50
Northeast	~48
Pacific	~45
Rocky Mountain	~22
South Central	~22

Graph Study
1. In which two regions does tourism bring in the most money?
2. In which two regions does it bring in the least?
3. About how many billions of dollars does the North Central Region receive from tourism?
4. About how many times greater is the Northeast Region's tourism income than the Rocky Mountain Region's?

Business and Transportation Centers

New York City is the main financial and trade center, not only of the Northeast, but of the whole United States. It ranks as one of the world's most important business centers. Many American companies have their main offices in New York. Banks and businesses from around the world also have offices there.

New York is served by three large airports. And ships from around the world sail in and out of its harbor. Boston, Philadelphia, and Baltimore are also important business centers and seaports. Railroads and major highways connect all four cities, linking them into one giant city.

The port of New York handles more than 150 million tons of cargo a year. It is one of the largest and busiest seaports in the United States.

Chapter Nineteen

South Central Region

Manufacturing

Much of the manufacturing in Texas, Oklahoma, and Louisiana is connected with the oil business. Factories called **refineries** turn crude oil into many useful products.

You already know about gasoline, motor oil, and heating oil. But the refineries also take out certain chemicals from the crude oil. These are used to make plastics, paints, fertilizers, and other products.

Many factories in the region make parts for oil wells. Others make parts for pipelines.

The region has other industries besides those related to oil. Aircraft building has long been important in the area near Dallas and Fort Worth. Arkansas produces many wood products. Texas, Oklahoma, and Arkansas have developed electronics industries. Fish, fruit, and vegetable products are also produced in the region.

Tourist Industry

Tourists flock to Gulf Coast beaches in winter. They visit historic sites, such as the Alamo in San Antonio. They go to the Johnson Space Center and attend basketball and football games at the Superdome, both in Houston.

Have you ever watched a space launch on TV? If so, then you have seen and heard workers at Mission Control, which is part of the Johnson Space Center.

Many tourists visit Indian reservations in Oklahoma. Others enjoy eating in French restaurants and listening to jazz in New Orleans.

Some tourists visit Arkansas to enjoy the baths at Hot Springs. Or they visit the Crater of Diamonds near Murfreesboro. It is the only major diamond field in the United States.

INCOME FROM RETAIL SALES	
Business	Billions of Dollars
Automotive dealers (including parts)	304
Food stores	289
Department and other general merchandise stores	164
Eating and drinking places	134
Gasoline stations	106
Building materials and hardware stores	75
Clothing and accessories stores	72
Furniture and appliance stores	69

Table Study
1. Which two kinds of retail businesses have the largest income?
2. What is the income of eating and drinking places?
3. Which two kinds of **retail** businesses have roughly equal incomes?

Business and Transportation Centers

The Dallas–Fort Worth area is the main financial, trade, and transportation center for the region. A giant airport serves both Dallas and nearby Fort Worth.

All forms of transportation are important to the region. Cattle are shipped in railroad cars. Oil and natural gas are shipped by pipeline, river barge, truck, and railroad car. Ships load up with food and oil products in New Orleans and Houston.

Dallas has the largest **merchandise mart** in the world. The mart has 3,400 showrooms in eight different buildings. Manufacturers from around the world display their products in the showrooms. Every year, about 600,000 buyers from other companies visit the showrooms and select products.

New Orleans handles almost 150 million tons of cargo a year. Houston handles more than 90 million tons. How does that compare with the amount of cargo handled in New York?

Southeast Region

Manufacturing

The textile industry has grown since moving from the Northeast to the Southeast in the period of time between the 1920s and the 1950s. Today, textile mills from southern Virginia to northern Georgia are making cloth and cloth products.

Another quickly growing industry is the making of plastics, paints, and fertilizers. These products are made from the crude oil that comes from fields in Louisiana and elsewhere.

Food processing is another important industry of the region. Fish, fruits, and vegetables are packed, frozen, and canned.

Furniture making is one of the oldest industries of the Southeast. Much of the furniture made in the United States comes from this region.

The Southeast also has an important steel center. It is located in Birmingham, Alabama.

Tourist and Retirement Industries

In winter, people from the cold northern states flock to Florida's warm beaches. All year round, Disney World and many other fun parks attract millions of tourists to the Orlando area. Not far away is the Kennedy Space Center, where visitors can learn about space travel.

Many older Americans retire in Florida. They relax in the year-round sunshine and enjoy fishing, golf, and other outdoor activities.

There are historic sites throughout the Southeast. In Williamsburg, Virginia, tourists can visit a whole village that looks just as it did back in the 1700s.

The Great Smoky Mountains and the Blue Ridge Mountains attract millions of visitors. They offer beautiful places to camp, hike, hunt, and canoe.

Spacecraft are launched at the Kennedy Space Center on Cape Canaveral, Florida. Once off the ground, they are controlled from the Johnson Space Center in Houston.

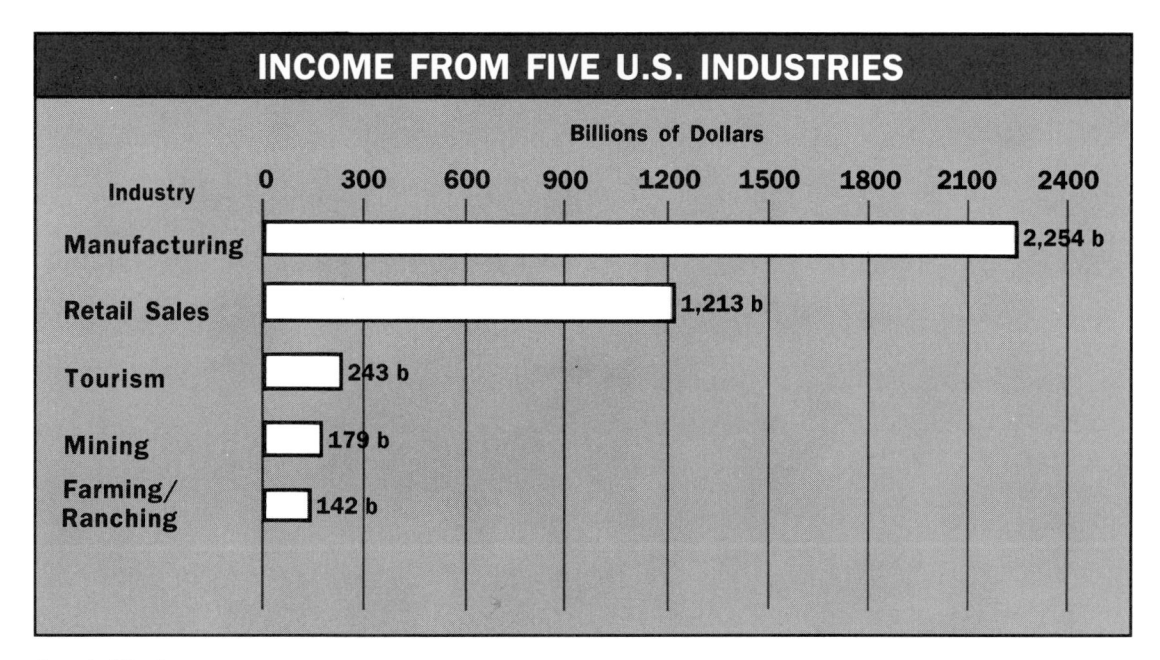

INCOME FROM FIVE U.S. INDUSTRIES

Billions of Dollars

Industry	Income
Manufacturing	2,254 b
Retail Sales	1,213 b
Tourism	243 b
Mining	179 b
Farming/Ranching	142 b

Graph Study
1. What is the yearly income from retail sales?
2. Which two industries have incomes greater than the incomes from tourism, mining, farming, and ranching combined?
3. How much larger is income from mining than income from farming and ranching?

Business and Transportation Centers

The main center for finance, trade, and transportation in the Southeast is Atlanta. The city has the second largest merchandise mart in the country. It also has the second busiest airport. And it is the main hub for rail and truck traffic in the region.

Three other cities are important seaports. Ships sailing between Mobile, Tampa, and Norfolk carry goods to and from the region's mills and factories.

Memphis is an important port for barge traffic on the Mississippi River.

Chapter Review

Summary

1. Some of the major products manufactured or processed in each region are:

    Pacific airplanes, satellites, computers, movies, food products

    Rocky Mountain mineral products, airplanes, machinery, food and wood products

    North Central autos and auto parts, steel, machines, flour, grain and meat

    Northeast paper, wood, leather, metal and electronic products, chemicals, steel, machines, submarines, and helicopters

    South Central chemicals, plastics, paints, fertilizers, oil well and electronic equipment, and airplanes

    Southeast textiles, plastics, paints, fertilizers, furniture, steel, and food products

2. Some major attractions in each region are:

    Pacific beaches, volcanoes, glaciers, mountains, movie and TV studios

    Rocky Mountain national parks, old mining towns, Indian reservations, resorts

    North Central Sears Tower, Gateway Arch, Mt. Rushmore, Minnesota lakes, Dakota Badlands

    Northeast historic sites, ski resorts, beaches, fall colors, New York City, Washington, D.C.

    South Central beaches, the Alamo, Johnson Space Center, Indian reservations, New Orleans

    Southeast beaches, fun parks, Kennedy Space Center, Williamsburg, mountains

3. The major business centers in the United States are Los Angeles, Denver, Chicago, Dallas, New York, and Atlanta.

4. The largest seaports in the United States are New York, New Orleans, and Houston.

5. The two U.S. industry groups that have the largest incomes are manufacturing and trade.

6. The two industry groups that employ the most people are services and trade.

246 Chapter Nineteen

Thinking and Writing

Answer these questions in complete sentences on a separate sheet of paper.

1. Give one reason why airports and seaports are especially important in Alaska and Hawaii.
2. Why are tourist attractions important to all the regions?
3. What are some jobs that may be plentiful in areas that have many tourist attractions?
4. Name one way a job in a hotel would be different from a job in a factory.
5. Why may it be said that the North Central Region is "the nation's butcher"?
6. Why do you think there are tire and auto glass industries in the North Central Region?

Questions to Discuss

1. What do you think an area needs in order to become a major manufacturing center?
2. What kinds of businesses earn money from tourists? How might these businesses be affected by weather, gasoline supplies, and rising prices?

Special Project

Look up your state in an encyclopedia. Find out what tourist attractions there are. Write a report about the tourist industry in your state.

Chapters 16–19

REVIEW

Answer these questions on a separate sheet of paper.

A. Key Words

electronics
exports
fossils
imports
material
pulpwood
refinery
cargo
textile
transport

Choose the word in the list on the left that best completes each sentence below.

1. Iron is a raw ____ used to make steel.
2. The U.S. ____ wheat to many other countries.
3. The U.S. ____ many cars from Japan.
4. Ships are used to ____ the wheat and cars.
5. The remains of plants and animals that lived millions of years ago are ____ .
6. Paper products are made from ____ .
7. The goods that are transported on a ship are that ship's ____ .
8. The ____ industry makes cloth.
9. Crude oil is made into useful products in a ____ .
10. Computers are made by the ____ industry.

B. Key Facts

Choose the word or words that best complete each sentence.

11. Two of the world's biggest producers of manufactured goods are ____ .
    a. India and Japan   b. China and the United States   c. the United States and Japan
12. Nigeria, Chad, and Zimbabwe are ____ .
    a. developed countries   b. developing countries   c. oil rich countries
13. Travel between the Atlantic and Pacific Oceans is made shorter by the ____ .
    a. Saint Lawrence Seaway   b. Panama Canal   c. Gulf of Mexico

14. The cheapest but also the slowest form of transportation is by ____ .
    a. land   b. air   c. sea
15. Today, most jet liners fly at speeds of ____ .
    a. 500–600 mph   b. 200–300 mph
    c. 600–900 mph
16. The nation's leading producers of lumber are Oregon, California, and ____ .
    a. Iowa   b. Nevada   c. Washington
17. The nation's leading producers of oil are Texas, Alaska, and ____ .
    a. Wyoming   b. Louisiana   c. Oklahoma
18. The region with the highest earnings from manufacturing is the ____ .
    a. Southeast Region   b. Pacific Region
    c. North Central Region
19. The two industry groups that provide the most income for businesses in the United States are ____ .
    a. trade and transportation   b. manufacturing and trade   c. service and construction
20. Fifty percent of U.S. workers are employed in ____ .
    a. service and trade   b. trade and manufacturing   c. service and construction

C. Main Ideas

Answer the questions below.

21. Give two reasons why the first U.S. factories were located in the Northeast.
22. Give two reasons why the steel industry started in the Great Lakes area.
23. Give two reasons why some countries have many industries while others have few, if any.
24. Compare ways of travel in poor countries with those in rich countries.

Chapter 20
Earth Has Billions of People

Eight million people live in New York, one of the world's largest cities.

Chapter Learning Objectives

1. Tell how early gatherers and hunters survived.
2. Name some discoveries and inventions that have affected life on Earth.
3. Explain how farming and herding affected early population growth.
4. Explain how towns and villages became cities.
5. Give reasons for the growth of the world's population in recent times.
6. Use a graph to study world population distribution.
7. Describe improvements that have been made in feeding the world's growing population. Describe problems that have yet to be solved in this area.

Words To Know

population the number of people that live in a place

sanitation the act of preventing disease by keeping things clean and safely getting rid of garbage and waste

There are more than 5 billion (5,000,000,000) people on Earth. If you were to count one person each second, it would take 150 years to count them all.

Early History

Gatherers and Hunters

Earth did not always have so many people. Back 10,000 years ago, its **population** was only about 10 million (10,000,000). In those times, people lived in small communities. Most were gatherers. They gathered wild seeds, berries, nuts, and other foods from plants and also hunted animals. Because of the limited amount of food in an area, not many people could live there. When there were no more plants to pick or animals to kill, the people had to move.

Cave drawing of a deer hunt.

Chapter Twenty   251

Discoveries

Is the building you live in heated? How? What form of energy is used to produce the heat? What form of energy is used to cook your food?

One of the things that greatly changed human life on Earth was the discovery of how to control fire. This helped people stay warm in cold places and protect themselves from wild animals. And it allowed them to cook their food.

People also learned how to make pots and baskets for cooking and storing foods. They built boats for travel on water. They found out how to make better tools and hunting weapons.

All these improvements led to small increases in the population.

Farmers, Herders, and Craftsworkers

Are crops grown in your area? Have they ever been? When? For how long?

In time, some people discovered how to grow plants. They became farmers and raised corn, wheat, rice, and barley.

People also learned to raise sheep, goats, and cattle. They became herders.

In time, people were able to produce more food by farming and herding than they could by hunting and gathering. As the food supply increased, so did the population.

At first, each community raised only enough food for itself. And the community made whatever it needed. But later, communities began to trade things. A community with extra wheat might trade some of it for a goat.

When farmers and herders got better at raising crops and animals, there was less need for everyone to be doing these things. Some people then became craftsworkers. They spent their time making tools, pottery, clothing, baskets, and other useful things.

A craftsworker could trade what he or she had made for food or for something that someone else had made. Later, money was invented. Then people could buy and sell things.

Big changes were also brought about when the wheel was invented. The wheel made it possible to move more things from one place to another.

How would your life be different if the wheel had never been invented?

The Growth of Towns and Cities

Villages of farmers and craftsworkers appeared in different places around the world. After a long time, villages grew into towns and cities. Here are just a few of the reasons some villages grew.
- They had good farmland that could support larger populations.
- They were near sources of water that could be used to water crops in dry seasons.
- They were near resources that could be used to build or make things.
- They were next to waterways and had places for boats to load and unload goods.

The ancient city of Babylon was founded on very fertile land between two rivers.

Chapter Twenty 253

Do you live in a large city? Have you ever visited one? Do you like cities? What do you like the most about them? What do you like the least?

Some places became cities because strong rulers built forts there. People came to live in the cities because they felt safer and could earn a living there. Later, cities offered other attractions as well, such as temples, theaters, and sports arenas.

People started building cities about 6,000 years ago. By that time, Earth's population had grown to about 85 million (85,000,000).

Recent Changes

The biggest growth in Earth's population has come in recent times. The growth came because people began to understand the importance of **sanitation.** Sanitation means safely getting rid of garbage and human wastes. Sanitation helped save lives by preventing disease. New medicines also helped save lives. By 1925 the population reached 2 billion (2,000,000,000).

Then scientists began to find ways to stop the spread of terrible diseases. The shot you were given as a child to keep you from getting smallpox is one example of this. Such diseases used to kill millions of people.

Shots, other improvements in health care, and larger food supplies kept more people alive. By 1975 the population doubled to 4 billion (4,000,000,000).

Since then, the number has grown by over a billion more.

The pie graph on the next page compares the size of each continent's population as of 1985. Except for some scientists, no one lives on Antarctica, so it is not included on the graph.

WHERE WE LIVE

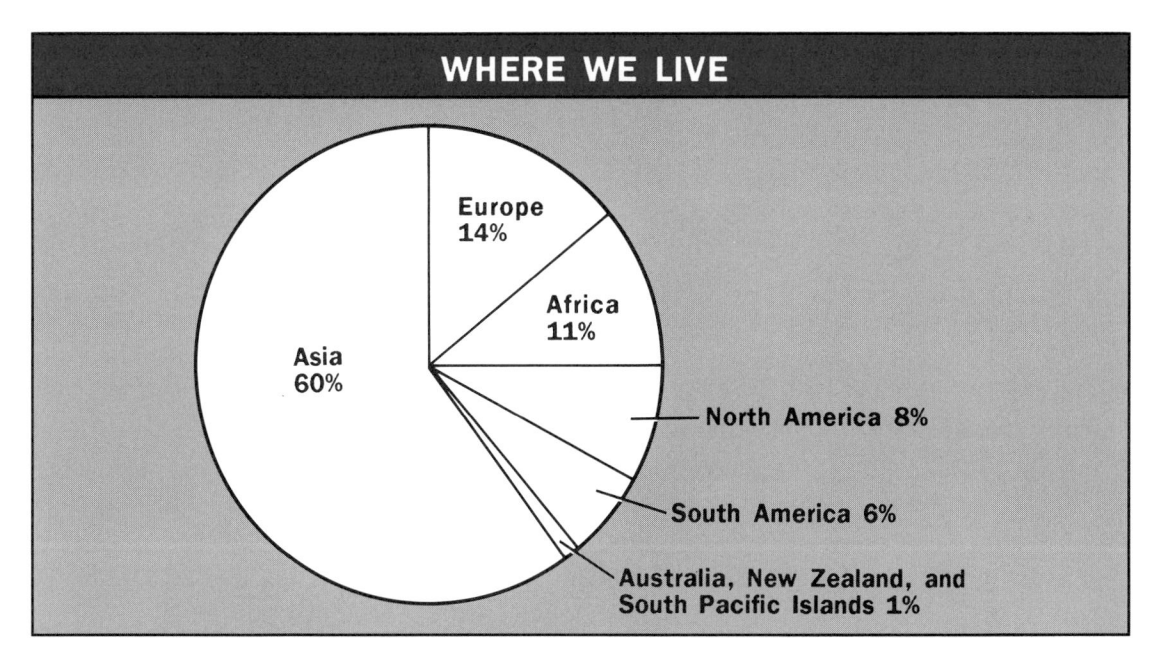

- Asia 60%
- Europe 14%
- Africa 11%
- North America 8%
- South America 6%
- Australia, New Zealand, and South Pacific Islands 1%

Graph Study
1. Which continent has the largest number of people?
2. What percent of the world's population lives there?
3. Do Asians make up more than or less than half of the world's population?
4. What percent of the world's population lives in North America?

Feeding the Growing Population

It takes a lot of food to feed more than 5 billion people. Where is it all coming from?

- Giant machines help farmers produce more than they could years ago.
- Science has found ways to get more food from corn, wheat, and rice plants. Some farmlands now produce more food.
- Some deserts have been turned into farmlands. This is done by piping in water from other places.
- Science has found ways to raise bigger animals that produce more meat.

Sometimes, there are famines in parts of the world. A famine is a severe food shortage. It can happen when a country gets much less rain than usual. It can happen when disease, floods, or war destroy crops. And it can happen when people do not have enough money to buy food.

Some people are worried. They say that if the population keeps growing as fast as it is growing now, there will not be enough food for everyone.

Others say that producing enough food is not the real problem. They believe that each country's farmlands could produce enough food to meet that country's needs. But too often, they say, farmlands are not used to raise crops that are needed. Instead they are used to raise animals and crops that can be sold for high prices, often to other countries.

Besides food, clothing, and shelter, what do you think people need the most?

A windmill helps pump water to a vegetable garden in Thailand.

The World's Largest Cities

City	Country	Millions of people
Tokyo-Yokohama	Japan	25
Mexico City	Mexico	17
São Paulo	Brazil	15
New York	United States	15
Seoul	Korea	14
Osaka-Kobe-Kyoto	Japan	14
Buenos Aires	Brazil	11
Calcutta	India	10
Bombay	India	10
Rio de Janeiro	Brazil	10

Table Study This table lists the world's most populated cities. *The numbers of people living in areas near the cities are included in the population figures.* In some city areas, two or more cities are listed. That is because the cities are close enough together to be counted as one.

1. Which city, or cities, has the largest population?
2. Which three countries have more than one city area with a population over 10 million?
3. Which three city areas have roughly equal populations?

Chapter Review

Summary

1. Thousands of years ago, people gathered wild seeds, berries, nuts, and other plant food. They also hunted animals. Earth's population was small then—about 10 million.

2. Life on Earth was affected by discoveries such as the control of fire and farming. It was also affected by inventions such as pots and baskets, tools, weapons, money, and the wheel.

3. As people found better ways to raise food, the population began to grow.

4. People became farmers, herders, and craftsworkers. They started to trade and set up villages. Some villages grew into cities.

5. Cities grew up in places that were near good farmland, water for crops and transportation, and resources for building and making things. Some places grew into cities because strong rulers built forts there. About 6,000 years ago, Earth's population had reached 85 million.

6. In more recent times, improved sanitation and new medicines led to longer life spans. By 1925 Earth's population had reached 2 billion.

7. In the next 50 years, Earth's population doubled to 4 billion. It has now reached more than 5 billion and is still growing. The main reasons for the growth are improvements in health care and increases in the food supply.

8. Some people worry that there will not be enough food to feed our ever-growing population. Others say that the problem is in how some farmlands are used.

Thinking and Writing

Answer these questions in complete sentences on a separate sheet of paper.

1. Which group probably had a larger population—farmers or gatherers? Why?
2. Tell two ways people could get things they needed before money was invented.
3. This chapter gives four reasons some villages grew into cities. Which of the four is *not* shown in the drawing of Babylon on page 253?
4. Give two reasons cities are often built beside rivers.
5. In the 20th Century, how long did it take for the world's population to double?
6. This chapter gives a number of reasons for population growth. Which ones seem to have had the greatest effect over the course of history?

Questions to Discuss

1. How does the way you and your family get food differ from the way gatherers and hunters got theirs?
2. Why do you think so many people choose to live in cities today?
3. What part has science and medicine played in helping Earth's population more than double since 1925?

Special Project

Find out the population of your town or city. Is the population increasing or decreasing? Try to find the reason for any changes.

Chapter Twenty

Chapter 21

People Live in Culture Groups

Soccer has become part of the American culture as more and more Americans play and watch the game.

Chapter Learning Objectives

1. Explain what culture is.
2. Show how food, sports, family life, language, and religion can differ from culture to culture.
3. Read a table describing changes in American family life between 1960 and 1985.
4. Explain how languages change.
5. Explain differences and similarities between popular religions.
6. Tell how migration has helped the United States become a nation of many cultures.

Words To Know

culture the ways in which a group of people think and act

language the words and sounds used by a group of people to express thoughts and feelings

migrate to move from one place to another

How We Live

People everywhere have the same basic needs. They need food, clothing, and shelter. They need love, friendship, and a sense of belonging.

But different groups of people meet their needs in different ways. Each group has its own **culture.** Culture is the way a group of people thinks and acts.

A culture group may include all the people who live in a country. Or it may be a small group that chooses to live a certain way.

In this chapter, you will read about some important cultural differences. There are others as well, such as clothing, music, and art. It is our differences that make us interesting.

Which culture groups do you belong to?

Food

Many Americans like fried, mashed, or baked potatoes with their main meal. That is part of the American culture. Most Asians prefer rice. Italians often prefer spaghetti or similar foods made from grain. That is part of their culture.

The ways people prepare food may also be very different. Most Americans cook the fish they eat. But most Japanese eat both raw and cooked fish. Today, Americans eat foods from many of the world's cultures. Do you eat pizza, bagels, or tacos? They were brought to the United States by people who came here from other countries.

Which foods are special to the culture you come from?

Chapter Twenty-One **261**

Sports and Games

Sports of some kind are played in most cultures. Many were started as a way to learn skills for hunting and war. For example, young children who played with wooden spears developed hunting skills they would need later.

Many cultures have games that call for the use of a bat and ball. Others have games that call for putting a ball through a hoop. From these games came the American sports of baseball and basketball.

Soccer was started in England. It became very popular in Europe and then spread to Latin America. Now soccer is being played by many Americans.

Latin America includes Mexico and all the countries south of it.

Family Life

In some cultures, only parents and their children live together. The parents provide for their children. The children may also help out as they grow older.

In other cultures, parents and their children may live together with other relatives. They may live with grandparents, aunts, uncles, and cousins. They may all live under the same roof or close by to each other.

How does living close to many relatives differ from living with only parents, brothers, and sisters?

In this larger family, all able grown-ups in the family help meet the family's needs. The older children may help on a family farm or in a family business. They may care for younger children and for family members who are sick or in need of help.

While many children live with both a mother and a father, others do not. Today, many children live with one parent. And some, of course, live with neither their mothers nor their fathers. The table on page 263 can tell us some things about family life in the United States between 1960 and 1985.

Related families gather for a reunion.

Families in the United States

Year	Total Number of Families*	Two-parent Families	Families Headed by Father	Families Headed by Mother
1960	45.11	39.33	1.28	4.50
1965	47.96	41.75	1.18	5.03
1970	51.59	44.76	1.24	5.59
1975	55.71	46.97	1.50	7.24
1980	59.55	49.11	1.73	8.71
1985	62.71	50.35	2.23	10.13

*all numbers are in millions

As the number of families increased, so too did the numbers of different kinds of families. However, the number of single-parent families increased faster than the total number of families. Also, in each year listed, there were many more single-parent families headed by women than by men.

What do stories do? Can listening to someone else's story tell you anything about your own life?

Language

Language is an important part of culture. Through it, people share their stories, ideas, and feelings. With language, they learn from one another.

There are about 3,000 different languages in the world. Some are spoken by only a few hundred people. Others are spoken by millions.

Which language do you think is spoken by more people than any other?

More people speak Mandarin, a form of Chinese, than any other language. The second most widely spoken language is English.

Most of today's languages started from a few main languages spoken thousands of years ago. As people spread out over Earth, they took their languages with them.

Over time, the sounds of some words changed. The meanings of some words also changed. Some words dropped out of the language because they were no longer used. New words were added as people discovered and did new things.

Other changes in language came when one country would take over another. This is how English started.

At different times, different European countries took over parts of England. Each time, the people living there had to learn the language of their new rulers. England's language became a mixture of French, German, and other European languages.

English was first brought to America by the people who came here from England in the 1600s. Today, American English has added many words from the languages of different culture groups that live here. For example, we get *tornado* from Spanish. *Pizza* comes from Italian. And *chow mein* is from Chinese.

A Buddhist temple

Religion

Many people belong to a religion. In North America, Christianity, Judaism, and Islam have the largest number of followers. There are also many followers of Hinduism, Buddhism, and Confucianism.

Though religions are different, they have some things in common.

Most religions have beliefs about how the world and its people were created. Some, but not all, believe in a god or gods who greatly affect life on Earth.

Most religions teach how people should act and how they should treat others. They usually promise everlasting peace and happiness for those who follow the teachings of the religion.

The teachings of most religions are set down in special writings. Christians have the Bible. Jews follow the Torah and the Talmud. Others follow the Koran or the Vedas. These writings often tell more than just the beliefs of the religion. They also tell about the history of the religion and about the lives of its leaders.

Each religion has its own way of praying. This may include singing, dancing, lighting candles, or leaving food or other gifts. Such things as birth, coming of age, marriage, and death are also celebrated in special ways.

Most of the world's popular religions were started by leaders with strong beliefs. While they were alive, these leaders traveled and taught. Later, many of their followers went out to spread the teachings.

That is one way some religions grew and spread. Another way was by people taking their religions with them when they moved to other lands.

People on the Move

People from many different cultures live in the United States. That is because people have **migrated** to America from all over the world. To migrate is to move from one place to another.

Migration is nothing new. Hunters and gatherers migrated to North America from Asia many thousands of years ago. They were looking for food.

About 500 years ago, people from Europe started migrating to North and South America. Many of them were looking for riches. Some were looking for freedom. Many wanted a chance to own land or to earn a better living.

Some people were forced to migrate. About 20 million people came to North and South America from Africa. They were brought here as slaves.

The Dust Bowl of the 1930s forced many American families to migrate from the Midwest.

Migration Is Still Going On

Today, there are still large migrations of people. Recent wars have forced millions of people to leave their homes in Southeast Asia, Central America, and the Middle East. Many of these people have migrated to the United States. And many people have come here from poor countries in order to find work.

All these people have brought with them their languages, religions, and other parts of their cultures.

Many people migrate within their own countries. They migrate from farms to cities. They migrate from one city to another in search of work. And they migrate from colder climates to warmer climates.

Have you ever migrated? Do you know anyone who has?

Chapter Twenty-One 267

Chapter Review

Summary

1. Culture is the way a group of people thinks and acts. Some of the things that may differ from one culture to another are: art, clothing, family life, games and sports, food, language, and religion.

2. Foods from different cultures have become part of the American diet.

3. Most cultures have sports and games. Many of them started as ways to develop special skills.

4. In some cultures, large groups of relatives live together or close by each other. They help one another.

5. Most languages come from a few main languages that changed as people spread out over Earth.

6. There are a number of different religions. They have different teachings, beliefs, ways to pray, and ways to mark events like birth and marriage.

7. Millions of people have migrated to the United States. Each new group adds something new to American culture.

Thinking and Writing

Answer these questions in complete sentences on a separate sheet of paper.

1. How does the number of today's languages compare with the number of languages thousands of years ago?

2. In North America, how does the number of Christians compare with the number of Buddhists?

3. This chapter tells three ways religions are spread. Which of the three is likely to have happened after the other two?

4. Think of a strong country taking over a weak country. How might the number of people speaking the strong country's language change?

5. How did the migration of people from Africa to the United States differ from other migrations here?

6. Tell two ways life in the United States would be different if everyone came from the same culture.

Questions to Discuss

1. What are some of the foods Americans eat that come from other cultures?

2. Tell why you agree or disagree with this statement: The mix of cultures in America makes life more interesting and enjoyable.

Special Project

Prepare a report about your family. Add pictures and maps. Write about the culture you come from. What are some of the beliefs, foods, games, and special events of that culture?

Chapter 22
People of the United States

People are the wealth of a nation.

Chapter Learning Objectives
1. Explain population distribution in the United States.
2. Name the two most crowded regions of the United States; explain how they became the most crowded.
3. Name the three fastest growing regions; explain why they are growing.
4. Explain why some cities are losing population.
5. Give examples of the different cultural groups found in each region.

Words To Know

urban of or relating to cities and large towns; an urban area is one with many cities and large towns

rural of or relating to the country or countryside; farms, ranches, forests, and mines are usually found in rural areas

density the measurement of how crowded a place is

dense crowded

suburb a living area close to a city

megalopolis an area with many large towns and cities crowded close together

decline a drop in amount; a city's population declines when more people move away than move in

---

Today, the United States is the fourth most populous country in the world. It has more than 240 million people. Only China, India, and the Soviet Union have larger populations.

Most of the people in the United States live in **urban** areas. An urban area is one that has been built up into large towns and cities.

Many cities are located on rivers or are found beside major bodies of water. In fact, by 1987 half the population of the United States lived within 50 miles of a seacoast.

Those who do not live in urban areas live in **rural** areas. In a rural area, people live some distance apart from each other. Most farm, ranch, forest, and mining lands are in rural areas.

Look at the pie graph at the right. What percent of Americans live in urban areas? What percent live in rural areas?

The United States is a land of different culture groups. In this chapter, you will read about six such groups. The groups are based on where people's ancestors lived. Our ancestors are the relatives who lived before us, our grandparents, great-grandparents, and so on. They are the people from whom we are descended.

Do you live in an urban or a rural area?

U.S. RURAL AND URBAN POPULATION

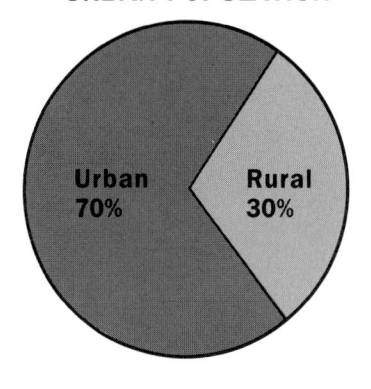

Urban 70%
Rural 30%

Chapter Twenty-Two   271

U.S. Culture Groups

Most of the people in these groups were born in the United States but have parents or ancestors who came from other places. However, the groups also include those who came here from other places themselves.

European Americans Americans whose ancestors lived in Europe

African Americans Americans whose ancestors lived in Africa

Hispanic Americans Americans whose ancestors lived in countries where Spanish is the main language, such as Mexico

Asian Americans Americans whose ancestors lived in Asia

Pacific Americans Americans whose ancestors lived on islands in the Pacific Ocean

Native Americans Americans whose ancestors lived in what is now the United States, long before other groups began settling there

Others There are some Americans who do not belong to any of the groups listed above. They are not listed separately because they do not form a large part of the population of the United States.

Pacific Region

California has more people than any of the other 50 states. Alaska has the fewest people, even though it is the largest of all the states in land area. Why do you think California has attracted so many people, while Alaska has attracted so few?

Climate, of course, has made the biggest difference. As you know, most of California is warm all year. Most of Alaska is cold. California also has large industries that provide jobs for millions of people. Alaska has far fewer opportunities for people to find work.

Most of the Pacific Region's people live in urban areas. There are more than 30 cities with populations of 100,000 or more people. Four of these cities have more than 500,000 people. All four are in California. Find them on the map on page 275.

Culture Mix

Most of the Pacific Region's people are European Americans. They began settling in the Pacific Region after gold was discovered in California in 1848.

Hispanic Americans make up the next largest group. Today, they form close to 20% of California's population. As a group, they are growing three times faster than the rest of the state's population.

Many Hispanic Americans are of Mexican descent. Their ancestors may have lived in California when it belonged to Mexico. Other Hispanic Americans are more recent arrivals from Mexico and from Central and South America.

Many of the people in California and Hawaii are Asian Americans and Pacific Americans. Their ancestors migrated mainly from China and Japan, and from the Philippines and other island nations in the Pacific Ocean. Many newcomers have recently arrived from those countries and from Vietnam, Korea, Laos, and Cambodia as well.

About 9% of the region's population is made up of African Americans. African Americans have been migrating west since the late 1800s.

About 10% of Hawaii's population is descended from Hawaii's first people, who were Polynesians. About 22% of Alaska's population is descended from the first Alaskans.

Be sure to study the chart on page 272 before reading this section.

Mexico owned all the land from Texas to the Pacific and from the Rio Grande to what are today Oregon and Idaho.

Asian and Pacific Americans make up more than 60% of Honolulu's population.

Rocky Mountain Region

Study the map on the next page before reading this section. All the cities on the map have populations of 500,000 or more.

As you can see from the map on the next page, most of the Rocky Mountain Region is lightly populated. In more than half of the region, the population averages five or fewer people per square mile.

The region has few large cities and they are far apart. Look again at the map. Which two cities in the Rocky Mountain Region have more than 500,000 people?

To find the average number of people per square mile, do this: Divide the number of people living in an area by the number of square miles in that area.

Most of the region's population live in urban areas. But many people live in small towns and in rural areas. In fact, many people moved to the region in order to get away from crowded city life.

But the liveable parts of the rugged Rocky Mountain Region may not remain uncrowded forever. Seven of the 10 fastest growing states in the United States are part of the region. They are Nevada, Arizona, Wyoming, Utah, Idaho, Colorado, and New Mexico.

What is attracting newcomers to those states? Most have moved there to find jobs in the growing mining, manufacturing, and tourist industries of the region. The warm, dry, climate of Nevada, Arizona, and New Mexico also draws many newcomers to those states.

Culture Mix

Most of the Rocky Mountain Region's population is European American. Gold and silver mining began attracting people back in the late 1800s. Later, others came to raise cattle, sheep, and wheat in the region's wide open spaces.

Hispanic Americans make up about 13% of the region's population. Most of this group is descended from Mexicans who lived in the region before it became part of the United States.

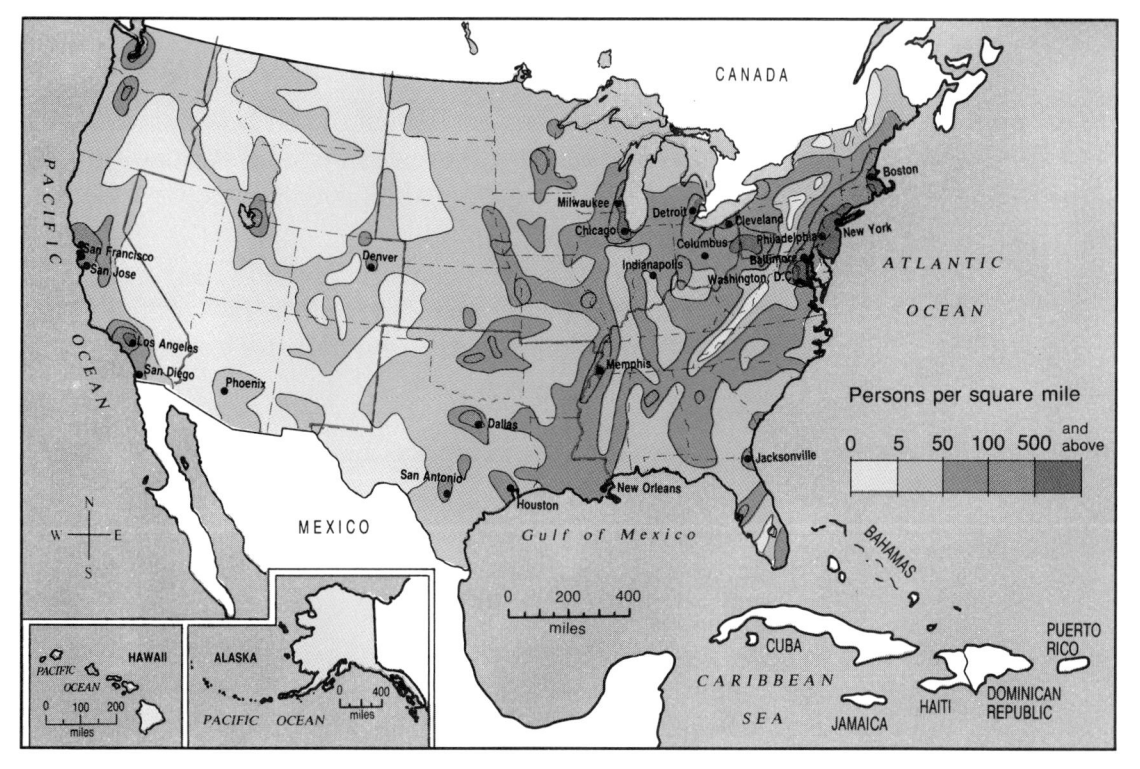

Map Study

Population Density

1. About how many persons per square mile live in most of the Rocky Mountain Region?
2. About how many persons per square mile live in the area around New York City?
3. Which three regions are the most crowded?

The third largest culture group in the Rocky Mountain Region is made up of Native Americans. Several tribes live in the region. The largest is the Navajo. Most of the people live on reservations, but many have moved into urban areas.

The Navajos have begun to build industries on their reservation. For a long time they have made beautiful jewelry and blankets. Now they also have a lumber mill and an electronics company. They have begun to mine coal on reservation land. And they have modern hotels and restaurants for tourists.

North Central Region

Look at the map on page 275. Which part of the North Central Region is most **densely** populated—the eastern half or the western half? How many cities in the region have more than 500,000 people?

As you can see from the map, most of the eastern half of the region is heavily populated. The rapid population growth began back in the late 1800s. That's when the growing iron and steel industry began attracting workers to the area.

The population swelled in the 1930s, when new farm machinery began to replace many farm workers. Southern farm workers moved to northern cities to find work in factories.

The eastern part of the region contains two of the six largest cities in the United States—Chicago and Detroit. Look at the graph on the right. About how many people live in Chicago? About how many live in Detroit?

The western half of the North Central Region is mostly rural. Most of the rural areas are farmlands where wheat and other grains are grown. However, there are a number of urban areas, too. The people live mainly in the urban areas, not on the farms.

Some of the region's larger cities are losing population, while some of the smaller ones are gaining. For example, St. Louis lost more than half its population between 1950 and 1980.

One reason for the change is that many businesses and factories moved to **suburbs** and rural areas. Costs are lower there. Also, many people moved out of the cities to escape such things as crowds, crime, noise, and dirt. Some just wanted to have their own homes with some grass and trees. They could not find or afford such places in the cities they were living in.

U.S. CITIES WITH LARGEST POPULATIONS

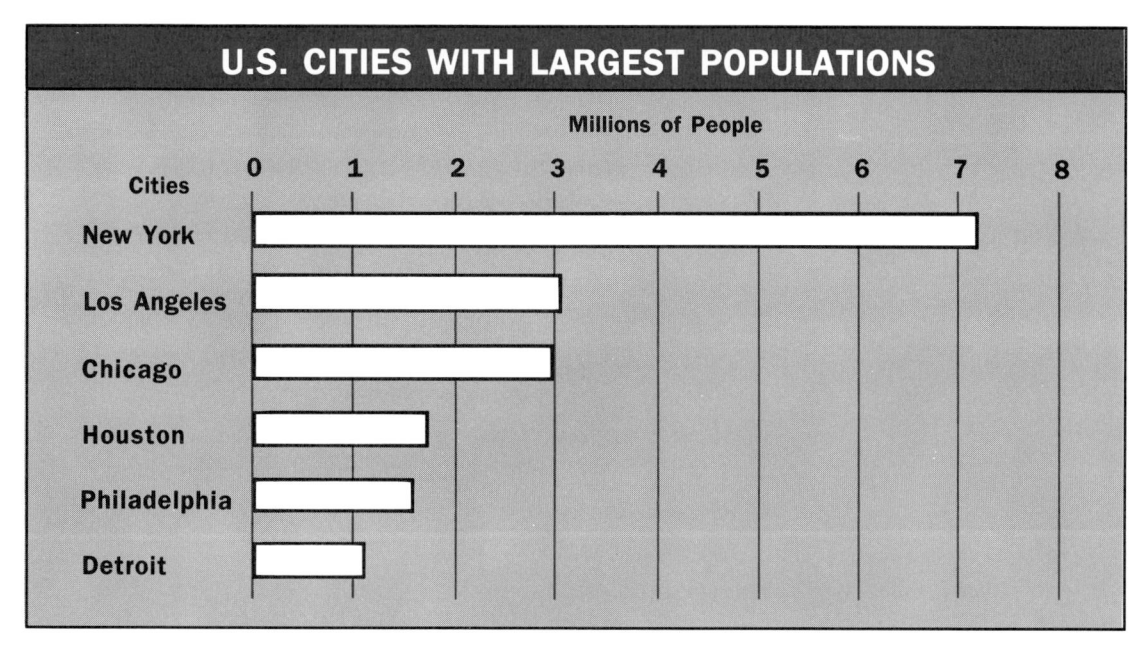

Millions of People

Cities	Population
New York	~7
Los Angeles	~3
Chicago	~3
Houston	~1.5
Philadelphia	~1.5
Detroit	~1

Graph Study
1. Which city has more people—Houston or Detroit?
2. Which two cities have about 3 million people each?
3. Which city has more than twice that number of people?

Culture Mix

During the 1800s, the fertile soil and flat lands of the region attracted farmers from northern Europe. Farmers also migrated from the eastern part of the United States. Farmland there was becoming expensive.

Later, the iron, coal, and steel industries attracted workers from the eastern states. But millions of workers also came from European countries.

During the 1920s and 1930s, many African Americans moved north from farmlands in the Southeast Region. They moved to Chicago, Detroit, and other large cities. They were looking for better jobs and a better life.

In more recent years, people from Central and South America settled in the region's larger cities.

Since 1820, more than 53 million people have migrated to the United States from all over the world.

Northeast Region

The Northeast is the most densely populated region in the United States. Look back at the map on page 275. How many cities in the region have more than 500,000 people? How many people are there per square mile in and around those cities?

The growth of this region began back in the 1700s, when settlers came from England. It grew more rapidly with the growth of factories in the 1800s. The factories needed workers. They came by the millions from Europe.

Later, farm machines began replacing farm workers. Many rural families then moved to the cities of the Northeast. They, too, went to work in the factories.

During the 1950s, the cities and suburbs of the Northeast grew at a rapid rate. The open spaces between them began to disappear. By the 1960s, the area between Boston and Washington, D.C., became like one giant city. Such an area, where many large towns and cities are crowded close together, is called a **megalopolis**.

In recent years, the population of some Northeastern cities has **declined**, or gone down. The reasons for the decline are the same as those you read about on page 276.

Culture Mix

Most of the Northeast's people are European Americans. Many of their ancestors arrived long ago from England, Germany, Ireland, Italy, and other European countries.

About 12% of the region's population is made up of African Americans. Ancestors of many of these people fled to the north during the days when slavery was allowed in the Southeast.

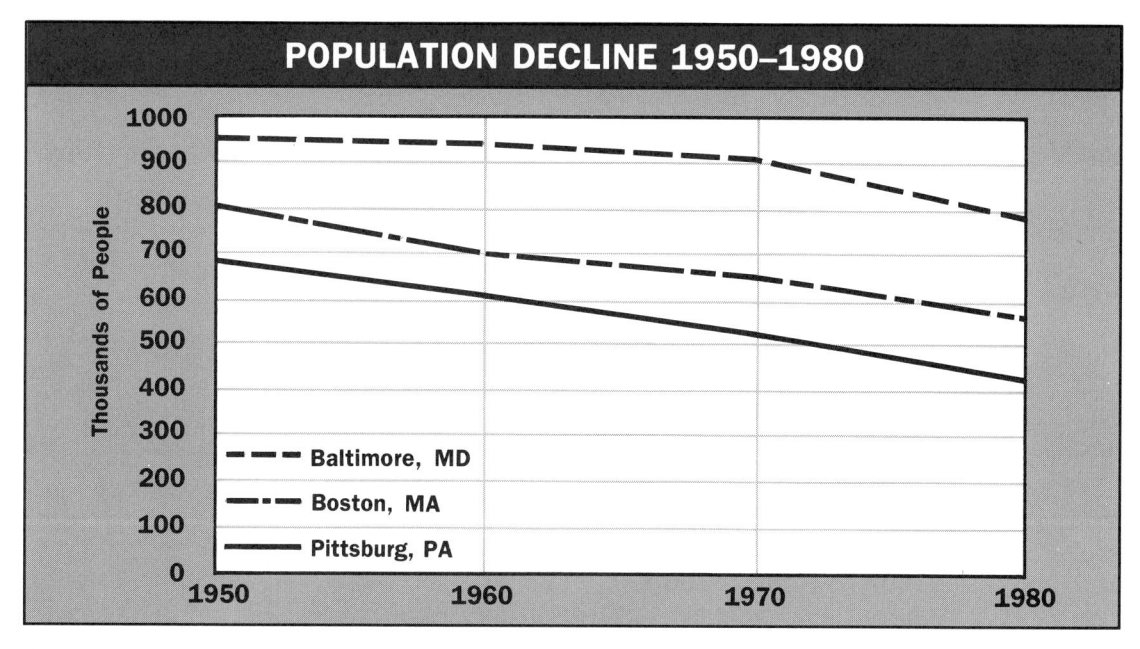

POPULATION DECLINE 1950–1980

(Graph showing Thousands of People from 1950 to 1980 for Baltimore, MD; Boston, MA; and Pittsburg, PA)

Graph Study
1. About how many thousands of people lived in Boston in 1950?
2. How many lived there in 1960?
3. The biggest decline in Baltimore's population came between 19___ and 19 ___ .

The United States took over Puerto Rico after a war with Spain in 1898. Most of the islanders were poor. For many years, Puerto Ricans have been moving to New York and other cities of the Northeast.

Thousands of African American families moved to the region later, during the 1920s and 1930s. Like those who migrated to the North Central Region, they were seeking better jobs and a better life.

Many other African Americans have migrated to the Northeast from Haiti and other islands in the Caribbean Sea.

About 5% of the region is made up of Hispanic Americans, mostly from Puerto Rico. Puerto Rico is also an island in the Caribbean Sea.

Find the island of Puerto Rico on the lower right side of the map on page 275.

South Central Region

Look at the map on page 275. How many cities in the South Central Region have more than 500,000 people?

Most of the western part of the region is lightly populated. Much of the area is grazing lands and oil fields. The major cities are in the eastern part of the region.

The region's urban areas began to grow rapidly after 1945. Much of this growth was due to the booming oil and gas industry. As it grew, trade, banking, service, and other industries also grew. This created many new jobs and attracted newcomers looking for work.

The population of some northern cities declined in the 1960s and 1970s. At the same time, some Texas cities doubled or tripled in size.

Except for Fort Worth and Dallas, most of the region's large cities are far apart.

Look back at the map on page 275. About how far is Dallas from Houston? About how far is Houston from New Orleans?

Culture Mix

European Americans began settling in Texas back in the 1820s, when the area belonged to Mexico.

After the United States took over the land, Mexicans continued to migrate there. Today, their descendants make up a large portion of the population. In recent years, both Mexicans and people from Central America have migrated to the area in large numbers.

Many people in the South Central region still speak Spanish. Many cities have Spanish names, such as El Paso and San Antonio. Mexican food, such as chili, is found in restaurants throughout the region. Many buildings in the area look like buildings in Mexico.

Louisiana is different from Texas. After it was settled by Native Americans, people from Spain and

This oil well is on the lawn of the Oklahoma state capital.

France settled there. They were later joined by people from Africa. Today, the city of New Orleans is a mix of all these cultures.

Large numbers of Native Americans live in the South Central Region. Many live on reservations in Oklahoma. More than 100 years ago, their ancestors were forced to move to the reservations from different parts of the United States.

More than 10% of Native Americans live in Oklahoma.

Chapter Twenty-Two   **281**

Southeast Region

The Southeast is one of the fastest growing regions in the United States. During the 1970s, about six million people moved there. Most were looking for jobs in the region's growing manufacturing and tourist industries. Many older people chose to retire there because of the warm climate. People are still moving in for the same reasons.

More than 500,000 Cubans have moved to the Southeast since 1960. Most have settled in Florida.

Not too many years ago, the Southeast was mostly rural. Today, most of the people live in urban areas. There are close to 40 cities with 100,000 or more people. Three cities have more than 500,000 people.

West Virginia has not changed as much as the other states in the Southeast. There, more than half the people still live in rural areas.

Culture Mix

Before the 1830s, the Southeast was the home of several Native American tribes. As settlers began spreading throughout the region, most of the Native Americans were forced out. Many were moved to reservations in Oklahoma.

Cotton had long been the main crop of the region. Farmers needed many workers to plant and pick the cotton. They bought slaves from slave traders.

The people who were taken from Africa, brought here, and sold as slaves numbered in the millions. In 1863, they were freed from slavery.

As you read earlier, many African Americans moved north during the 1920s and 1930s. Now many have moved back to the Southeast because of the improved opportunities there.

Look back at the map on page 275. Find the three cities in the Southeast that have more than 500,000 people.

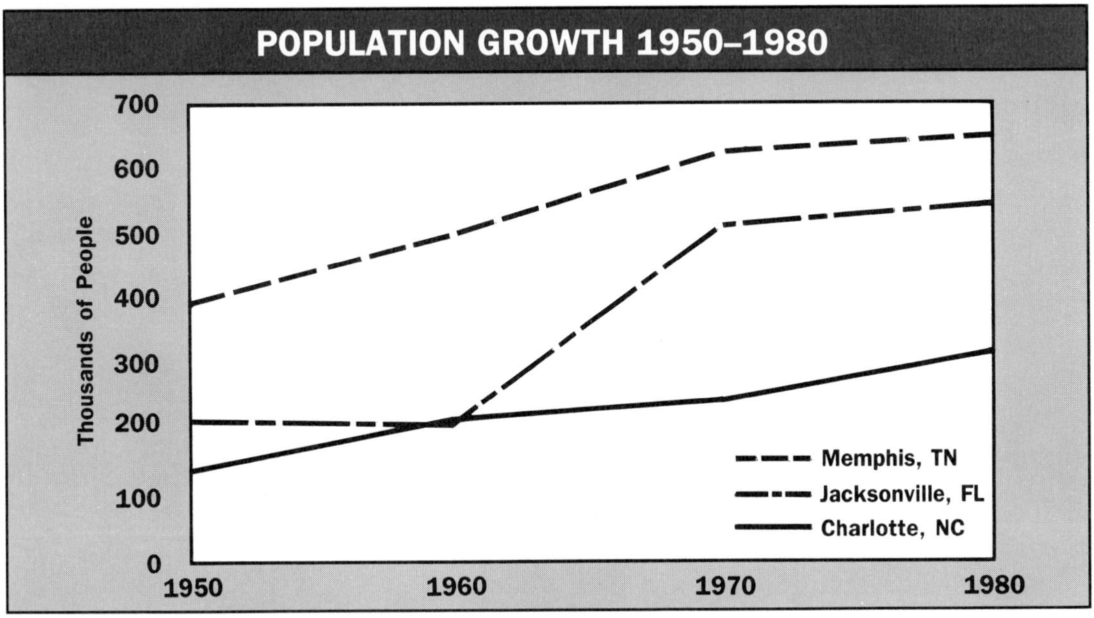
POPULATION GROWTH 1950–1980
Thousands of People
700
600
500
400
300
200
100
0
1950
1960
1970
1980
Memphis, TN
Jacksonville, FL
Charlotte, NC

Graph Study

1. About how many people lived in Memphis in 1950?
2. About how many people lived there in 1980?
3. Which of the three cities had the greatest growth between 1950 and 1980?

These same opportunities are drawing people from other groups as well. You read about the large migration of Cubans, mostly to Florida. Other Spanish-speaking people have moved to the region from Central and South America. Large numbers of people from Haiti have also moved to the Southeast.

Chapter Review

Summary

1. The United States has the fourth largest population in the world. About 240 million people live here. About 70% of the people live in the large towns and cities of urban areas. Most of the other 30% live in rural farm and grazing areas.

2. The two most crowded regions of the United States are the Northeast and the North Central Regions. The great number of factories there attracted millions of workers from Europe during the late 1800s and early 1900s. Later, millions of farm workers moved north to find jobs in the factories.

3. The three fastest growing regions of the United States are the Southeast, the South Central, and the Rocky Mountain Regions. Warm climate and the growth of industries are the main attractions.

4. Many businesses and factories have left the big cities and moved to smaller cities, suburbs, and rural areas. Many workers have followed. In addition, many other people have chosen to move out of the big cities and into the suburbs.

5. Each region is a mix of several cultures.
   - European Americans make up the largest group in all the regions.
   - African Americans form a large part of the population in the Southeast, Northeast, and North Central Regions.
   - Hispanic Americans form a large part of the population in the southern parts of the Pacific, Rocky Mountain, South Central and Southeast regions. There are also many Hispanic Americans in some North Central and Northeastern cities.
   - Asian and Pacific Americans form a large part of the population in the Pacific Region, especially in Hawaii and California.
   - Most Native Americans live in the western regions of the United States.

Thinking and Writing

Answer these questions in complete sentences on a separate sheet of paper.

1. What is the difference between an urban and a rural area?
2. In the 1800s, the United States attracted millions of European workers. Why did they come here?
3. How did changes on American farms lead to further growth of northern cities?
4. Has the population of the southern part of the United States increased or decreased in recent years? What has caused the change?
5. Name two problems that you think cities with rapid growth may be facing.
6. In what way is the population of Texas today similar to the way it was in the early 1800s?

Questions to Discuss

1. Until recent times, most people stayed in one place for all or most of their lives. Now, many people move from place to place. What is good about staying in one place? What is bad? What is good about moving from place to place? What is bad?
2. What does the United States gain from having a mix of culture groups?

Special Project

Make a poster that shows the six main culture groups you have read about. Draw or cut out pictures to show people from each group. Add information about where most of the people in each group live.

Chapters 20–22

REVIEW

Answer these questions on a separate sheet of paper.

A. Key Words

ancestors
descendants
declines
density
language
sanitation
migrate
population
rural
urban

Number your paper from 1 to 10. Then read each sentence below. Find the word in the list on the left that best completes each sentence. Write that word next to the proper number on your paper.

1. The number of people who live in a place is that place's ____ .
2. Population ____ is a measure of how crowded a place is.
3. Garbage trucks are operated by ____ companies.
4. Areas that have many towns and cities are ____ areas.
5. Areas that have few towns and cities are ____ areas.
6. The ____ of most people in the United States came from Europe.
7. We are our great-grandparents' ____ .
8. Without ____ , we could not share our thoughts.
9. People ____ in order to find jobs or better living conditions.
10. When the population of a place drops, it ____ .

B. Key Facts

Number your paper from 11 to 20. Next to each number, write the word in parentheses that best completes each sentence below.

11. Back 10,000 years ago, people were hunters and (sailors/gatherers).
12. The first big increase in world population came when people became farmers and (herders/craftsworkers).

13. In 1988, there were 5 (million/billion) people in the world.
14. The second most widely spoken language in the world is (Spanish/English).
15. In North America, the religions with the largest followings are Christianity, Judaism, and (Islam/Buddhism).
16. In recent times, many people have migrated to the United States from Central America and Southeast (Africa/Asia).
17. The United States is the (fourth/sixth) most populous country in the world.
18. Most of the U.S. population lives in (urban/rural) areas.
19. The most densely populated region of the United States is the (Northeast/Southeast).
20. Since the 1820s, more than (five/fifty) million people have migrated to the United States.

C. Main Ideas

Answer any five questions below. Number your paper with the same numbers as the questions you choose.

21. Give two reasons why the world's population was very small about 10,000 years ago.
22. About 6,000 years ago, some towns and villages grew into large cities. Give two reasons why this happened.
23. Name three things that led to the rapid growth of the world's population during the 1900s.
24. Name two ways that life in the United States is affected by the nation's mix of many cultures.
25 Name two things that most religions have in common.
26. Give two reasons why the Northeast and North Central Regions are densely populated.

Review 287

Atlas

North American political map
World political map
United States political map

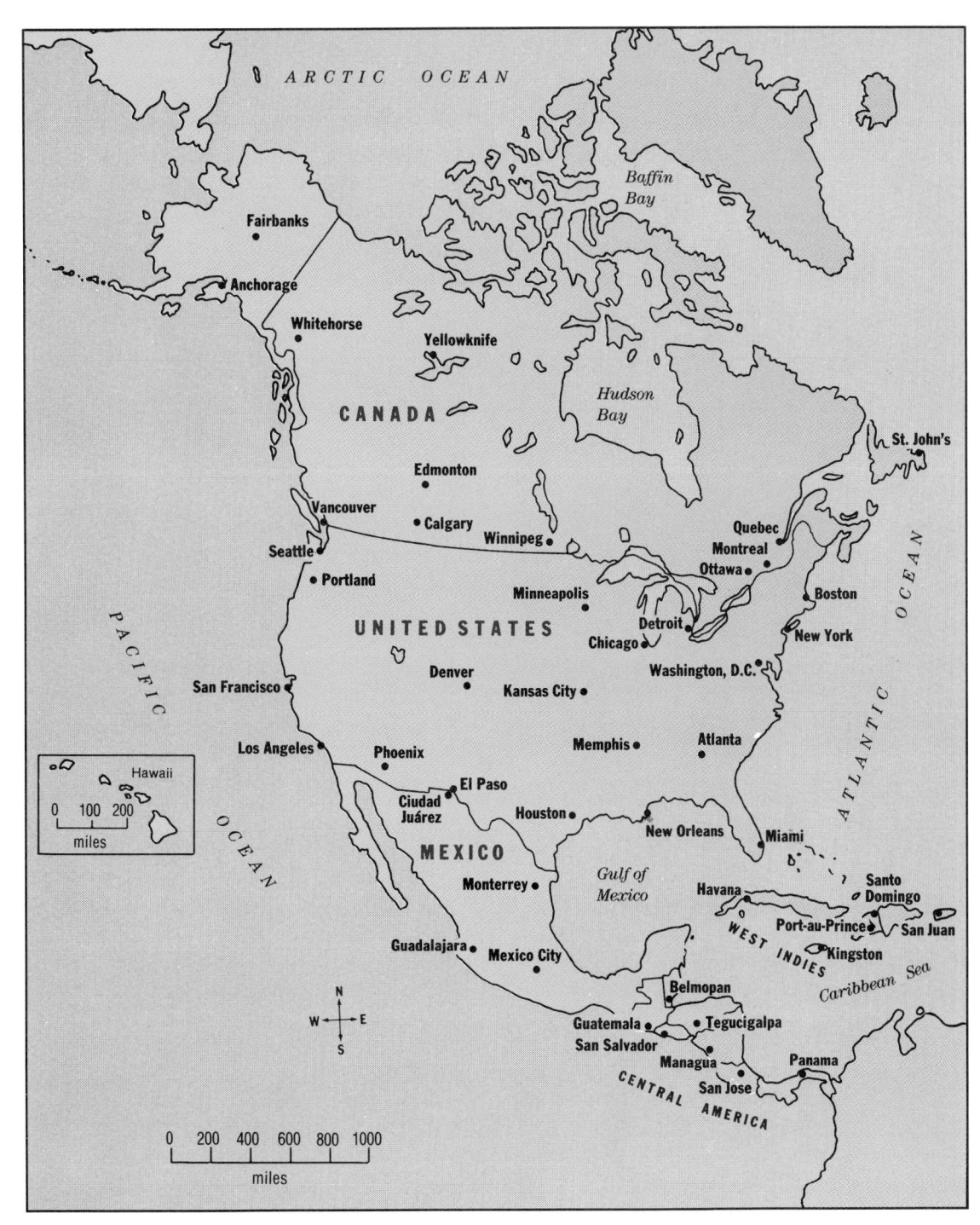

NORTH AMERICAN POLITICAL MAP

WORLD POLITICAL MAP

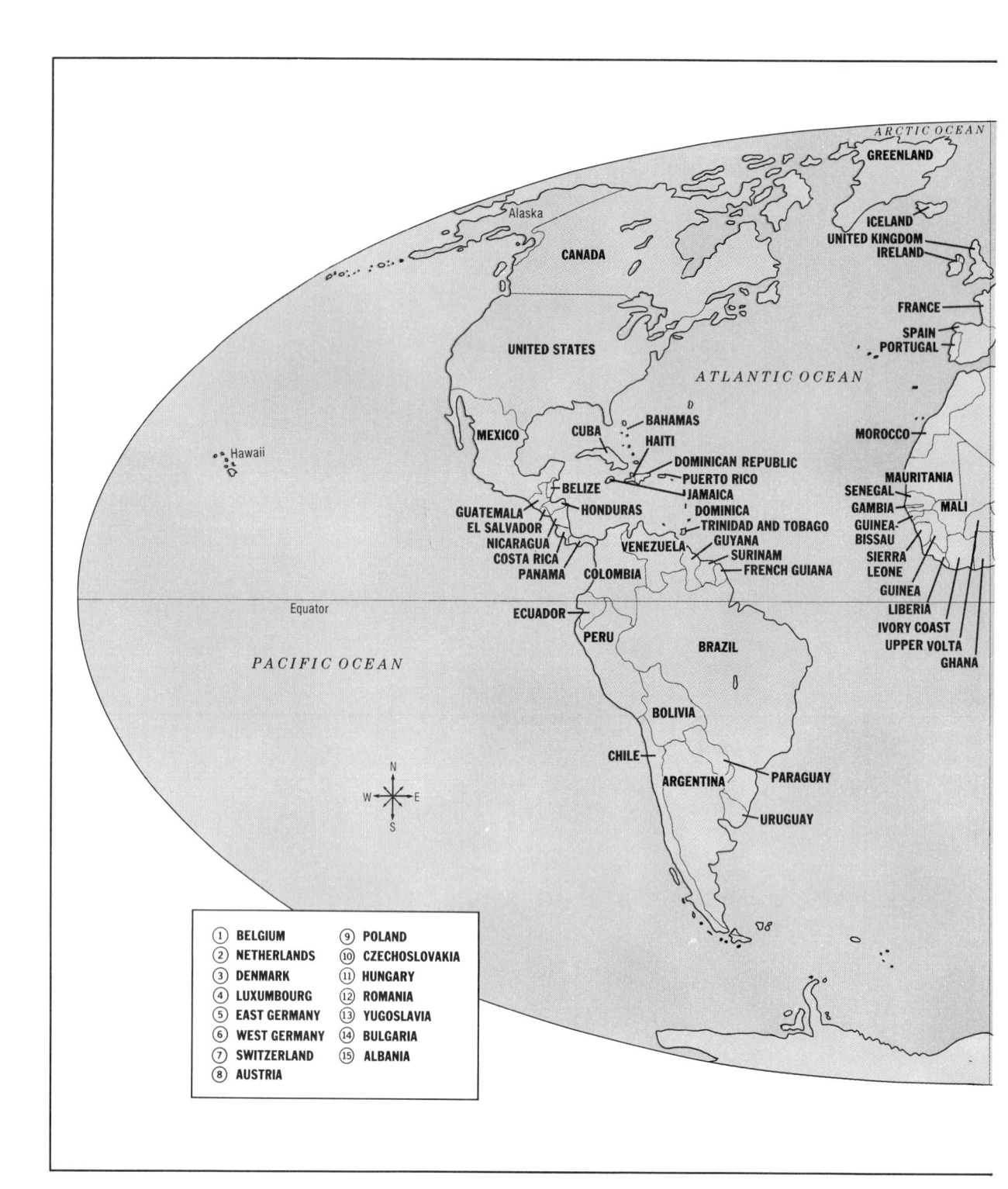

Americas, Western Europe, and West Africa shown.

Labeled locations:

- Arctic Ocean
- Atlantic Ocean
- Pacific Ocean
- Equator
- Greenland
- Alaska
- Canada
- United States
- Hawaii
- Mexico
- Cuba
- Bahamas
- Haiti
- Dominican Republic
- Puerto Rico
- Jamaica
- Belize
- Guatemala
- Honduras
- El Salvador
- Nicaragua
- Costa Rica
- Panama
- Dominica
- Trinidad and Tobago
- Colombia
- Venezuela
- Guyana
- Surinam
- French Guiana
- Ecuador
- Peru
- Brazil
- Bolivia
- Chile
- Paraguay
- Uruguay
- Argentina
- Iceland
- United Kingdom
- Ireland
- France
- Spain
- Portugal
- Morocco
- Mauritania
- Senegal
- Gambia
- Guinea-Bissau
- Mali
- Guinea
- Sierra Leone
- Liberia
- Ivory Coast
- Upper Volta
- Ghana

Legend:

1. Belgium
2. Netherlands
3. Denmark
4. Luxumbourg
5. East Germany
6. West Germany
7. Switzerland
8. Austria
9. Poland
10. Czechoslovakia
11. Hungary
12. Romania
13. Yugoslavia
14. Bulgaria
15. Albania

Map of Eastern Hemisphere

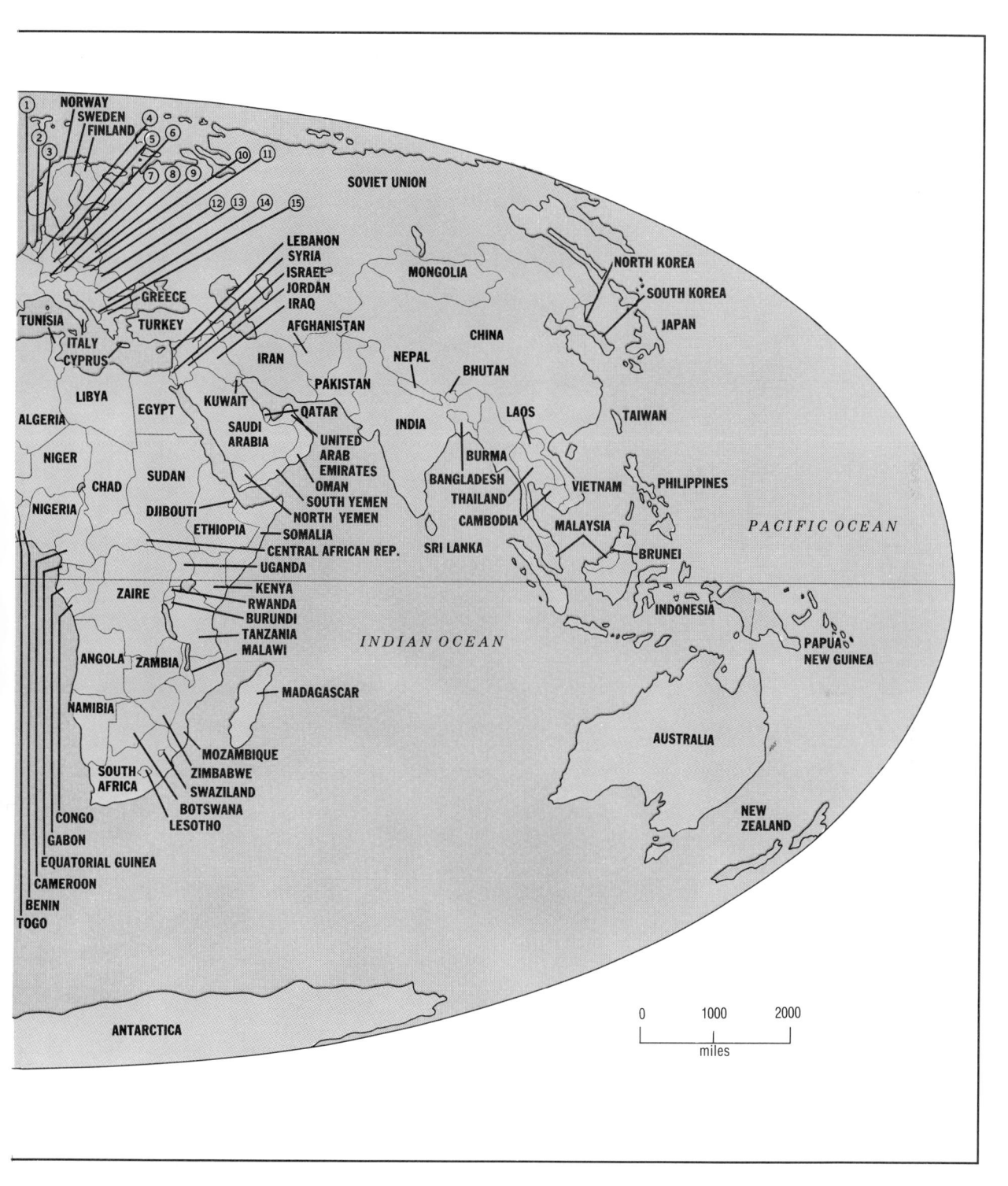

Labeled countries and regions:

- NORWAY
- SWEDEN
- FINLAND
- SOVIET UNION
- MONGOLIA
- NORTH KOREA
- SOUTH KOREA
- JAPAN
- TUNISIA
- ITALY
- CYPRUS
- GREECE
- TURKEY
- LEBANON
- SYRIA
- ISRAEL
- JORDAN
- IRAQ
- AFGHANISTAN
- CHINA
- LIBYA
- ALGERIA
- EGYPT
- IRAN
- PAKISTAN
- NEPAL
- BHUTAN
- TAIWAN
- NIGER
- KUWAIT
- QATAR
- INDIA
- LAOS
- SAUDI ARABIA
- UNITED ARAB EMIRATES
- OMAN
- BURMA
- BANGLADESH
- THAILAND
- VIETNAM
- PHILIPPINES
- CHAD
- SUDAN
- SOUTH YEMEN
- NORTH YEMEN
- NIGERIA
- DJIBOUTI
- ETHIOPIA
- SOMALIA
- SRI LANKA
- CAMBODIA
- MALAYSIA
- CENTRAL AFRICAN REP.
- UGANDA
- BRUNEI
- ZAIRE
- KENYA
- RWANDA
- BURUNDI
- TANZANIA
- INDONESIA
- PAPUA NEW GUINEA
- ANGOLA
- ZAMBIA
- MALAWI
- NAMIBIA
- MADAGASCAR
- MOZAMBIQUE
- ZIMBABWE
- SOUTH AFRICA
- SWAZILAND
- BOTSWANA
- LESOTHO
- CONGO
- GABON
- EQUATORIAL GUINEA
- CAMEROON
- BENIN
- TOGO
- AUSTRALIA
- NEW ZEALAND
- ANTARCTICA

Oceans: PACIFIC OCEAN, INDIAN OCEAN

Numbered locations (1–15)

Scale: 0 — 1000 — 2000 miles

UNITED STATES POLITICAL MAP

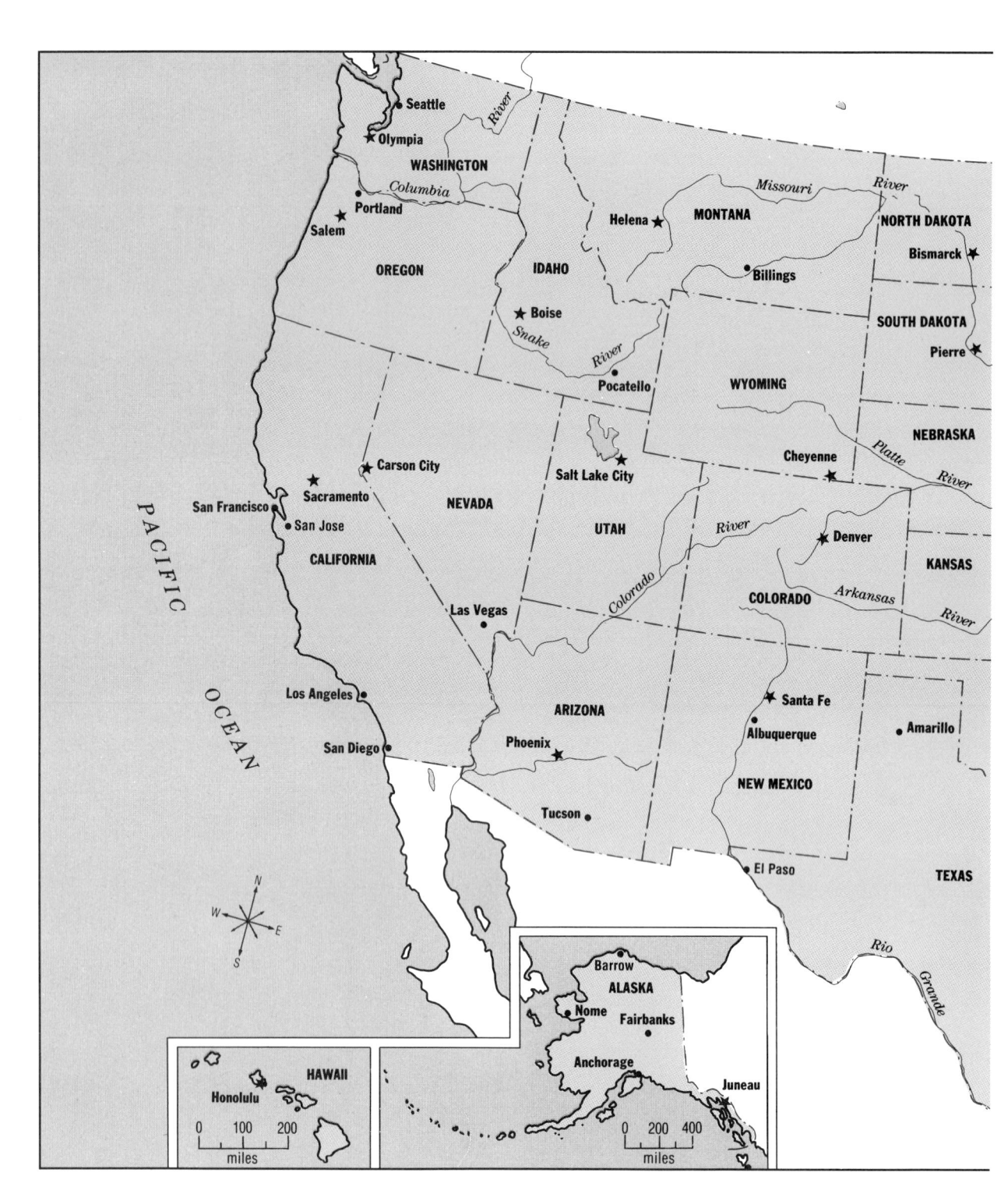

LAKE SUPERIOR
LAKE MICHIGAN
LAKE HURON
LAKE ONTARIO
LAKE ERIE
MAINE
Augusta
Montpelier
NH
Portland
Concord
VT
Albany
MA
Boston
Plymouth
Providence
RHODE ISLAND
CT
Hartford
NEW YORK
Buffalo
New York
NJ
Trenton
PENNSYLVANIA
Philadelphia
Pittsburg
Harrisburg
Baltimore
MD
Dover
DE
Annapolis
Washington, D.C.
VIRGINIA
Richmond
Williamsburg
Norfolk
WEST VIRGINIA
Charleston
OHIO
Cleveland
Columbus
Cincinnati
MICHIGAN
Lansing
Detroit
INDIANA
Indianapolis
Gary
ILLINOIS
Chicago
Springfield
WISCONSIN
Milwaukee
Madison
MINNESOTA
Fargo
Minneapolis
St. Paul
Sioux Falls
Sioux City
IOWA
Des Moines
Omaha
Lincoln
Missouri
Mississippi
River
Topeka
Kansas City
Jefferson City
St. Louis
MISSOURI
Wichita
Tulsa
ARKANSAS
Little Rock
Oklahoma City
OKLAHOMA
Ohio
River
Louisville
Frankfort
KENTUCKY
Nashville
TENNESSEE
Memphis
Winston-Salem
Raleigh
NORTH CAROLINA
SOUTH CAROLINA
Columbia
Charleston
Tennessee
River
Birmingham
Atlanta
MS
ALABAMA
Jackson
Montgomery
GEORGIA
Savannah
Dallas
Fort Worth
LOUISIANA
Mississippi
River
Baton Rouge
New Orleans
Mobile
Tallahassee
Austin
Houston
San Antonio
FLORIDA
Tampa
Miami
GULF OF MEXICO
ATLANTIC
OCEAN
0
100
200
300
400
miles

Glossary

acid a chemical substance that wears away other substances

acre a unit of measure; an acre of land is about the size of a football field

agriculture the growing of crops and raising of animals

alfalfa a plant grown as food for horses and cattle

atmosphere the layers of air above Earth's surface

average the most common or usual amount; to find the average of two numbers, add them and then divide the sum by two

bale a large bundle; one bale of cotton weighs about 480 pounds

barge a large flat-bottomed boat used to carry heavy loads, such as coal or oil

basin a wide area of land that dips downward from nearby mountains and plateaus

bay an inlet of an ocean or other body of water, usually smaller than a gulf

blizzard a blinding, windy snowstorm

boron a kind of metal used to harden steel; it is also used in making glass

broadleaf a kind of tree with wide leaves rather than needle-shaped leaves

bushel a measurement that equals about 32 quarts

canal an inland waterway that has been dug by people rather than by nature

canyon a deep valley with very steep walls, such as the Grand Canyon

carbon dioxide a gas that is breathed out by animals and taken in by plants

cargo the goods carried on a ship or plane

cement a mixture of several minerals that can hold sand and pebbles or crushed stone together

cereals grains that can be used as food; also, a kind of food made from these grains

citrus a type of fruit that includes oranges, grapefruits, lemons, and limes

climate the usual yearly weather of a place

compass rose an aid to finding directions on a map

continent a very large body of land; Earth is divided into seven continents

continental shelf land at the edge of a continent that gently slopes beneath the ocean

core the center of Earth

cranberry a red berry from eastern Massachusetts

crude oil oil from under the ground before it is made into a product, such as gasoline

crust Earth's outer layer

culture the ways in which a group of people think and act

current a part of a large body of water that moves in a particular direction

dairy milk and milk products

decline a drop in amount; a city's population declines when more people move away than move in

delta islands and sandbars made from sediment dropped by a river

dense crowded

density the measurement of how crowded a place is

desert a barren, often sandy, area of land that receives very little rain

dune a hill of sand

earthquake the shaking of part of Earth's crust caused by breaking or slipping rock within the crust

electricity a form of power used to make light and heat and to run machines

electronic having to do with radios, televisions, computers, and similar products

elevation the height of the land above sea level

energy the power to do work

equator an imaginary line that circles Earth halfway between the North and South Poles; the line on a globe that stands for that imaginary line

erosion the carrying away of weathered rock

evaporate to turn into tiny droplets that are too small to be seen

export to sell goods to other countries

fault a deep crack in Earth's crust

fertile able to produce; good for growing crops

fertilizer a substance added to soil to provide nutrients

finance the use of money

fossil remains of plants and animals that lived thousands or millions of years ago

fuel any material that is burned to provide energy

glacier a very large moving body of ice and snow

gorge a narrow canyon

grain any grass plant grown for its seeds

gravel small pieces of rock

gravity a strong pulling force from inside Earth

graze to allow cattle to feed on open grassland

gulf   an inlet of an ocean or other large body of water, usually larger than a bay

hail   small balls of ice

hemisphere   half of a ball

hill   a landform that is similar to a mountain but not as high

hub   the center of a wheel; also a center for business or other activities

humid   full of moisture

humus   dead plant and animal matter that provides plants with nutrients

hurricane   a strong storm that has fast-moving winds and often heavy rain

import   to buy goods from another country

industry   a group of companies that make similar products or that offer similar services

inlet   any body of sea water that extends inland from the sea

interior   the inland or central part of a country

interstate highway   a highway that runs from one state to another

irrigation   the use of water from a river or well to raise crops

island   a landform that is surrounded on all sides by water

lake   a body of water surrounded on all sides by land

land form   a feature of Earth's surface, such as a mountain, hill, plateau, or plain

language   the words and sounds used by a group of people to express thoughts and feelings

lava   melted rock from inside Earth that flows over the land when a volcano erupts

lock   the part of a canal used to raise or lower ships from one height to another

magma   the melted rock below Earth's crust

mainland   the largest part of a country that is separated from one or more other parts by water or land

mantle   the layer of very hot rock between Earth's crust and outer core

manufacture   to make a product by hand or machine

megalopolis   an area with many large towns and cities crowded close together

menhaden   a kind of fish used mainly in animal feed and fertilizer

merchandise mart   one or more large buildings with showrooms where manufacturers show their products to buyers

migrate   to move from one place to another

mineral   a usable substance, such as coal, oil, or iron, that is found in Earth's crust

moisture   wetness

molybdenum   a metal used to strengthen blends of other metals

mountain   a landform that rises very high above sea level and the surrounding land

mouth   the place where a river flows into a larger body of water

needleleaf   a kind of tree that has leaves shaped like needles

nutrient   a substance in soil that gives plants what they need to grow

ocean   the largest body of salt water on Earth

orchard   an area of land planted with fruit trees

ore   rock that contains metals such as iron, copper, or gold

oxygen   a gas that is released by plants and breathed in by animals

pass   a low gap, or opening, in a mountain range

peak   the highest part of a mountain

peninsula   a piece of land that reaches out into the water from a larger body of land

per capita   for each person

phosphate   a mineral used in fertilizers

plain   a large area of mostly flat land

planet   any of the large bodies in space that circle the sun, such as Mercury, Venus, and Earth

plate   a huge piece of Earth's crust that moves slowly across the mantle

plateau   a large area of flat land that is higher than sea level

polar   having to do with areas near the North or South Poles

pollute   to make unhealthy, as in polluting the air and water

population   the number of people that live in a place

port   a city where ships pick up and deliver goods

potassium   a mineral used in the making of fertilizers and liquid soaps

poultry   animals such as chickens, ducks, and turkeys that are raised for their meat or eggs

prairie   treeless area with tall grass

precipitation   wetness that falls from the sky as rain, snow, sleet, and hail; fog is also a form of precipitation

prime meridian   an imaginary line that circles Earth, running through the North and South Poles; the line on a globe that stands for that imaginary line

projection   a way of showing all or parts of round Earth on flat paper

public utility a company that provides telephone, electric, or gas service

pulpwood a mash made from ground-up logs; it is used to make paper

quarry a large pit where stone is removed from the side of a hill or mountain

range a row or line of mountains; a large group of mountains

raw materials the things from which a product is made, such as leather, rubber, and glue in shoes

refinery a factory that turns crude oil into usable products

refuge a safe place

region a group of places that have one or more things that are alike

reservation an area of land set aside by the federal government for American Indians to live on

resort a place to relax and have fun in

resource something we need or can use

retail having to do with selling directly to the public; supermarkets are retail stores

river a large stream of fresh water

rotate to spin or turn around

rural of or relating to the country or countryside; farms, ranches, forests, and mines are usually found in rural areas

sanitation the act of preventing disease by keeping things clean and safely getting rid of garbage and waste

savanna a grassland found in warm climates that have both wet and dry seasons

scale a number of evenly spaced points used for measuring

sea a large body of salt water that is smaller than an ocean. Seas are partly surrounded by land.

sea level the point at which the ocean meets the land

season a time of year, such as summer or winter

sediment the loose rocks, stones, sand, and soil carried away by streams and rivers

seismograph a sensitive machine that records movements within Earth's crust

shale a kind of rock that is formed mostly from hardened clay

sleet rain that has partially frozen

smog dirty air made of fog, smoke, and chemicals

soil very fine bits of weathered rock mixed with living matter and the remains of plants and animals

source the place where a river begins

soybean the seed of the soybean plant; it can be used as food or as a source of cooking oil

steppe a grassland found in cool dry climates

suburb a living area close to a city

sulphur a pale yellow mineral used to make matches and other products

swamp an area of soft wet land

temperate not too hot and not too cold

temperature how hot or cold something is. In the United States, temperature is usually measured on the Fahrenheit scale.

textile any woven cloth

thunder a sound caused when air suddenly heats and expands

tide the rise and fall of the surface of the sea. It is caused by the pull of the moon and the sun's gravity.

tornado a violent, fast-moving column of air that extends downward from a cloud

tourist a person who travels for sightseeing and pleasure

transport to carry

tributary a river or stream that flows into a larger river or stream

tropical having to do with the tropics, the warm moist regions around the equator

troposphere the layer of the atmosphere closest to Earth

tsunami a fast moving wave started by an earthquake or a volcanic eruption

tundra a cold, treeless land where only tiny plants can grow in summer

uranium a mineral used as fuel in some power plants

urban of or relating to cities and large towns; an urban area is one with many cities and large towns

valley a lowland between two mountains or mountain ranges

vapor very tiny droplets of water or other liquid floating in the air

vegetation the kinds of plants that grow in a place

volcano a break in Earth's surface through which melted rock flows

weather day-to-day changes in air temperature, winds, and precipitation

weathering the softening and wearing away of rock

Glossary **299**

Index

A

Acid rain, 169
Air, 151
Airplanes, 209, 234, 236, 242
African Americans, 272, 273, 277, 278–279, 282
Agriculture
    in the Northeast Region, 140–141
    in the North Central Region, 140
    in the Pacific Region, 138
    in the Rocky Mountain Region, 139
    in the South Central Region, 142
    in the Southeast Region, 142–143
Akron, Ohio, 238
Alabama, 143, 228, 229
Alamo, 242
Alaska
    agriculture in, 138
    climates of, 104, 116
    landforms of, 66
    oil in, 219
    tourist industry in, 234
    vegetation in, 129
Alaska Range, 66
Alaskan Pipeline, 210
Aluminum, 165
Appalachian Highlands, 72
Appalachian Mountains, 49
Arizona, 127, 139, 274
Arkansas, 120, 142, 226, 242
Asian Americans, 272, 273
Atlanta, Georgia, 245
Atlantic Coastal Plain, 72
Atlantic Ocean, 121
Atmosphere, 22–23
Automobile industry, 192

B

Badlands, 238
Baltimore, Maryland, 241
Barrow, Alaska, 104
Bay of Fundy, 81
Bell, Alexander Graham, 211
Bering Sea, 218
Birmingham, Alabama, 244
Bismarck, North Dakota, 35, 119
Black Hills of South Dakota, 44
Blue Ridge Mountains, 72
Bodies of water, 7
Boone, Daniel, 72
Boston, Massachusetts, 241
Brooks Range, 66
Buddhism, 265
Buffalo, 71
Buffalo, New York, 89, 119
Business and Transportation Centers
    in the North Central Region, 239
    in the Northeast Region, 241
    in the Pacific Region, 235
    in the Rocky Mountain Region, 237
    in the South Central Region, 243
    in the Southeast Region, 245

C

California
    agriculture in, 138
    manufacturing in, 234
    oil in, 219
    tourist industry in, 234
    vegetation, 127
Canada, 193, 196
Canals, 88, 89, 208
Canal locks, how they work, 88
Caribbean Sea, 121
Carlsbad Caverns, 71
Cascade Range, 66, 67
Cattle, 138, 139, 140, 143
Caverns, 71, 72
Central America, 11
Central Valley, 67
Chesapeake Bay, 224, 228
Chicago, Illinois, 192, 238, 239
Christianity, 265
Cities
    development of, 253–254
    world's largest, 257
Citrus fruits, 138, 142, 143
Cleveland, Ohio, 89, 192
Climate
    explanation of, 97–107
    in the Northeast Region, 118–119
    in the North Central Region, 118
    in the Pacific Region, 116
    in the Rocky Mountain Region, 116–117
    in the South Central Region, 120–121
    in the Southeast Region, 121

Coal, 162–163
Coast Ranges, 66
Coastal Lowlands, 72–73
Colorado, 70, 139, 274
Colorado Plateau, 56, 70
Colorado River, 56, 85
Columbia Plateau, 70
Columbia River, 85
Communication, 210–213
Compass rose, 11
Computers, 213
Confucianism, 265
Continental Shelves, 79
Continents, 5
Connecticut, 240
Connecticut River Valley, 140
Copper, 165, 166
Corn, 140, 142
Cotton, 139, 142, 143, 155, 282
Cuba, 282
Cumberland Gap, 72
Culture groups
    classification of U.S., 272
    explanation of, 261–266
    in the North Central Region, 277
    in the Northeast Region, 278–279
    in the Pacific Region, 273
    in the Rocky Mountain Region, 274–275
    in the South Central Region, 280–281
    in the Southeast Region, 282–283

D

Dairy farming, 138, 140, 141
Dallas, Texas, 242, 243
Death Valley, 70
Delaware, 119, 141
Delaware Bay, 224
Denver, Colorado, 236, 237
Deserts, 116, 127
Detroit, Michigan, 238
Developing nations, 196–199
Direction, 10, 53
Distance, 29
Dust bowl, 267

E

Earth
    faults, 46
    layers of, 21
    movements of, 31–32
    plates, 45–47
    population of, 251
    size of, 3–4
Earthquakes, 41–42, 45–47, 52
Eastern Hemisphere, 26
Equator, 13, 15, 35
Elevation, 100
El Paso, Texas, 280
Energy, 151, 162, 170
Erosion, 56–61
European Americans, 272, 273, 274, 278, 280
Everglades, 73
Exports, 193

F

Factories, first U.S., 191
Family life, 262–263
Famines, 256
Farmers, the first, 252
Farming. *See* Agriculture
Farmland, decreasing U.S., 180–181
Fishing
    in the North Central Region, 222
    in the Northeast Region, 224
    in the Pacific Region, 218
    in the South Central Region, 226
    in the Southeast Region, 228
Florida
    agriculture in, 143
    climate of, 105
    products of, 228, 229
    tourist industry in, 244
    vegetation of, 128–129
Forestry
    in the North Central Region, 222
    in the Northeast Region, 224
    in the Pacific Region, 218
    in the Rocky Mountain Region, 220
    in the South Central Region, 226
    in the Southeast Region, 228
Forests, 156–157, 169–170, 176
Fort Worth, Texas, 242, 243
Fossil fuels, 217
Furniture, 244

G

Garden of the Gods, 71
Gas, natural, 217

Gatherers, 251
Georgia, 143, 228
Glaciers, 58–60
Globes, 12–15
Gold, 165
Government
    land-use control by, 182–183
    pollution-control by, 170
Grand Canyon, 56–57
Gravity, 23
Great Basin, 70
Great Lakes
    canals between, 88–89
    fish in, 222
    formation of, 59
    industries nearby, 191–192
    size of, 88
Great Plains, 71
Great Smoky Mountain National Park, 228
Gulf Coastal Plain, 72
Gulf of Mexico, 84, 121, 226

H

Hail, 101, 102
Haiti, 283
Hawaii
    agriculture in, 138
    climate of, 116
    culture groups of, 273
    landforms of, 44, 66
    tourist industry in, 234
    vegetation, 127
    volcanoes of, 66

Health care, improvements in, 254
Hemispheres, 26
Herders, 252
Hinduism, 265
Hispanic Americans, 272, 273, 274, 277, 279, 280, 283
Hogs, 140
Honolulu, Hawaii, 235, 273
Hot Springs, Arkansas, 242
Houston, Texas, 243
Hudson River, 85
Hunters, 251
Hurricanes, 103, 121

I

Idaho 127, 139, 274
Illinois, 222
Imports, 193
Indiana, 222
Industry, growth of U.S., 191–192
Industries, U.S. *See* Fishing, Forestry, Manufacturing, Minerals, and Tourist Industry
Interior Plains, 71–72
Inventions, 211–213
Iowa, 128, 140
Irrigation, 86, 87, 138, 139, 142
Iron, 164, 166
Islam, 265
Islands, volcanic, 44

J

Japan, 193, 194, 196
Judaism, 265

K

Kansas, 104, 141
Kansas City, Kansas, 238
Kansas City, Missouri, 99, 100
Kentucky, 229

L

Lake Erie, 89
Lake Huron, 89
Lake Michigan, 88
Lake Ontario, 88
Lake Superior, 88
Landforms
    kinds of, 6–7
    of United States, 64–75
Land use, 174–184
Language, 264
Latin America, meaning of term, 262
Lead, 165
Los Angeles, California, 234, 235
Louisiana, 120, 142, 226, 242
Lumber, 218, 219

M

Maine, 119, 125, 140, 224, 240
Manufacturing
    in the North Central Region, 238
    in the Northeast Region, 240
    in the Pacific Region, 234
    in the Rocky Mountain Region, 236
    in the South Central Region, 242
    in the Southeast Region, 244
Maps, 12–13, 15–17
Map skills,
    locating states and cities, 28
    understanding directions, 10, 53
    understanding hemispheres, 26–27
    understanding projections, 16–17
    using map keys, 68–69
    using scale of miles, 29
    see also list of Geography Skills in table of contents
Mariana Trench, 78
Maryland, 119, 141
Massachusetts, 141, 240
Mauna Loa, 52
Meat-packing, 238
Megalopolis, 278
Memphis, Tennessee, 245
Mesabi Range, 222
Metals, 163–165
Meteor Crater, 71
Mexico, 273
Miami, Florida, 105
Michigan, 140, 192, 222
Mid-Atlantic Ridge, 49
Migration,
    of African Americans, 267, 273, 277, 278–279, 282
    to the United States, 266–267, 277
    to individual regions, 273, 274, 277, 278, 279, 280–281, 282–283
    rural to urban, 267
Minerals,
    in the Northeast Region, 224–225
    in the North Central Region, 222
    in the Pacific Region, 218–219

in the Rocky Mountain Region, 220–221
in the South Central Region, 226
in the Southeast Region, 228–229
Mining, 162–163, 169, 176
Minneapolis, Minnesota, 238
Minnesota, 118, 192, 222, 238
Mississippi, 143, 228, 229
Mississippi Delta, 73, 84
Mississippi River, 84, 86, 245
Missouri, 222
Missouri River, 84
Mobile, Alabama, 245
Montana, 139
Mountains
    formation and kinds of, 48–49
    Mauna Kea, 66
    Mauna Loa, 52
    Mount McKinely, 66
    Mount Mitchell, 72
    Mount Saint Helens, 44, 52
    Mount Whitney, 67
Movies, 234

N

Native Americans, 275, 281, 282
Natural resources,
    non-renewable, 160–172
    renewable, 148–158
    problems, 168–171
    See also fishing, forests, and minerals
Nebraska, 128
Nevada, 274
Navajo, 275
New England, 118, 140, 224, 240
New Hampshire, 224, 225
New Jersey, 119, 141, 240
New Mexico, 139, 274
New Orleans, Louisiana, 242, 243
New York, 141
New York City, New York, 240, 241, 250
Nigeria, 194
Norfolk, Virginia, 245
North America, countries of, 11
North Carolina, 228
North Central Region
    agriculture, 140
    business centers, 239
    climate, 118
    industrial growth, 191–192
    fishing, 222
    forestry, 222
    manufacturing, 238
    minerals and fossil fuels, 222
    population, 276–277
    states in, 113
    transportation centers, 239
    tourist industry, 238
North Dakota, 238
Northern Hemisphere, 26, 34
North Pole, 14
Northeast Region
    agriculture, 140–141
    business centers, 241
    climate, 118–119
    industrial growth, 191
    fishing, 224
    forestry, 224
    manufacturing, 240

minerals and fossil fuels, 224–225
population, 278–279
states in, 113
transportation centers, 241
tourist industry, 240

O

Oak Creek Canyon, 71
Oklahoma, 120, 142, 226
Oceans, 5, 78–83, 99
Ocean currents, 82–83, 100
Ohio, 222, 238
Ohio River, 86, 87
Oil, 161–162, 167, 169, 227
    formation of, 161
    in United States, 227
    refining of, 242
    transporting of, 86, 210, 243
    uses of, 162
Oil shale, 220–221
Oklahoma, 142, 226, 242
Omaha, Nebraska, 238
Open pit mines, 163
Oregon, 138, 218
Orlando, Florida, 244
Ozark-Ouachita Highlands, 72

P

Pacific Americans, 272, 273
Pacific Ranges, 66
Pacific Region
    agriculture, 138
    business centers, 235
    climate, 116
    fishing, 218
    forestry, 218
    manufacturing, 234
    minerals and fossil fuels, 218–219
    population, 272–273
    states in, 113
    transportation centers, 235
    tourist industry, 234
Painted Desert, 71
Panama Canal, 208, 209
Peanuts, 143
Pennsylvania, 141, 224, 240
Philadelphia, Pennsylvania, 119, 241
Pineapples, 138
Piedmont, 73
Pipeline, Alaskan, 210
Pittsburgh, Pennsylvania, 192
Planning, city, 182–183
Plymouth, Massachusetts, 240
Pollution, 168–169, 170
Population
    changes in U.S. urban, 276, 278, 279, 280, 283
    density, U.S., 275
    feeding Earth's growing, 255–256
    growth of Earth's, 251–254
    of North Central Region, 276–277
    of Northeast Region, 278–279
    of Pacific Region, 272–273
    of Rocky Mountain Region, 274–275
    of South Central Region, 280–281
    of Southeast Region, 282–283
    of United States, 271
    urban/rural distribution, U.S., 271
Portland, Oregon, 235

Potatoes, 139, 140, 141, 142
Poultry, 138, 140, 141, 142
Prairies, 128
Precipitation
    explanation of, 101–102
    in the Northeast Region, 119
    in the North Central Region, 118
    in the Pacific Region, 116
    in the Rocky Mountain Region, 117
    in the South Central Region, 120
    in the Southeast Region, 121
Prime meridian, 15
Pueblo Benito, 71
Puerto Rico, 279
Pulpwood, 218, 222, 224, 228

Q

Quarries, 224

R

Radio, 212
Railroads, 207
Rain, 101, 102
Ranching, 139
Red Rocks Park, 71
Redwood trees, 218
Refineries, oil, 242
Regions
    climate, U.S., 106–107
    geographic, U.S., 112–113
    landform, U.S., 68–69
    temperature, 98
    vegetation, U.S., 132–133
Religion, 265–266
Reservations, Native American, 236, 242

Rio Grande, 85
Rivers, U.S., 84–87
    Arkansas, 71
    Columbia, 85
    Colorado, 56–57, 85, 86
    Connecticut, 87
    Cumberland, 87
    Hudson, 85
    Mississippi, 84
    Missouri, 84
    Ohio, 86, 87
    Rio Grande, 85, 86
    Sacramento, 86
    San Joaquin, 86
    Savannah, 85
    Snake, 86
    Susquehana, 87
    Tennessee, 87
Roads and highways, 203–205
Rocky Mountain Region
    agriculture, 139
    business centers, 237
    climate, 116–117
    forestry, 220
    manufacturing, 236
    minerals and fossil fuels, 220–221
    population, 274–275
    states in, 113
    transportation centers, 237
    tourist industry, 236
Rocky Mountains, 70–71
Royal Gorge, 71

S

Sacramento Delta, 76
Saint Lawrence River, 89
Saint Lawrence Seaway, 89
Saint Louis, Missouri, 238
Salt Lake City, Utah 236
San Andreas Fault, 46, 47
San Antonio, Texas, 242, 280
San Diego, California, 235
San Francisco, California, 99, 100
San Jose, California, 234
Savannas, 128
Saw mills, 218
Sea level, 7
Sea life, 83
Seasons, 33–34
Seattle, Washington, 235
Sheep, 138, 139, 142
Sierra Nevadas, 48, 49, 66, 67
Silver, 165
Sleet, 101, 102
Smog, 168
Snow, 101, 102
Soil, 56, 130, 157
Solar energy, 170
South Carolina, 143
South Central Region
   agriculture, 142
   business centers, 243
   climate, 120–121
   fishing, 226
   forestry, 226
   manufacturing, 242
   minerals and fossil fuels, 226
   population, 280–281
   states in, 113
   transportation centers, 243
   tourist industry, 242
South Dakota, 222, 238
Southeast Region
   agriculture, 142–143
   business centers, 245
   climate, 121
   industrial growth, 244
   fishing, 228
   forestry, 228
   manufacturing, 244
   minerals and fossil fuels, 228–229
   population, 282–283
   states in, 113
   transportation centers, 245
   tourist industry, 244
Southern Hemisphere, 26, 34
South Pole, 14
Soybeans, 140
Space exploration, 244
Space industry, 234
Steel, 164, 165
Steel industry, 191–192
Strip mining, 163
Suburbs, 276
Sun, 3, 4, 31, 32, 33, 151
Sugarcane, 138, 142
Swamps, 73

T

Telegraph, 211
Telephone, 211
Television, 212
Temperature
    in North Central Region, 118
    in Northeast Region, 119
    in Pacific Region, 116
    in Rocky Mountain Region, 116
    in South Central Region, 120
    in Southeast Region, 121
    regions, 98–99
    things that affect, 33–35, 98–101
Tennessee, 143, 228
Texas
    agriculture in, 142, 143
    climate, 120
    fishing, 226
    manufacturing in, 242
    oil and gas in, 226
Tides, 81
Tobacco, 140
Toledo, Ohio, 238
Tornadoes, 103, 120, 121
Tourist Industry
    in North Central Region, 238
    in Northeast Region, 240
    in Pacific Region, 234
    in Rocky Mountain Region, 236
    in South Central Region, 242
    in Southeast Region, 244
Trade, 193–194, 235

Transportation,
    airplanes, 209
    barges, 86
    cables, 210
    canals, 88, 89, 208
    early forms of, 203–204, 208
    interstate highways, 204, 205
    pipelines, 210
    railroads, trains, 207
    roads and highways, 203–204
    ships, 208
    trucks, 206
Tree farming, 228
Tundra, 129

U

United States
    agriculture in, 136–144
    climate of, 114–122
    industries of, 216–230, 232–246
    landforms of, 64–74
    natural resources of, 216–230
    population of, 270–284
Uranium, 220
Urban areas, 271
Utah, 139

V

Vegetables, 138, 139, 140, 141, 142
Vegetation, 125–133
Vermont, 141, 224
Virginia, 143
Volcanoes, 42–45, 52

W

Washington, 138, 234

Washington, D.C., 240

Water, 152, 169, 170, 177

Water cycle, 101–102

Waves, 80

Weather, 97

Weathering, 55

Western Hemisphere, 26

West Virginia, 126

Wheat, 128, 138, 139, 140

Williamsburg, Virginia, 244

Winds, 103

Wisconsin, 140, 222

Wyoming, 139

Wyoming Basin, 70–71

Y

Yukon River Valley, 66